SEABIRDS BEYOND THE MOUNTAIN CREST

Seabirds beyond the Mountain Crest

The history, natural history and conservation of Hutton's shearwater

Richard J. Cuthbert

OTAGO

For my father, recalling our many long walks in the Warwickshire countryside that instilled in me a love of wildlife and the outdoors.

Published by Otago University Press
Level 1, 398 Cumberland Street
Dunedin, New Zealand
university.press@otago.ac.nz
www.otago.ac.nz/press

First published 2017

ISBN 978-0-947522-64-3

Editor: Imogen Coxhead

Cover image: Detail of a painting by Austen Deans, courtesy of Geoff Harrow.

Printed in China by Asia Pacific Offset

CONTENTS

He is lucky who, in the full tide of life, has experienced a measure of the active environment he most desires.

– **Eric Shipton**, *Upon That Mountain*, 1943

Acknowledgements

This book and my time in the Kaikoura mountains could not have come about without the support of several key organisations and a great many individuals. Among the former I am grateful to the Commonwealth Scholarship Commission, the University of Otago and the Department of Conservation Te Papa Atawhai, which enabled my time in New Zealand. A large number of colleagues, friends and volunteers supported the fieldwork and helped collect the data presented in this book. I regret I cannot list everyone who helped, but I am particularly grateful to Erica Sommer, Mike Dunlop, Caren Genery, Sheryl Hamilton, Geoff Harrow, Justine Ragg and Al Wiltshire for their time in the field; to Dave Armstrong, Faith Barber, Keith Dunlop, Mike Morrissey and Dave Walford for the logistical help that made the fieldwork possible; and to Professor Lloyd Davis, Peter Gaze and Kath Walker, whose guidance and advice were fundamental in bringing me to New Zealand and making the project a success.

Ongoing efforts to ensure the survival of Hutton's shearwater have been driven by a number of dedicated people and the creation of the Hutton's Shearwater Charitable Trust. The work of Geoff Harrow, Paul McGahan, Mike Bell, Nicky McArthur, Jodie Denton, Dennis Buurman, Lindsay Rowe, Teri Sonal, Gina Solomon, Phil Bradfield and Mike Morrissey has been essential to the recent conservation gains of this species.

Writing this book has involved the support of many key people. In particular I would like to thank Tim Corballis for our shared mountain adventures and for his literary knowledge and guidance that helped bring my writing ideas into reality. I am very grateful to Geoff Harrow and Erica Sommer who commented on early drafts and provided constant encouragement; to the book's scientific reviewers, Graeme Taylor and Colin Miskelly, who helped clarify some key aspects; to Paul

McGahan for reviewing the book's cultural references; to Lindsay Rowe for checking facts around the new peninsula colony. Any remaining errors are my own. I am grateful to the Alexander Turnbull Library, Wellington, New Zealand; the American Museum of Natural History, New York; BirdLife Australia; CSIRO Publishing; the Natural History Museum, London; the National Library of Australia; and to Colin Miskelly for assistance in obtaining and using historical images. I am also extremely grateful to Rachel Scott and Imogen Coxhead at Otago University Press, whose patient editing and support have made this book a reality.

Finally, I would like to thank my mother and sister for their ever-present support; Geoff and Lyndsey Harrow for 20 years of friendship and inspiration; and my wife and greatest friend, Erica, whose support was fundamental during our time in the Kowhai Valley and in many subsequent adventures.

Prologue

On the corner of the desk three stuffed birds lay side by side on their backs. Small cardboard labels, carefully tied with cotton thread, trailed from each of the birds' legs. Stacks of books and a wooden box of birds were piled high upon the desk, along with two manuscripts awaiting submission. I looked through the labels on the birds' legs before carefully picking up one bird and carrying it to the window for a closer view. It was light, stuffed with dried grass, and in the curiously elongated sausage shape that all museum bird specimens seem to take. The long slender beak and dark grey feathers on its otherwise white upper breast instantly confirmed the species' identity. Three rectangular labels were attached to the bird: the plainest was fashioned from thin brown card with two clipped corners, and on it was written, in ink in a neat hand, the words 'Puffinus Gavia' and the scientific symbol for a female. Below them in the same hand were the words 'Snare Isl' in pencil. A faded green label, dated 20 May 1912, bore the word 'TYPE', while a red label bore the inscription 'AMNH 527761'. Outside the window the low November sun filtered weakly through the trees in a scene familiar to me from dozens of films. From my vantage point I looked down at the hustle of New York's distinctive yellow cabs as they braked and honked, stopping to drop off and collect passengers on Central Park Avenue.

The bird in my hand was the holotype of Hutton's shearwater, a small seabird that breeds at only two remote sites on the New Zealand mainland, and I held it with a sense of reverence akin to that reserved for a holy artefact or priceless work of art. A holotype – also called a 'type specimen' or simply a 'type' – is unique, for it is the single individual used to define and classify a biological species. While taxonomists and biologists may measure and study dozens, if not hundreds, of specimens in order to separate and define one species from another, when the time comes to formally name and distinguish a species a single specimen is put forward. This procedure applies whether it is a bird, mammal, butterfly, or even the fossil remnant of a dinosaur: in all cases the species is formally defined by a single holotype. Further specimens – paratypes – are held by museums and help to define the size range and other variations within the species, but the holotype remains unique and priceless. Museums such as the American Museum of Natural History, which kept the type specimen AMNH 527761 that I held in my hands, carefully preserve holotypes as the crown jewels of their collections.

Quite what the remains of a small seabird from New Zealand were doing in a museum in the middle of Manhattan is a complex story. Like many aspects of Hutton's shearwater, the history of the holotype remained for many years a mystery made more complicated by the passage of time, the characters involved, the sometimes rather shady practices of bird collectors in New Zealand in the late nineteenth century, and the convoluted description of the species. Uncovering the exact circumstances of the holotype's collection would take more than 120 years of detective work.

But the history of the holotype is only one aspect of the extraordinary Hutton's shearwater story, for even after the species was formally described it remained an enigma. Another 50 years would pass before the whereabouts of the species' breeding grounds was uncovered, not by the ornithological or scientific communities but by a middle-aged mountaineer and amateur ornithologist who, ignoring perceived wisdom and following local accounts and knowledge, tracked down the species to where it was least expected to occur.

Fifty years on I stood holding the holotype of Hutton's shearwater in my hands in the American Museum of Natural History in New York. It was in part a professional visit, but perhaps more of a personal pilgrimage – to see and hold a specimen that had so influenced my life. Raising the bird to my nose, I sniffed gently and inhaled the curious musty aroma that is characteristic of all albatrosses and petrels, an odour that took me instantly back to a mountainside in New Zealand; to the species' description, discovery, natural history and conservation; and to a place where, for three years and all too briefly, I had the privilege of living.

1. Arrival in the Kowhai Valley

I crouched down and shielded my eyes and ears from the blast of snow and the accelerating whine of the helicopter's blades until, in a final crescendo, the craft lifted, turned and dropped behind the steep ridgeline. The noise abated suddenly and all was still apart from the dull roar of the river in the valley below. Picking myself up, I gazed awestruck at the surrounding view: a snow-covered landscape of bluffs, cliffs, valleys and mountains soaring high above me and dropping away to river-filled gorges below. It was an intimidating sight – and it was going to be home for the next three years.

Mike Dunlop and I stood in the heart of the Kowhai Valley in the Seaward Kaikoura mountains, in the midst of the Kowhai colony, the largest of the two remaining Hutton's shearwater colonies, at the start of my first field season in September 1996. Funding from New Zealand's Department of Conservation (DOC) and a Commonwealth scholarship to study at the University of Otago had placed me there, along with my own passion for all things to do with mountains, wild places, wildlife and conservation. The continued presence of Hutton's shearwaters in the valley was a mystery, for they appeared threatened on all sides, and most critically by introduced stoats. My task over the next three years was to try to understand the magnitude of these threats and help to develop a plan for conserving the species.

Gradually the mounds of gear in the snow encroached upon my reverie and I turned to the urgent need to start unpacking while the weather remained calm. Surrounding me were rucksacks, boxes of food, equipment, fuel, ropes, climbing gear and skis – all that Mike and I would require to live and work in the valley over the next few months. Mike was a good friend, and our shared passion for climbing and mountains had brought us to the Kaikoura ranges. Although we had only been acquainted for a couple of months, we knew each other well, since the need for total trust while mountaineering has a way of either forging or breaking friendships.

A few metres from the boxes and bags of gear stood a small tin bivouac, and we began the improbable task of packing our kit inside: wedging bags and boxes under the bunks and, when the space ran out, piling them along the one free wall. When the bivvy was full we were forced to stack the remaining gear and canned food outside in the snow or in the nearby long-drop. A plastic barrel set in the snow served as a fridge, and we stuffed our fresh food, cheese and bread inside.

The light was nearly spent, for it was early September and the days were short. The shadows cast by the mountains on the eastern side of the main valley lengthened before our eyes, creeping inexorably up the snow slopes like an incoming tide. Clouds swept across the jagged peaks to the south, and a harrier soared upwards on the wind, circling high with stiff wings spread like a crucifix, using the last updrafts to return to its roosting site down the valley. As the light left the landscape, the cliffs and buttresses became dark brooding shapes and only the summit of Manakau, the highest peak in the Seaward Kaikoura Range, remained lit by the sun, glowing like a beacon before fading softly into shadow.

After our first evening meal in the bivvy we retreated to our bunks with a large mug of Milo and a good book each, and settled in to wait. For the first two hours nothing happened. No sound but the dull roar of the river and the odd rustle as Mike turned a page of his book on the bunk below. At 11.15 I thought I heard something. Jumping down from the bunk I pulled on my boots and stepped outside into the snow. Nothing; perhaps I had imagined it? I waited again and then heard it: a sound like a gasping inhalation followed a fraction of a second later by a low-pitched trill, like a purring cat. The sound was repeated, once higher up and then again in the valley below. It was the magical sound of Hutton's shearwaters flying in to visit the snow-covered colony.

Grabbing our hats, down jackets, torches and gloves, Mike and I walked over the small ridge crest separating the bivouac from the nearest sub-colony of birds and sat down in the middle of it. More and more birds called overhead, and a sudden rush and flutter of wings made us duck as a bird swooped low overhead. By shining our head torches up into the sky we revealed birds at multiple altitudes, some circling low over the sub-colony as they found their bearings prior to landing, others high overhead flying in a straight line to sub-colonies further up the valley. One bird landed on the snow four metres from me, hitting the ground with an audible thump and a scattering of snow. More began to arrive, raining out of the sky like a meteorite shower. After landing, each bird sat still, as if surprised by its own abrupt arrival, before making a headlong dash along the ground in search of its burrow.

Like most petrels, Hutton's shearwaters are built for life out at sea. A flock of shearwaters skimming across the surface of the waves is an awe-inspiring sight, the birds just centimetres from the water effortlessly banking from one side to the other in a flash of white bellies and white under-wing coverts. On dry land, however, the birds are clumsy, stumbling across the ground in short, ill-balanced bursts, as if against a strong wind.

Gradually the number of arrivals dwindled, then ceased. The birds were visible on the snow, some alone and others in pairs. A chorus of manic hooting and braying filled the air, the sound of shearwaters reuniting with their breeding partner from the previous year or searching for a new one. After two hours of sitting on the snow we were cold, so with frozen feet and numb hands we stood and headed back to the bivvy. We hadn't caught, weighed or banded any birds – there were plenty more nights of that to come – but had simply wanted to experience our first night on the shearwaters' home ground.

The next morning dawned bright and clear, and after a large bowl of porridge and two cups of coffee each it was time to get out and explore our surroundings. The Kowhai Valley sits high on the southern flank of the Seaward Kaikoura Range, which, along with the Inland Kaikoura Range, runs northeast and parallel with the coast for 100 kilometres. Between them, the Clarence River runs northeast before breaking out to the coast in a 90-degree turn at the northern end of the Seaward Range, where it deposits its sediments into an ever-growing alluvial delta.

The Seaward and Inland Kaikoura mountains are the northernmost extension of the Southern Alps and were created along the Marlborough Fault System,[1] pushed up during the Kaikoura orogeny – the most recent period of mountain building in New Zealand – from 24 million years ago to the present.[2] The ranges continue to rise at 6–10 mm per annum.[3] Such a rate of change would swiftly (in geological terms) raise the Kaikoura ranges to challenge Mt Cook and the Southern Alps in height, were it not for the Weet-Bix-like texture of the sand and mudstone of which they are generally formed. The combined actions of wind, rain and frost-heave are enough to erode the mountains at the same rate they are rising. Higher up in the Inland range the rate of erosion is so fast that 'glaciers' of scree and rock are slowly formed and grate their way downhill, carving their way through the mountains. Unlike their counterparts that accumulate from snowfall, these rock glaciers are fed by the constantly eroding high peaks above, and the added weight of this erosion and the permafrost conditions in the arid highest ranges continues to feed and push the rock glaciers towards the coast. The uplift and these soft rocks, past ice glaciers, current rock glaciers, streams and rivers have together created towering mountains, huge banks and runnels of scree, and deeply carved valleys and watercourses. Even relatively small streams have, over thousands of years, been powerful enough to cut through these rocks. The Kowhai Valley itself is guarded to the south by two gorges and high waterfalls that have been eroded by the Kowhai River.

From the bivvy site a steep snow- and tussock-covered slope dropped sharply to the main river valley below. From there the Kowhai Valley ran northwards for two kilometres before steepening to a fringeing cirque of mountains, with Mt Manakau, at 2608 metres the highest peak in the Seaward Kaikoura Range, visible four kilometres to the north. To the east the ground rose steeply to a small peak, beyond which was a dizzying mass of slopes and near-vertical faces ending directly above us in the scree-covered dome of Mt Uwerau, the summit of which was out of sight. To the west, more peaks rose from the main valley.

Moving 10 metres down the hill from the bivvy brought the roaring Kowhai River into sight and sound. Dark wet rock faces climbed directly from the river valley, and opposite the bivvy a single vertical waterfall tumbled freely from the cliffs and fell 80 metres into a gorge that it had cut. Above the waterfall the ground eased and snow slopes rose more gently to the summit of Mt Saunders and the western skyline. A long thin ridge ran away to the south, hemmed in by the Kowhai River on the right and a smaller valley to the left. The top of the ridge was covered in snow and tussock, but lower down it was smothered with an ankle-wrenching scrub of snow tōtara and coprosma. In the more sheltered areas of the two flanking valleys, stands of mountain ribbonwood trees were able to dominate, the one area in the upper Kowhai where these trees were substantial.

The main valley ran away from us to the south, allowing an uninterrupted view across the hills to the coast, the ocean and the distant horizon, where the snow-covered hills of Banks Peninsula were visible. The landscape was wilderness and the only sign of a human hand was a radio mast over 20 kilometres south, just visible through binoculars on a clear day.

Over the next few weeks Mike and I began to explore the valley and our surroundings, each day providing new sights, sounds and experiences and a further small step in our knowledge. As we skinned up the valley on skis, smaller valleys and streams appeared beyond each ridge or low peak. Higher up, a pile of avalanche debris lay heavy and jumbled across the main valley floor, and we nervously looked around at the snow-covered slopes and cliffs to assess whether it was safe to continue. The ever-present Kowhai River tumbled down the main valley, in places covered by snow bridges that we crossed cautiously, and in others running free and cutting a dark line through the snow-covered land.

The tracks of animals were everywhere in the valley, a tangled hieroglyphic alphabet that told its own story. One morning the prints of a stoat were clearly

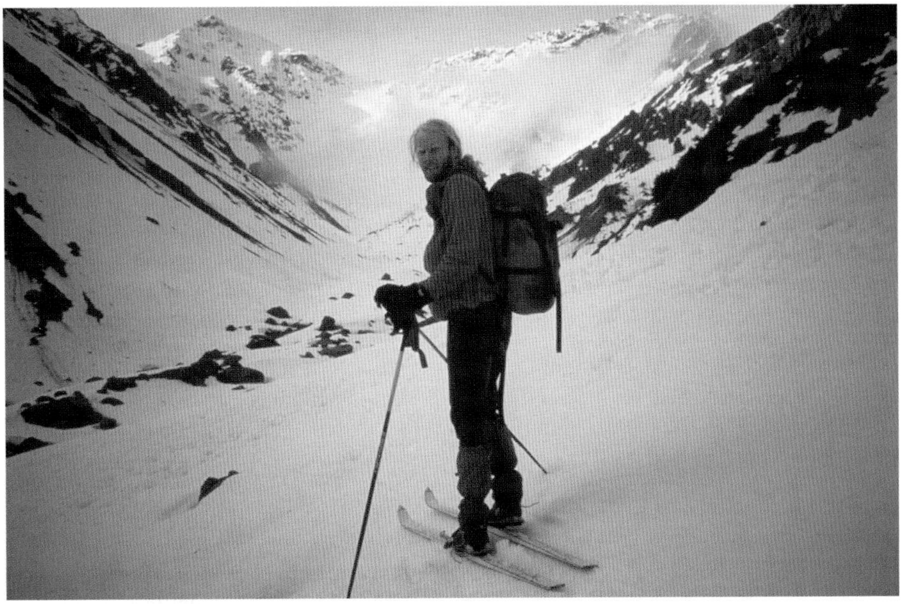

Mike Dunlop skiing up the valley during the first visit. Author photo

defined in the snow around the bivvy. Having circled us during the night the stoat had departed, leaving two small yellow stains on the snow's surface as a mark of its territory. Shearwater footprints and guano lay thick on the ground in each sub-colony, visible signs of the presence of thousands of courting and calling birds on the surface during the preceding night. A soft patch of snow at the edge of a sub-colony held the impression of a shearwater's wingtips as it ran down the hillside, accelerating for take-off. The tracks of a kea, two toes forward and two to the rear, marched like a set of capital Ks from the frayed stem of a mountain toatoa to a scattering of soil and moss where the bird had dug through the snow in search of food. The prints of a hare headed purposefully across the valley, the front paws landing together leaving one single print and the back legs swinging past on either side in a fluid triangle of motion, scattering a rough-edged powder of snow forward with its momentum.

Two sets of chamois tracks led down the mountainside and crossed the valley floor before climbing to another patch of colony high on the other side of the main valley. Further on, the tracks of a single animal came to a stop in the shelter of mountain ribbonwood trees, the flattened snow and scattered black pellets revealing where the chamois had rested for the night. The hoof prints were large – probably those of an immature and solitary male roaming the mountains until he was old

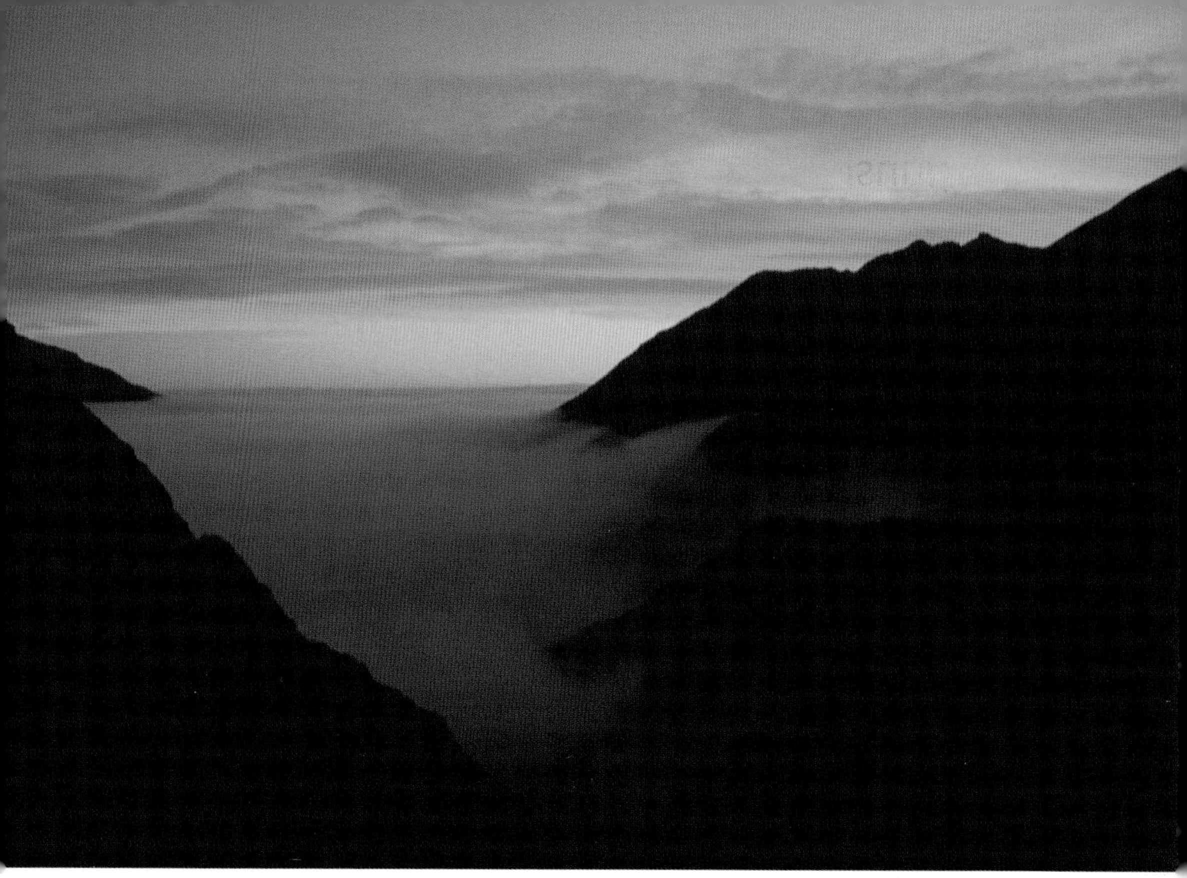

Sunset looking down the valley. Author photo

enough to secure and hold a harem of females. The prints of a stoat bounded across the snow's surface and disappeared into a dense patch of snow tōtara. We found the tracks of another stoat at the top of a nearby sub-colony, intermingled with guano and the odd feather. The stoat's prints led down and through the colony, and further on there was a flurry of pawmarks and a patch of blood on the snow's surface.

Arriving back at the bivvy each day in the fading afternoon light, we would immediately put a brew on and start digging through the boxes of food in the snow for an evening meal. We were often joined by a lone kea, an adult male bird that would strut across the tin roof of the bivvy, his claws screeching horribly, before stopping and peering over the edge to gaze intently at us sitting inside next to the stove. No alarm clock was necessary, for at dawn (and sometimes earlier) the kea would land on the roof with a metallic clump and then apparently proceed to sharpen his bill on the metal roof edge. Ten minutes of screeching metal torture was always enough to see me out of my sleeping bag and opening the door to the start of another day.

2. A gunshot off the Snares Islands

In the ninth century the Māori leader Rakihouia and the crew of the *Uruaokapuarangi* (*Uruao*) migration canoe reached a low-lying peninsula jutting from the eastern coast of Te Wai Pounamu (the greenstone waters – New Zealand's South Island).[1] Rakihouia's own father, Rākaihautū, had left him at Whakatū (Nelson) in the northern reaches of Te Wai Pounamu and set off to travel overland down the length of the unexplored land. Māori legend recalls that Rākaihautū travelled with his kō, or digging stick, and dug many rivers and lakes including Whakamātau (Coleridge), Rotorua, Pūkaki, Ōhau, Wānaka, Tekapo and Hāwea, during his journey.

While Rākaihautū journeyed overland, Rakihouia continued his journey south by sea in the *Uruao*. Off a low-lying peninsula his pregnant wife, Tapuiti, was craving eggs, and seeing the tens of thousands of pakahā tītī (shearwaters) at sea, Rakihouia sent his crew ashore to climb the slopes in search of eggs from the nests. They landed in a Garden of Eden, for they were the first people to set foot on this land. The seas surrounding the peninsula abounded in kōura (crayfish), kekeno (fur seals) and paikea (sperm whales), and the thick forest rang with the calls of kōparapara (bellbirds), riroriro (grey warblers) and pīwakawaka (fantails). Among the forests giant moa paced, and above the treeline, perched on a rocky outcrop, the great eagle pouakai waited silently, ever ready to swoop on an unwary moa. As night fell the forest came alive to the booming calls of kākāpō and the doleful shrieking of whēkau, the laughing owl. Later that night when the fires had dimmed, the yelping calls of seabirds flying overhead kept Rakihouia and his crew from sleeping. Over the next days the men climbed up through the forest until the vegetation thinned and they emerged onto steep tussock-covered slopes, where they found the tītī nests and were able to collect eggs for Tapuiti.

Over the coming centuries Rakihouia's people and other migrations of Māori passed through and settled on this eastern peninsula, but to all of them and particularly to the Ngāti Kuri and Ngāi Tahu people, the tītī were a taonga or treasure, for the fat chicks could be caught in abundance high in the mountains before the winter snows and preserved in bags of rimurapa (bull kelp) to sustain the people through the winter. In turn, Rakihouia's descendants became the birds' kaitiaki or guardians, responsible as protectors of the tītī.

With the arrival of the European Pākehā over 800 years later, Ngāti Kuri and Ngāi Tahu's land and traditional practices changed, and as the lowland forests were felled and burned and the seals and whales were slaughtered, knowledge of the tītī and their location waned. By the early nineteenth century only a few of the eldest Māori, the kaumātua, could remember the practice of collecting chicks beyond the mountain's crest, and as these men and women died one by one, so the knowledge of the mountain tītī was lost. Only the names remained: the steep mountain slopes called Te Whatakai-o-Rakihouia – 'the food storehouse of Rakihouia' – and the peninsula with its abundance of crayfish, named Kaikōura.

On 9 January 1890, a thousand years after Rākaihautū and Rakihouia's arrival in the South Island, a gunshot sounded from the deck of the New Zealand government steamer SS *Hinemoa* as it lay off the Snares Islands to the south of New Zealand. The shot came from one of the ship's passengers; the unfortunate target was a small black and white seabird skimming and turning along the wave's crests in the flight pattern characteristic of shearwaters. That shot heralded the scientific genesis of a new species.

The species in question was Hutton's shearwater and the bird was the very one that I examined in the American Museum of Natural History, more than 120 years later. One of many significant specimens in the museum, it is important not only because it is the holotype of the species – carefully locked in a vaulted 'type room' within the museum's ornithological wing – but also because of what it reveals about the naturalists and scientists involved in collection in the late nineteenth century. The collection of the type specimen of Hutton's shearwater remained clouded in mystery for over a century while museums and science historians debated the question of who collected the first bird, and when and where.

The formal scientific description of New Zealand's fauna and flora began with the arrival of Captain Cook in 1769 and the work of the botanist Sir Joseph Banks, and continued in the following century most notably, for ornithology, in the work of Walter Buller and his seminal publication *A History of the Birds of New Zealand* in 1872–73. These scientists formally described and gave European names to the wide variety of species already known and named by New Zealand Māori – species that were important cultural sources of food and clothing for all Māori tribes. Buller's publication came at the zenith of the Victorian obsession with natural history collecting, and New Zealand's unique avifauna, with its curious flightless kiwi, kākāpō parrots and fossil remains of moa, was an irresistible lure for museums and collectors around the world. No longer was collecting simply undertaken by scientists for the purpose of scientific description; now, a small but select group of professional collectors secured a somewhat perilous living from the trade in rare or new forms of wildlife from New Zealand.

By the late nineteenth century collectors were venturing to ever more remote areas of New Zealand and its subantarctic islands in order to find and collect new species. Among the professional collectors and dealers of birds, plants and fossils, two names began to turn up regularly: many specimens were collected by Danish-born Sigvard Jacob Dannefærd and Englishman Henry Hammersley Travers. The men were rivals, although on occasion they may have collaborated. Dannefærd (1853–1920) came to New Zealand at the age of 20 and remained for 47 years. He ran an establishment in Rotorua selling curios and 'travelled all over the world, especially as a naturalist in search of rare plants'.[2] He was also an art and jewellery connoisseur, and his expertise was often sought by the authorities to settle disputes in this area.

Henry Travers (1844–1928) arrived in New Zealand as a boy in 1850, the son of the lawyer and prominent Nelson, Christchurch and Wellington politician William Travers, himself a respected explorer and naturalist and one of the founders of the New Zealand Institute.[3] Henry Travers was educated at Nelson College and, following in his father's footsteps, was admitted to the New Zealand bar as a lawyer in Wellington in 1876. He married in 1869 and had five children. Although the law was his main occupation, Travers appears to have been more interested in his passion for natural history collecting and taxidermy. Early explorations and collecting trips around the Nelson region with his father were later followed by independent visits to the Chatham Islands, where he collected the first specimens of the black robin, *Petroica traversi*, which was named after him by F.H. Hutton, curator of the Canterbury Museum.[4] In fact Travers appears to have been more successful as a collector than a lawyer, as he lost his law practice in 1900. Although appointed as the curator of the Newtown Museum in November 1913, a job that would seem to have suited his background and interests, he failed to prosper and was dismissed in 1915.[5]

Between them, Travers and Dannefærd collected the type specimens of the black robin, Snares Island fernbird and tomtit, and the now extinct Chatham Island rail,

Sigvard Dannefærd, one of the main early collectors who sent the type specimen to Lord Rothschild. Photo courtesy of Dianne Dannefærd, via Te Papa Tongarewa

Henry Travers, who collected the type specimen. *Annual Journal of the Royal NZ Institute of Horticulture* No. 16, 1989, p. 60. Photo courtesy of Hocken Collections

South Island snipe and Stephens Island wren. Controversy has dogged the work of both men, however, and both were notorious for their poor records, a fact that for decades has frustrated museum staff who are still trying to untangle which man was responsible for collecting the many specimens from New Zealand.

The situation should have been clear, for each man used unique labels to distinguish his specimens: Travers' collection labels were rectangular with a distinctive curved bottleneck shape at one end and tied with pink cotton thread, whereas Dannefærd's were rectangular with two clipped corners and tied with black or white thread.[6] For many years museum collectors relied upon this difference in labelling styles to determine who had collected each specimen. Over time uncertainty grew, however, as dates and localities revealed increasing inconsistencies. Specimens were being identified from localities where the men had not or could not have visited at the time of labelling. The handwriting on their distinctive labels also varied greatly, to the point that museum staff began to doubt that either man had written his own. Over 100 years later Colin Miskelly, curator of terrestrial vertebrates at New Zealand's Te Papa Tongarewa museum, sought expert assistance. Forensic analysis of the handwriting confirmed his suspicions that both Travers and Dannefærd had handed out their distinctive labels for other collectors to fill in and then passed these specimens off as their own.[7] The analysis also revealed that on at least one occasion both Travers and Dannefærd – whether wittingly or unwittingly – were employing the same third party to collect birds in their own names, for the same handwriting appears on both men's labels. It also showed that at least one of Travers' most important type specimens could not have been collected by him: the now extinct South Island snipe, collected from Stewart Island and long credited to Travers, was actually collected by an unknown person whose writing is on Travers' label.

Both Travers' and Dannefærd's names are linked to the type specimen of Hutton's shearwater, and details of the collection of this bird have been debated since the 1950s. The first written records concerning the species are dated 16 May 1895, when an inventory of specimens sent by Dannefærd to Lord Rothschild in England indicated that a '*Puffinus Gavia Snare Isl*' had been included.[8] The ascribed scientific name, *Puffinus gavia*, refers to the related but already well-known fluttering shearwater, but the bird would later be described as 'Hutton's shearwater'. Dannefærd's decision to sell it to the wealthy Lord Rothschild suggests that he was well aware that the bird in question was not the familiar fluttering shearwater. The bird was marked with Dannefærd's clipped labels, and the writing of both the scientific name and the locality were in his own hand. In sum, the evidence that he himself had collected the bird should have been conclusive – but for one small fact: Dannefærd had never visited the Snares Islands, or indeed any of New Zealand's subantarctic islands. While Henry Travers is clearly implicated in some creative mislabelling of specimen localities,[9] no previous evidence indicates that Dannefærd followed the same practice. But if Dannefærd were honest with his labelling, yet never visited the Snares, then who did collect the birds?

The next mention of the birds was in *A Monograph of Petrels (Order Tubinares)*, published in 1907–08, which states that these Snares shearwaters were collected by Henry Travers.[10] To add to the confusion, a paper from 1948 indicates a collection date for the Snares birds of January 1890 – five years earlier than Dannefærd's correspondence with Lord Rothschild – and again lists Henry Travers as the collector.[11]

In 2010, in a bid to resolve the mystery behind the collection of the holotype of Hutton's shearwater and also other type specimens purported to have been collected from the Snares by Dannefærd, New Zealand ornithologists and museum curators Alan Tennyson and Colin Miskelly and American Museum of Natural History

The bird on the right is the Hutton's shearwater type specimen in the American Museum of Natural History. Author photo

A close-up of Dannefærd's label on the type specimen. Author photo

curator Mary LeCroy began searching through early editions of New Zealand newspapers.[12] The three were looking for reports of the voyages of the New Zealand government steamers that made regular visits to the southern islands to search for castaways and replenish depots stationed for shipwreck survivors. Travers and other collectors utilised these voyages to visit the Snares and other subantarctic islands. After weeks of careful searching the researchers found what they were looking for. The *Otago Daily Times* of 21 January 1890 held an account of the return of the government steamer SS *Hinemoa* to Port Chalmers:

> The S.S. *Hinemoa* returned early yesterday from her periodical visits to the islands after having searched the Snares, Auckland Island, Campbell Island, Antipodes Island and the Bounty Islands for traces of castaways, and having inspected the various provision depots and boats stations maintained by the Government in these remote groups. The vessel carried several passengers round, among them Professor Kirk, Messrs Martin Chapman and F.R. Chapman, Mr H.D. Bell, Mr Russell, Mr H. Travers, and several boys … A number of people visited the *Hinemoa* in the course of yesterday afternoon to see the albatrosses and penguins which Captain Fairchild had brought home for various museums.[13]

While uncertainty persists over much of Henry Travers' collecting, the article clearly records a Mr H. Travers on the vessel that visited the Snares in the month and year that '*Puffinus Gavia Snares Isl*' is reported to have been collected. How long the *Hinemoa* remained at the Snares is unrecorded, but given the fine weather reported during the voyage, and the ship's itinerary, it is likely it was there for a single day, making it probable that the bird was collected by Travers on 9 January 1890. Yet intriguingly it was Dannefærd who ended up with the specimen and who sold it on to Lord Rothschild five years later. Perhaps the shaky state of Travers' legal practice necessitated a quick sale and the bird that would become the holotype of Hutton's shearwater was traded to his great rival, Sigvard Dannefærd.

Thus, in 1895, the Hutton's shearwater most likely collected by Travers ended up in the hands of Lord Walter Rothschild, who was among the world's most pre-eminent private natural history collectors. Like Travers, Rothschild was more interested in his zoological pastime than the family business. While he spent 18 years employed as a partner at the family's London bank (a period for which no record of his banking work exists[14]) he devoted himself to being a full-time zoologist, a passion he had held since childhood when he reportedly declared to his parents, 'Mama, Papa, I am going to make a museum …'[15]

Unlike Travers, however, Rothschild had the immense wealth of the family's banking dynasty to support his passion. From 1892 until his death in 1937 he

Portrait of Lord Walter Rothschild (c. 1910) by Joszi Arpad Koppay, Baron von Dretoma. Natural History Museum, London, 004269

BELOW: Lord Walter Rothschild (c. 1895) proving a point about zebras. Natural History Museum, London, 002847

bought and traded specimens from around the world. He amassed the world's largest private natural history collection – over 300,000 bird skins, 144 giant tortoises, 200,000 bird eggs and more than two million butterflies and moths – and with other zoologist curators described more than 5000 new species of animal in a torrent of more than 1200 books and papers.[16] Rothschild also had a modest zoo in the

grounds of the family estate at Tring in Hertfordshire that contained, among other animals, zebras, wild horses, a tame wolf, kangaroos, emus, rheas, cassowaries, a flock of kiwi, giant tortoises, pangolins, capybara and a giant anteater.[17] When he acquired the shearwater specimen from Dannefærd in 1895 he was six years into his banking career but already buying and trading hundreds of specimens on the side. A famous photo of Rothschild taken in the same year shows him – suitably bewhiskered for the Victorian era – in a carriage pulled by zebras that he drove to Buckingham Palace to prove that the zebra could be tamed.

At some point in the next few years Rothschild chose to exchange the Snares Island shearwater with Australian taxonomist Gregory Mathews, who made the first formal description of this bird in 1912. Then in 1920 Rothschild, presumably making a financial offer that Mathews couldn't refuse, purchased Mathews' entire collection of bird skins – including the Hutton's holotype. The shearwater would undoubtedly have remained in Rothschild's collection and would now reside in the Britain's Natural History Museum at Tring, were it not for a scandal. The details are opaque, but it appears to have involved the long-term extortion of Rothschild following an affair with a 'charming, witty, aristocratic, ruthless blackmailer',[18] who was clearly more than a passing distraction from his butterfly collecting. In 1932 the financial pressure of the blackmail became too much. In urgent need of cash for a settlement, Rothschild was forced to sell the majority of his bird collection to the American Museum of Natural History.[19] Along with thousands of other bird skins, the original Hutton's shearwater specimen from the Snares ended up making a journey to the Big Apple, where it remains today.

Gregory Macalister Mathews was born in 1876 at Merrygoen, New South Wales, and had a typical boyhood passion for collecting birds' eggs. After working on a cattle station for six years he became an orchardist, and in 1902 married a wealthy widow. Along with her two children, the couple sailed for England where Mathews, supported by his wife's income, lived the life of a country squire, with rounds of hunting, racing and horse shows.[20] Following a visit to the British Museum, however, he was inspired to follow his childhood interest and determined to produce the definitive work on Australian birds. Mathews became obsessive, amassing a collection of over 30,000 bird skins and 5000 books, and wrote the 12-volume *The Birds of Australia*, which was published from 1910 to 1927. In 1912, in the second volume of *Birds of Australia*, Mathews formally described, for the first time, the Snares shearwater collected by Henry Travers. Dannefærd had labelled the bird *Puffinus gavia*, the scientific name for the related fluttering shearwater that was well known to collectors and ornithologists and bred at numerous islands around

Portrait of Gregory Macalister Mathews (1929) by B. Gotto. National Library of Australia, nla.obj-134322450

Frederick Wollaston Hutton, curator of the Canterbury Museum. Photograph by E. Wheeler and Son. Alexander Turnbull Library, MNZ-0474-1/4-F

the North Island and in the Marlborough Sounds. Mathews correctly identified the relationship to the fluttering type species, but recognised this as a distinct new form and gave it the scientific name *Puffinus gavia huttoni* and the common name Hutton's shearwater, in honour of the English-born Frederick Wollaston Hutton, former curator of the Canterbury Museum in Christchurch who had died in 1905.[21]

Mathews' description and naming of Hutton's shearwater in 1912 should have cemented this bird as a new species and invited ongoing interest and research. Unfortunately, not many people took notice of the new description for the simple reason that Mathews was known as an enthusiastic 'splitter'. While it is a simplification, taxonomists can usually be clustered into 'lumpers' – those who group different forms into a single species – and 'splitters' – those who separate even the most minor of different forms into distinct species. Mathews was firmly in the latter camp: his *Reference List to the Birds of Australia* (1912) almost doubled the number of recognised forms from 800 to a staggering 1500 species. Some of these splits are still accepted, although the number of bird species in Australia recognised today stands at 705,[22] hinting at the scale of his over-ambition.

So the scientific and ornithological community largely ignored Mathews' description, and tantalising glimpses of Hutton's shearwater that occurred over the next decades were equally unsuccessful in advancing scientific knowledge of the species. In January 1916 Captain S.A. White set out on a cruise in the waters of the St Vincent and Spencer gulfs off Adelaide, Australia, in pursuit of 'a strange white-breasted Petrel' that he had previously seen 'but never identified'.[23] Captain White saw more of these birds on his cruise, but rough seas thwarted attempts to shoot and collect them. Further Hutton's shearwaters were seen by the American Whitney South Sea Expedition, which journeyed through the Pacific 1920–32 – the longest ornithological voyage in history[24]– and members of the expedition even collected some off Banks Peninsula on 28 and 29 January 1926.[25] The significance of these specimens was lost among the more than 40,000 birds this expedition collected, however, and the 'mixed catch' of Hutton's and fluttering shearwaters were once again grouped together as the better-known fluttering shearwater.[26]

Twenty-five years after Mathews' description, Hutton's shearwater came into scientific view again when a dead bird was found washed ashore on a beach at Bunbury in southwestern Australia. The bird was collected by a keen ornithologist and collector, Lawson Whitlock, on 23 April 1937. Despite careful observation

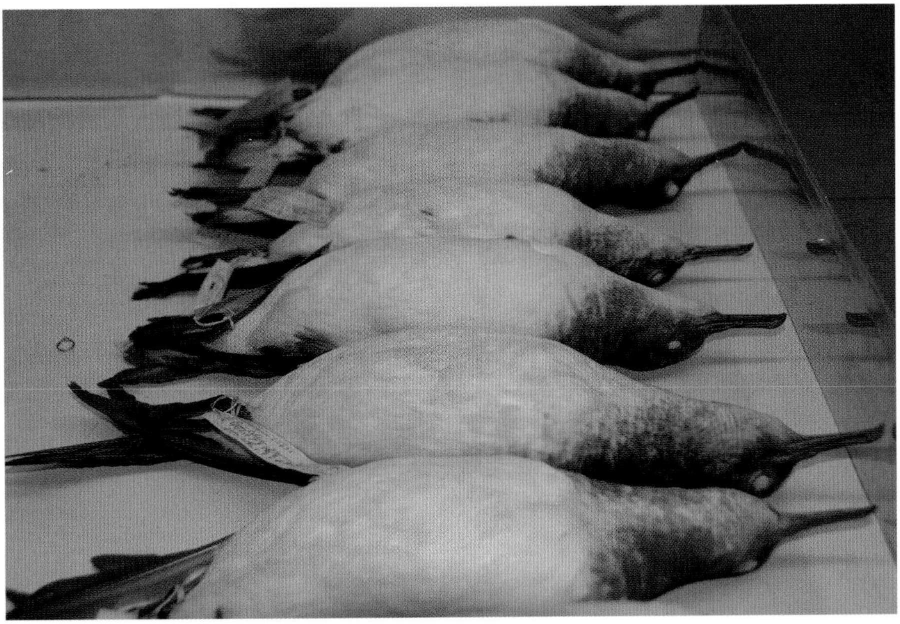

Hutton's shearwaters collected by the American Whitney South Sea Expedition in 1926, which were incorrectly classified as fluttering shearwaters. Now in the American Museum of Natural History. Author photo

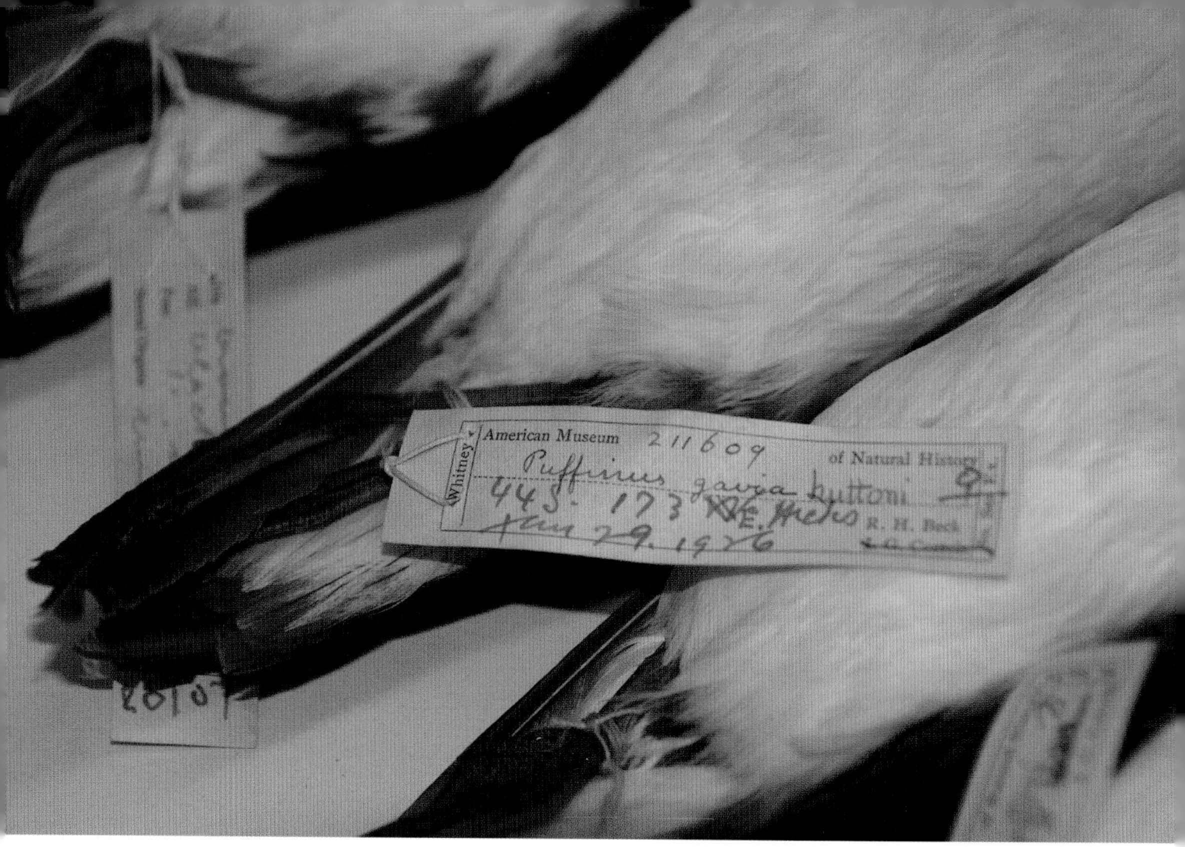

A close-up of the label on a bird collected in 1926, revealing the incorrect identification as '*Puffinus gavia*', with '*huttoni*' added later by another hand. Author photo

and comparison with published guides, Whitlock was only able to classify it as belonging to the shearwater group of species,[27] so he sent the bird to England to the eminent authority on Australian birds – none other than Gregory Mathews. On the 30 June 1937, within weeks of receiving the bird, Mathews published a note and fuller description of the Bunbury bird as another new species, hailing in immodest fashion the find of the 'slender-billed shearwater *Puffinus leptorhynchus*' as 'probably the most important this century'.[28] A beautiful illustration of the 'new' species in Whitlock's account,[29] however, highlights its dark underwing coverts and relatively long and slim bill – features that are all characteristic of Hutton's shearwater. Mathews was never afraid to trumpet a new species, and his work in creating new taxa – often on the most tenuous grounds – has been described by modern museum curators as 'carelessness to the point of serious professional incompetence'.[30] In his haste, Mathews had overlooked the crucial fact that the 1937 bird from Bunbury matched Travers' bird from the Snares that he had in 1912 described as Hutton's shearwater.

The 1937 image of Hutton's shearwater in Whitlock's paper, incorrectly assigned to another species by Mathews. From *Emu* 37, 1937, plate 16, pp. 116–17. Courtesy of BirdLife Australia

It took two years for the situation to be corrected. In February 1939 the Australian ornithologist Don Serventy collected two small black and white shearwaters from among a large flock of petrels flying at sea off Kangaroo Island, South Australia. Based on their size and plumage Serventy correctly identified these as Hutton's shearwaters, and pointed out that Mathews' 1912 description and his 1937 description were of one and the same species.[31] It had taken a long time, but Serventy's resolution of the true species status of Hutton's shearwater, nearly 50 years after the collection of the first birds from the Snares Islands, finally alerted scientists and ornithologists to the fact that there was another small black and white shearwater present in Australian and New Zealand waters. In 1937 two questions remained, however: where did Hutton's shearwater occur, and where did it breed?

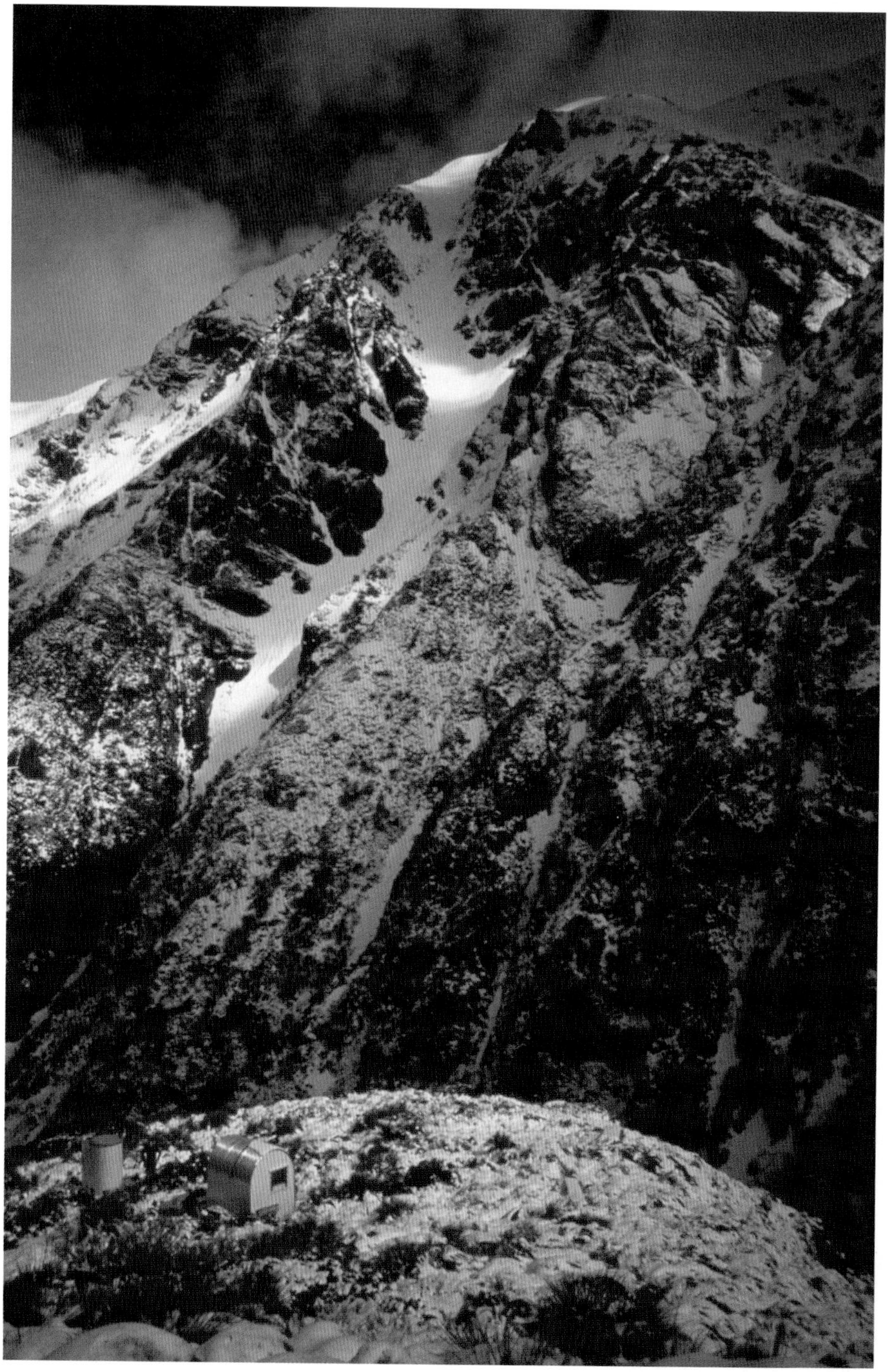

View of the bivvy and the snow-covered shearwater sub-colonies beyond. Author photo

3. Explorations amidst shearwaters

It is difficult to describe the excitement of my first days in the valley, but exploring and getting to know every wrinkle of this landscape gave me an impossible excess of energy and a visceral thrill. Despite the kea's early wakeup calls I would rise each day fresh and eager to search out another feature of the area.

The exhilaration of those weeks was tempered by the nature of our overnight accommodation, for we were living in what became known simply as 'the biv'. The bivouac was shaped like an overgrown baked-bean tin, and was made from a hoop of corrugated iron with one-centimetre-thick plywood walls at either end, a door and two small vented windows. The whole structure was around 2 metres long by 1.5 metres wide and its highest point was a few centimetres lower than my height. A frayed and rather optimistic-looking wire cable looped over the roof, held taut by two waratah stakes driven into the ground. Inside, two narrow bunk beds ran along one wall and a stack of wooden stoat traps formed rudimentary shelving along the other. A small galvanised tin-covered table, upon which sat an ancient and evil-smelling kerosene stove, was levered into the remaining space. Everything we possessed was stored in the nooks and crannies that were left over: clothes, waterproofs, gloves, boots, cameras, binoculars, notebooks, field-guides, papers, banding gear, a single-sideband (SSB) radio, ropes, crampons, ice axes, skis and food – and last, but by no means least, a couple of bottles of whisky.

Our cramped living conditions were exacerbated by the weather in those early days; during the three years that I lived in the Kowhai I never again experienced such a continuous spell of southerly squalls. Each cold front brought a fresh layer of snow and frustrated our efforts to dig the foundations for the planned research hut. Leather boots would freeze, water left in the billy would be solid ice in the morning, and the windows and door let in a steady stream of spindrift that covered every surface with a fine layer of snow. By morning we looked like two ash-coated bodies from Pompeii, mummified by snow and our sleeping bags. A down jacket and an occasional medicinal swig of whisky would induce enough warmth and clarity to get the stove going and save us from a similar fate.

Unfortunately, lighting the stove was a double-edged sword. Designed for use in a well-ventilated space, its only redeeming feature was its capacity to be lit with a single arm thrust from the warm depths of a sleeping bag. The stove consisted of a cylindrical glass flagon that held a couple of litres of kerosene. Gravity and a copper tube led the kerosene to two circular wicks that were opened by the spin of a wheel. As the kerosene exited and air entered, the bottle would glug noisily like a parched throat gulping down a beer. A couple of minutes later the stove would produce two 30-centimetre-high sooty yellow flames, along with clouds of acrid black smoke. The top of the biv would rapidly become unbearably hot and smoke-filled while the bottom remained bitterly cold, and whoever was on the top bunk would be fighting to open the door while at the same time removing layers of clothing.

Only a northwest wind could offer respite from the southerly fronts, but the warm norwesters would arrive in ferocious gusts that howled down the valley. Twice the sheer strength of these lifted me clean off my feet, on one occasion dumping me onto a nearby snowdrift, and on another into a stream that I was jumping across. The bivvy didn't enjoy these winds either, and the whole structure would rattle and vibrate with each gust. On one sleepless night a gust of wind shifted the bivvy 10 centimetres closer to the coast in a sickening lurch before the wire tie-downs sang taut in the wind. The next day, to avoid another such experience, I got out another cable and banged in two more waratahs.

Communication with the outside world was provided through the SSB radio. Using the radio was simple except that the 20-metre aerial had to be laid out and taken in each time we used it. The aerial was bright orange, a colour the kea found irresistible; by the end of the season it was multi-coloured with insulation-tape repairs, reminders of occasions when we were too slow in chasing away an inquisitive beak.

Each night we would attempt to talk to the Kaikoura DOC office to reassure them that we were alive. Radio waves prefer to travel in straight lines, however, and Mt Fyffe lay directly between us and the Kaikoura field centre. More frequently we indulged in a game of 'Chinese whispers', relaying messages to Kaikoura via the West Coast, Murchison or Stephens Island and back again. Later in the season we would share the airwaves and chat with a couple of hunters who were employed culling goats and other feral animals in the Kaikoura ranges. Each night we switched on the radio to hear the latest results, like rugby scores from some newly named provincial

The crammed bivvy at the start of the first season. Author photo

teams: 'Goats 48 – Deer 9'; 'Cows 1 – Sheep 3'. Every once in a while we would also hear the guys reporting they had got one or two of the disturbingly named 'others'. In addition to transmitting the hunting tally, both hunters had long nightly chats with their wives over the radio. This was fine except for the litany of home improvements that were being undertaken in their absence – we would endure 20 minutes of debate over whether to have brass or silver door fittings, or order a rounded or Arabesque arch for the living room. Occasionally we chipped in with less than useful suggestions that usually cleared the airwaves for just long enough to allow us to tell Kaikoura that we were fine.

While we needed to explore our immediate surroundings, the mountains were also calling. The Kaikoura mountains lack the height of New Zealand's Southern Alps, but they still offer plenty of challenges. Our first climb in the valley had been up a frozen waterfall nearly 70 metres high that had formed in a steep and shaded gully. We discovered the waterfall on one of our first days of exploring, and two weeks later we returned. An hour on skis steadily skinning uphill with a heavy rucksack of ropes, crampons, ice axes and ice-screws served as a good warm up. The climbing was uneventful but steep, with the last 20 metres of vertical ice offering no chance of a rest. It was with burning forearms and pumped calves that I struggled up the last few metres. Near the top a strange wētā lay frozen on the surface of the snow. I quickly grabbed it and shoved it down the back of one of my gloves while I hung from one firmly planted axe. It was worth the effort, for it turned out to be a perfectly preserved ground wētā, complete with giant back legs like an overgrown grasshopper, and a species never before recorded from the Kaikoura ranges.[1]

While the ice climb had been adrenalin boosting, we were keen to tackle a mountain route. Opposite the bivvy lay an obvious challenge: a steep snow gully curled upwards in the shape of a long, lazy question mark, starting at the height of the Kowhai River and stretching 1000 metres to the crest of the skyline. From here a ridge ran for six kilometres to the summit of Manakau at 2608 metres.

We set off at 3am, the early start necessary to minimise the risk of avalanche and rock fall as the morning sun thawed the walls of the gully. Floundering down the ridge to the river in deep snow, by the light of my head torch, I cursed the fact that we had not beaten a trail in the light of the previous day. After nearly an hour of frustrating descent, intermittently getting tangled in thickets of ribbonwood and bluffed by vertical sections, we made it down to the main river. Directly opposite us on the other side of the river the start of the snow gully hung in the darkness. The river was bridged in places by drifts of snow, and through the open spots we could see and hear the Kowhai roaring, a dark mass of shifting water, sediment and grit that 20 metres downstream fell in a waterfall that marks the boundary of the upper Kowhai Valley.

We tiptoed across a snow bridge, my mind not even wanting to contemplate an early-morning plunge into the freezing water, nor the vertical drop just downstream of us. Ten metres of frozen rubble separated us from the start of the gully and after a nerve-wracking scramble I sank my ice axes into the snow. I shouted gleefully to Mike, for the névé was in perfect condition – not so soft that you would sink in up to your knees, nor so hard that you had to fiercely kick your crampons just to gain a tentative purchase. Instead, the weight of my step was sufficient to drive my crampon points in securely, and grasping both axes near their heads I punched them like daggers into the frozen snow. Glancing at Mike, I saw him grin and a nod and we started climbing. The ropes were still coiled in our rucksacks but on such perfect snow we were both confident to climb without them. I settled into a steady rhythm of movements: two steps of the feet and then a quick left-right punch with my axes, my breath following deeply but not laboured, my mind focusing solely on the rhythm.

We were gaining ground rapidly, both of us climbing at a steady rate and with no ropes or gear placements to hinder us. Glancing down I saw that Mike was moving at a similar pace to me, and I was thankful for a good winter's activity that meant I was fit. The gully rose steadily, the snow surface smooth apart from the occasional crater and channel created by the gouging impact of a falling rock. As we gained height we moved out of the shadows and into the soft glow of a late-rising moon. Pausing for the first time to extinguish my torch, I became fully aware of my surroundings. The gully fell below in a dizzying sweep, with the dark line of the Kowhai River visible in places through the snow. Opposite and now far below us a sliver of moonlight reflected off the tin roof of the bivvy. On either side, dark near-vertical walls of rock leaned menacingly over the gully, effectively preventing any escape and committing us to the climb. Looking upwards I could see the gully widening into a sweeping amphitheatre of snow; above, in the clear mountain air, the stars hung so vividly that the familiar constellations were drowned in a vast backdrop of more distant stars. On the opposite side of the valley Mt Uwerau hung in deep moon-shadow, with only the Milky Way defining the jagged skyline. Both sides of the gully were flanked by shearwater sub-colonies where thousands of courting birds whooped, screamed and yelped in a symphony of exultation. Mike had also stopped climbing and was absorbing the scene. Looking across, I saw him shake his head in disbelief: nothing needed to be said.

We carried on climbing, torn between wanting to stop and absorb the perfection of the moment and the need to get out of the gully before the sunrise made it into a bowling alley of falling rocks. It was one of those rare climbing days when the timing was perfect: as we crested the skyline a thin crescent of fire broke over the sea beyond the Kaikoura Peninsula and the rising sun hit us with palpable warmth. By this stage we had been moving and climbing continually for four hours and we were more than happy to sit and wait as the petrol stove roared and turned a billy of snow into a hot brew. A mug of tea helped wash down a thick wedge of cold Christmas pudding, and we were ready to go again.

From where we stood the ridge rose gently to Mt Saunders and then continued for over five kilometres to Manakau. It was a vertical gain of over 300 metres to the summit of Saunders at 2146 metres, and nearly another 500 metres to the peak of Manakau. The going was easier now and we both climbed with just one axe and a ski pole. As we gained ground, the initially broad ridge became narrow and fell steeply on both sides; in places, windblown snow had settled on the lee side of the ridge in the shape of a breaking wave, creating a tempting flat surface overhanging the ridge's crest that could collapse at any moment. We moved slowly, sticking to the steeper slopes and avoiding the cornice.

Midway between Saunders and Manakau I stopped suddenly, for there on the snow, in a trail along the very crest, was a set of stoat prints – at 2100 metres, across terrain that we were negotiating with ice axes and crampons while wrapped in thermals, fleece and waterproofs. Testament, indeed, that the shearwaters were up against a remarkable predator and one perfectly suited to this environment.

We climbed steadily towards the shoulder where the ridge joined the summit mass of Manakau. The snow was becoming softer and the going heavier, and after 10 hours of climbing we were both beginning to flag. At 2pm we reached a bulging mound of snow that hung in the lee of the mountain and blocked off the final 300-metre climb. The snow bulge looked poised to collapse. To either side the drop was vertical and this unstable bank of snow was the only way up. Mike drew the short straw and, after getting the rope out for the first time, set off climbing gingerly onto the pillow of snow. My precaution – of belaying off a spike of rock instead of tying into the rope – did not inspire Mike with any extra confidence, but if it collapsed it would be better for both of us if I were not attached to the system.

Mike made it with the snow intact and I swiftly followed, 'thinking light' for the whole climb. For another 200 metres the narrow ridge rose steeply to the summit. The climbing was now straightforward, albeit with dizzying exposure on either side. Only the clinging snow hindered us; softened by the sun to the consistency of porridge, it stuck to our crampons with each step, creating heavy balls underfoot that would slip crazily on the surface. Every step had to be followed by a sharp tap to the foot with an ice axe to get rid of the balling snow and allow the crampon points to bite firmly. It was no place to slip.

The summit was abrupt: a sharp pyramid of three ridges converging to a single peak. Beyond the mountain's crest the Inland Kaikoura Range lay like a topographic map, and further away the northernmost peaks of the Southern Alps were visible, the summits blurred by a distant haze. Tapuae-o-Uenuku dominated the scene, its flanks deeply covered with snow and with a stream of spindrift peeling from the summit. To the southwest of 'Tappy' the shark's tooth of Mt Alarm validated its name. The whole of the Clarence Valley was cloaked in snow and I imagined the musterers, in its days as an active sheep station, cursing the need to go out searching for stock. Now, however, the scene was one of wilderness, and only a line of poplars visible through my binoculars betrayed the past presence of a human hand. Running through the scene, the Clarence River cut a dark contrasting course in the valley. To the north along the Seaward Range the summits of Mt Uwerau and Te Ao Whekere lay ahead of us begging to be climbed; beyond them, a brown smudge of land and covering cloud marked the southern extremes of the North Island. To our south the Kowhai Valley suddenly looked very small, the tin bivouac a silver speck in the snow visible only through binoculars. The scale of the surroundings emphasised the vulnerability of the Kowhai Valley and of Hutton's shearwaters themselves. It was an awe-inspiring scene, and turning back to look over the Clarence Valley and Inland Kaikoura Range I was seized with the complete conviction that I was going to explore as much of this land as was physically possible.

The descent from the summit of Manakau was one of numbed tiredness as we concentrated fiercely to remain focused, well aware that a simple slip is the main cause of accidents in the mountains – and that most slips occur on the way down. With one near-out-of-control standing glissade we rapidly lost height, and three hours after standing on the summit we crawled up the steep rise from the valley to the bivvy in the penumbra of the fading sun. The evening was swift and all I can remember was consuming a vast bag of salt and vinegar chips with several mugs of tea, and the vivid snap of a piece of river-ice cracking in a large whisky.

The New Zealand Alpine Club Himalayan Expedition team at the end of the 1954 trip. Front row from left: Charles Evans, George Lowe, Colin Todd and Da Tensing; centre row: Norman Hardie, Bill Beaven and Geoff Harrow; back row: Urkien, Kuncha, Ang Dawa and Ang Temba. From *East of Everest* (Hodder & Stoughton, 1956).

4. An ornithological mystery

In 1954 Sir Edmund Hillary led the New Zealand Alpine Club's Himalayan Expedition to the Barun Valley in Nepal. Lying between the giant peaks of Everest and Makalu, the Barun Valley had seldom been visited and was largely unmapped. It also contained many of the Himalaya's unclimbed peaks in country that, in Hillary's words, was 'a confused mass of icepeaks and hidden valleys'.[1] Hillary had explored the outer fringes of this area in 1951 with the legendary explorer and mountaineer, Eric Shipton. After attempts to climb the peak of Cho Oyu had failed in 1952, Hillary, Shipton and future Everest team members Charles Evans and George Lowe had entered the Barun Valley for the first time and climbed three snow peaks. While there they spied another peak, 'one of the loveliest mountains I have seen,' according to Hillary, and, as his companion George Lowe described it, 'worthy of an expedition'.[2] The team called it Baruntse.

In 1952 Hillary and fellow New Zealander George Lowe had formed plans for an expedition to climb Baruntse, and the Nepalese authorities had granted permission to return for the attempt in 1954. In the meantime, the year 1953 'was one of some importance to George and me', as Hillary wrote in understated fashion a few years later.[3] It was, of course, the year when Hillary and Sherpa Tensing made the first ascent of Mt Everest, supported by Lowe, Sir John Hunt and a large team of climbers and Sherpas. On his return to New Zealand Hillary was a global celebrity, in an age when fame was still tied to genuine achievement. After just six short weeks at home, Hillary set off back to the Himalayas as the leader of the 1954 New Zealand expedition.

Accompanying Hillary on the expedition were two British climbers: Charles Evans – an experienced hand from Everest and other Himalayan trips – and the expedition doctor, Michael Ball. Selected from a large number of applicants, the

Geoff Harrow, Norman Hardie & Bill Beaven at a reunion of survivors of the 1954 New Zealand Alpine Club Barun expedition, c. 2014. Photo Colin Monteath/Hedgehoghouse.com

largest component of the expedition came from New Zealand and consisted of Hillary's long-term friend and Himalayan climber George Lowe, as well as Bill Beaven, Norman Hardie, Jim McFarlane, Colin Todd, Brian Wilkins and a young climber from Christchurch named Geoff Harrow.

It is fair to say the expedition was not Hillary's finest hour. While surveying the Barun Glacier McFarlane and Wilkins fell into a deep crevasse. Besides a cut forehead and some bruises, Wilkins was uninjured, and after a desperate scramble was able to climb out of the crevasse and descend to the camp, leaving the injured and immobile McFarlane where he lay. On reaching camp Wilkins alerted Hillary, who immediately ascended the glacier with five Sherpas in order to undertake a rescue before darkness fell. Unable to climb down Wilkins' route, Hillary was lowered on a rope by the Sherpas into the glacier's depths, but could not reach McFarlane. In his haste Hillary tied the rope straight around his waist, and as the Sherpas pulled him back up, the rope rode up and tightened around his chest and ribs. It then cut through the lip of the crevasse, jamming Hillary underneath. He was eventually pulled around the crevasse's overhanging edge, but at the cost of three broken ribs.[4] McFarlane was rescued the next morning and evacuated with severely frostbitten hands and feet. Hillary remained at the camp but, with his injuries, was limited in what he could accomplish.

The expedition continued and began to reconnoitre a route up the slopes of Makalu, the world's fifth-highest peak. The climb was going well: four camps were established on the mountain and the leading team had reached 23,000ft with good ground to the summit ahead of them. Unable to contain his frustration at resting in base camp, Hillary joined the team on the mountain. It proved to be a mistake. With his broken ribs and possibly also suffering from malaria he collapsed, and the attempt on the peak was replaced with the urgent task of carrying him back to lower altitude. Hillary's expedition was over and he returned to Kathmandu with McFarlane and the expedition's doctor.

The other team members stayed on. Although efforts to climb Makalu were now called off, in a burst of activity they climbed a series of peaks (bringing the expedition's total to 19 peaks over 20,000ft), surveyed the upper Barun plateau, and made the first direct crossing of the Barun–Imja watershed. The expedition's ultimate objective, the 23,497ft peak of Baruntse, was summited on 30 May 1954, the last 1500ft a steep and difficult ice ridge. Hillary and Lowe's book on the expedition, *East of Everest*, was published in 1956 and the cover features a striking photo of two tiny figures above a yawning drop, slowly cutting steps along the steep slope of the summit ridge of Baruntse. The two figures in the photo, and the first to reach the summit, were New Zealanders Colin Todd and Geoff Harrow.

Geoff Harrow's interest in the mountains had been kindled when he was 14 years old by a visit to the Carrington Hut at the head of the Waimakariri Valley in Arthur's Pass, where he encountered members of the Canterbury Mountaineering Club. He soon became a member himself and developed a passion for tramping and climbing; over the coming years he climbed many new peaks and routes in New Zealand. One of his most notable efforts was in January 1953 when he climbed the east face of Mt Sefton, a peak that rears up and dominates the view from Mount Cook Village. In 1969 an article reviewing developments in New Zealand climbing over the previous decades, published in the prestigious *Alpine Journal* of the Alpine Club of London, described this as a breakthrough for a new climbing generation, one that sparked off the modern phase of New Zealand mountaineering. It was the first such climb by a guideless party and 'the first occasion on which a face of such steepness and exposure had been attempted in New Zealand', causing climbers in New Zealand to rethink what was technically possible.[5]

After Baruntse in 1954 Geoff returned to New Zealand to fatherhood and a steady job. While these changes spelled the end to his time in the highest mountains, they did not hamper his other pursuit – a passion for wildlife. As a boy growing up

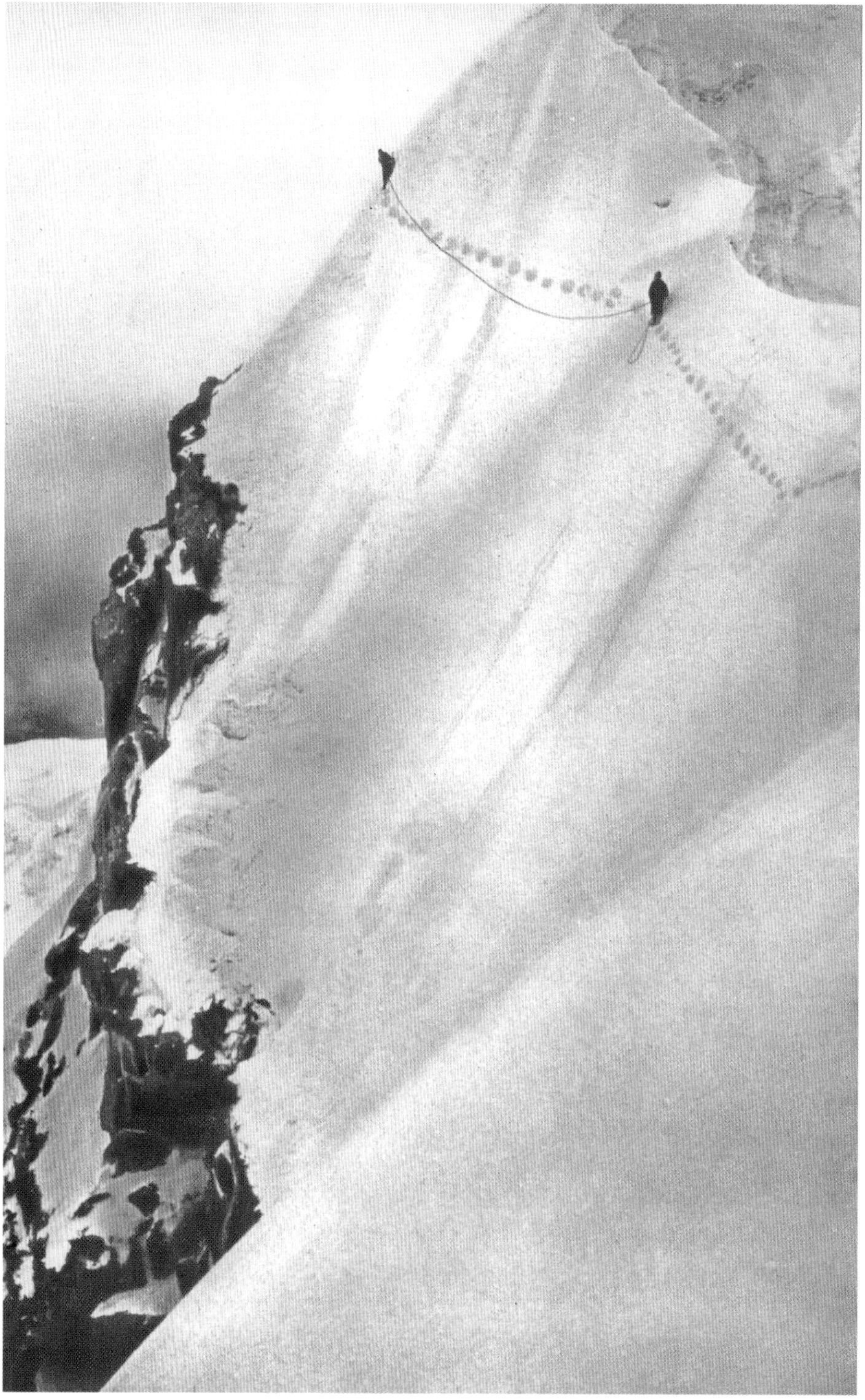

A young Geoff Harrow, 1954, during the New Zealand Alpine Club Himalayan Expedition. From *East of Everest* (Hodder & Stoughton, 1956)

OPPOSITE: Colin Todd and Geoff Harrow on the summit ridge of Mt Baruntse, 1954. Photograph by Bill Beaven, from *East of Everest* (Hodder & Stoughton, 1956)

in Christchurch Geoff had developed a keen interest in wildlife. He and a number of school friends were members of the Canterbury Museum Bird Club, which met after school on Fridays. The club hosted regular talks by staff from Canterbury Museum, and occasional visits by the renowned ornithologist Dr Robert Falla (later Sir Robert Falla), whose exploits included being a member of Douglas Mawson's 1929–31 Antarctic expedition, and manning one of the secret observation posts established on New Zealand's subantarctic islands to watch for German ships during World War II.[6] While Geoff was interested in all forms of natural history, as a boy he was hooked on ferns and spent several summers trying to find and identify every fern species growing in Christchurch's Port Hills. After Baruntse he still visited the hills to fish or bring back venison for the table, trips that kept alive his enthusiasm for the mountains he loved and for being in and among New Zealand's wildlife and wild places.

In December 1964 Geoff's work took him to the small coastal town of Kaikoura on the east coast of the South Island. Today Kaikoura is famous around the world for the whales and wildlife that attract thousands of tourists each year, and, more recently, for the devastating earthquakes of 2016, but back in the 1960s it was a small country town. Geoff stayed in the town's first motel, run by brothers Ivan and Archie Hislop. The Hislops supplied vegetables, fruit and honey to many shops and households; they also worked as deerstalkers and knew Kaikoura's surrounding hills and ranges well. Geoff had seen the burrows of sooty shearwaters on Banks Peninsula and on Stewart Island, and while chatting to Ivan at the motel one evening he casually remarked that the Kaikoura Peninsula and headlands off the Kaikoura coast looked like ideal places for sooty shearwaters to nest.

'Do you mean muttonbirds?' Ivan replied, using the generic name for the shearwater chicks that are traditionally hunted by Māori and are still served in fish-and-chip shops of New Zealand's South Island. Geoff nodded and Ivan continued, 'Not at sea level, no. They're way up in the mountains at five to six thousand feet, up by the snow line.' Geoff was surprised, but Ivan carried on: 'There are burrows there and dead birds. We never actually saw any live ones, just the burrows and all the feathers and dead birds – plenty of them.'

Geoff spent the night at the motel scratching his head and feeling sceptical of Ivan's talk of the burrows in the hills, especially as the memories were more than a decade old. The idea of muttonbirds right up by the snow line was bizarre – the environment would have been utterly alien as a breeding habitat for any New Zealand seabirds. The next morning he decided to speak to Archie Hislop, who was next door with his beehives, to see if he could confirm his brother's tale. Archie's reception surprised Geoff, for they had met several times before and Archie had always been really friendly. This time his response was the opposite. 'No, I'm not telling you anything about them at all. They are doing all right as they are and don't need any interfering. People are often asking about them and I know what they want – they want to harvest them.'

Geoff drove back to Christchurch puzzling over what he had been told. Ivan and Archie's contrasting answers both somehow supported the concept that there was truth to the story. As baffling as it seemed, Geoff believed them.

Over the coming weeks he discussed what he had heard with New Zealand bird photographer and author M.F. Soper. Soper knew of no seabird that nested at such a great height but said it could explain why the nesting sites of Hutton's shearwaters had never been found.[7] Gregory Mathews – not unreasonably, given the species' first collection site – had suggested the Snares Islands as the likely breeding site.[8] But visits to the Snares in 1947 and careful searches over two weeks at the height of the likely breeding season had failed to find any trace of the birds. The great American seabird researcher Robert Cushman Murphy, who was among the visitors to the Snares in 1947, concluded that it must nest further south.[9] Don Serventy's observations of flocks of Hutton's shearwaters off Kangaroo Island and earlier records off Adelaide suggested that the bird could be breeding off Australia, but searches of likely islands there had revealed nothing.

In 1947 several dead birds were found near Pukerua Bay on the southwest coast of New Zealand's North Island. These birds and another, 'a somewhat moth-eaten, dried, flat skin from Kapiti Island', held in the Dominion Museum since 1934, hinted that Hutton's shearwaters might well occur in New Zealand.[10] Further observations came in the 1950s, mostly of Hutton's shearwaters that had crash-landed in the lights of the Lyttelton–Wellington ferry.[11] These included recently fledged and immature birds, further suggesting that the breeding colonies were located somewhere in New Zealand.

Interest in finding the breeding site of Hutton's shearwater was spurred on by the discovery in 1948 of the takahē, a giant flightless rail, in the remote Murchison Mountains in Fiordland in the South Island. The discovery caused a sensation at the time, as the takahē had not been seen for 50 years and was believed extinct. The bird was known only from four specimens collected between 1848 and 1898, and two lithographs by Johannes Gerardus Keulemans included in Walter Buller's *A History of the Birds of New Zealand*.

Like the takahē, the nesting site of Hutton's shearwater was one of New Zealand's great, unsolved natural mysteries. It was, in fact, the only New Zealand bird whose breeding biology remained unknown. In 1965 Dr Robert Falla wrote, 'Of the search for nesting places up to 1965 all that need be said here is that every accessible islet and stack from Banks Peninsula to Cook Strait had been examined by several field parties with no result.'[12]

M.F. Soper encouraged Geoff Harrow to return to Kaikoura and follow the lead he had been given.

Looking up the Kowhai Valley from close to the bivvy. Author photo

5. Planning the fieldwork and a research hut

The morning after our climb of Manakau I awoke with sore legs and a dull dehydration headache. I pulled on my down jacket and a hat and staggered stiff-limbed from the bivvy. It was another superb clear day. The morning sun glowed on Manakau's eastern flank and a plume of snow unfurled itself from the summit: it seemed unbelievable that we had been up there the day before. While the Kowhai Valley had looked small and vulnerable from the summit, now that I was in it again the size and complexity of the landscape in front of me was truly impressive. But the question that was beginning to worry me was: how on earth was I going to collect meaningful information on the shearwaters and stoats? That was the real reason for being here, and as I stood outside the bivvy surrounded by this fierce landscape, across which stoats moved effortlessly, and where shearwaters bred in their tens of thousands in areas I couldn't even reach, the enormity of what I had got myself into struck me with force. It was a daunting prospect.

The other major concern was accommodation. The bivvy was only a temporary solution, and although it provided a shelter to sleep and eat in, it was too cramped to work in efficiently. Anyone who has spent more than a few days away in the wilds with a tent will know what it's like. Simply making a cup of tea involved checking the fuel, lighting the stove and waiting for the sooty flames to dissipate, not to mention the 10-minute trip to fetch water from the stream or the interminable wait for snow to melt. The transcription of data from field notebooks had to be done by the light of a head torch while wearing a down jacket, hat and gloves, sitting in a sleeping bag with paper and books crammed onto the bunk – whereas back in Kaikoura I had solar panels and a laptop computer. A proper hut would greatly improve the efficiency of our work, as well as the comfort of doing it.

During the months before beginning my first season I had visited numerous huts around New Zealand in the course of fieldwork and climbing trips, and had gleaned various ideas about the way a hut should be put together. I had put forward a suggested layout to DOC staff in Nelson and Kaikoura: a closed-off area for sleeping, loads of benches and shelves for working and as many windows as possible. The hut was duly built, and by rights it should already have been in the valley, but an early, heavy autumnal dump of snow on the mountains had put paid to flying the materials in before the winter. Now that the snow was beginning to melt, the gear had arrived and I was keen to get things started.

Mike emerged from the bivvy looking similarly stiff and sore. After another coffee, enjoyed while seated on a pile of timber that had been dropped off by the helicopter the previous week, we began working. With spades in hand we walked 20 metres from the bivvy to the site marked out for the hut and began clearing the last snow from the area. Next we measured out and marked spots for each of the hut's 18 foundation holes. More digging followed, first of all to uproot and topple the biggest snow tussocks, which we rolled down the slope out of the way, after which we tackled the tough and bristling speargrass. Despite our leather gloves and thick clothes, these found ways of spiking our hands, legs and arms no matter how carefully we approached them. The speargrass plants left deep, starchy and sweet-smelling tap-roots that we struggled to pull out. Within the roots fat grubs writhed in the light, larvae of the speargrass weevil whose adult forms appeared each evening and methodically, like small clockwork toys, made their way up and down the bivvy walls.

With the smallest possible area cleared we began digging foundation holes, each 50 centimetres square and up to a metre deep: having felt the bivvy shake and move in the ferocious northwest winds that hit the valley, we knew solid foundations were definitely in order. As we dug we discussed work options for the forthcoming field season, for now that the snow was beginning to melt the birds would soon be back in their burrows and egg-laying would follow. Our first few weeks during September had given us a feel for the valley; although there were still many areas to explore and daunting challenges ahead, I knew we had enough of the picture to start planning the coming study.

Any fieldwork study has three essentials. First and perhaps most important is to define what the study aims to find out. The key issue for Hutton's shearwaters was to evaluate the impact of introduced stoats on the population and determine what factor, or factors, had caused the restriction of range to two small, high-altitude sites in the Kaikoura ranges. Second, any study stands on the shoulders of previous knowledge. The prior studies of both Hutton's and related species undertaken by

DOC and, before that, by Geoff Harrow, were vital for setting a baseline and the priorities for what would come next. Third, and as important as the first two, is the need to be adaptable. My experience of fieldwork had taught me that no matter how much careful planning, reading and preparation you have done, the reality is always different. Biological fieldwork is simply like that; having the wherewithal to spot where the work is diverging and to maximise the opportunities presented is essential.

The key task was to examine the productivity and survival of Hutton's shearwaters, and to measure how many eggs, chicks and adult birds were being killed by stoats. These questions had to be answered within the challenging physical environment of the valley and also, critically, within the constraints of the shearwaters' breeding cycle. Geoff Harrow's previous work and knowledge of the phenology of other shearwater species had provided a clear picture of this cycle.

After spending the winter in waters off Australia, Hutton's shearwaters return to the Kaikoura mountains in the early spring. Throughout September and October they alternate between flying in to the mountain breeding sites at night and spending time at sea off Kaikoura feeding on the area's rich marine resources. During this period birds are courting and establishing or re-establishing the bonds between breeding pairs. Once the snow has cleared, the birds visit the colonies for several days at a time, busily digging out their burrows and creating enlarged nesting chambers. Females lay a single egg in late October or early November and thereafter the pair take turns: one member spends up to a week incubating while its partner returns to sea to feed, before they swap places. After nearly two months, the egg hatches and both 'parents' spend the next three months flying out to sea at dawn to find food and returning every fifth to seventh night to feed the growing chick. Finally, around mid-March, the shearwater chicks and adults depart to sea. The adults spend five months away and return the following spring; the young birds remain at sea for three to four years before those that survive return to the colony to begin breeding.

It was now early October. In the two weeks since our climb the winter snows had melted from the shearwater-burrowed tussock slopes and egg-laying was about to start. Mike and I needed to choose a sample of burrows to monitor in order to be able to calculate the breeding success of the birds within the valley. We had a head start on this, as the work of DOC's Alison Davis and Brian Paton had provided an estimate of breeding success in the Kowhai colony. While that information was vital it was also limited, because it came from only three out of around 30 sub-colonies and, more critically, from small patches within each of these three sub-colonies. It wasn't clear how representative these results were, given the sub-colonies' varying altitudes and aspects, with some of them covered in a tangle of trees and others in sparse tussock grasses.

The need to accurately monitor a wider area was especially important considering the level of threat posed by stoats, and the patchiness of their hunting. For example, a female stoat might set up her den site in the middle of a sub-colony and proceed over the season to eat every egg, chick and adult bird in every burrow in a 50-metre radius, while not touching a single burrow in the surrounding area. Anyone measuring breeding success and adult survival from a sample of burrows close to the den site would conclude an ecological disaster was under way. Conversely, if they had sampled burrows 100 metres from the stoat's den, they might conclude that stoats were having zero impact on the shearwaters. The reality, as always, likely lay somewhere between these extremes, meaning we needed to monitor the impact of stoats across as wide an area as possible.

We decided to expand the number of sub-colonies to be monitored from three to nine, and to select sites across a range of different vegetation types, aspects and altitudes to better reflect the entire breeding colony. We would also continue to monitor the small areas within the three sub-colonies that had been checked previously, but include other burrows from across the wider area of these three sites. Data from all of the burrows would provide estimates on the number of pairs that went on to lay an egg, as well as the success of hatching, fledging and overall breeding. In addition, checks of burrows would provide an estimate of the number of adults and large chicks that were being killed by stoats; unlike the smaller chicks and eggs, which stoats would remove completely, the remains of the larger birds were left in the burrow after they had been killed and fed upon.

Another unknown was the number of adult birds being killed on the surface of the colony at night. Estimating the level of these mortalities required a different approach, so we decided to establish a series of transect lines traversing seven spatially distinct sub-colonies. Dead birds, or the remains of dead birds, were likely to remain on the ground for several weeks at a time in the snow, so by carefully walking along the same transect lines every two weeks we would be able to identify new mortalities and estimate their numbers.

Over the coming weeks we continued our exploration of the valley and began selecting the sub-colonies to monitor. We avoided any that were too fragile to walk on regularly, or not safe to approach; after one harrowing visit to two particularly steep colonies on the opposite side of the gorge, we christened these areas 'Death' and 'Double Death' and made sure we never returned. Within the selected colonies we began to mark transect lines using spray-painted bamboo poles and knotted tussocks, and we marked individual burrows to be monitored with poles and numbered metal tags that we stamped in the evenings back at the bivvy.

During two days of murky weather, when the mist was too thick to set up transects, we completed digging the hut foundation holes and radioed Kaikoura that they were ready. A week later the helicopter reappeared with another load of timber. Also on board were Keith Dunlop and Dave Walford from the Kaikoura DOC office, who quickly assembled the foundation frame and piles for the hut. With the weather due to pack in, the helicopter came early the next morning to pick the guys up and brought us 16 bags of cement. The bad weather failed to materialise, however, and we made the most of the opportunity to mix and shovel concrete, a job not made easier by the need to collect water from Col Stream in two 20-litre jerrycans and carry it back. We mixed the concrete in a plastic barrel-mixer, which we rolled back and forth between the tussocks before pouring the mix into the foundation holes and firmly packing it down around the piles. The physical work felt good and we completed the job in an afternoon: all 16 bags were empty and the foundations and frame well and truly anchored.

Ten days later Keith and Dave came up once more to put the final bolts in the frame and double-check the measurements. Everything was ready for the arrival of the hut. As the two sections of the hut were too heavy for the normal helicopter DOC used, we were relying on assistance from the New Zealand Air Force, who had agreed to do the lift as a training exercise. The day was set, but the evening before, the weather began to turn, and tell-tale clouds of a gusty norwester appeared above the summit of Manakau at the head of the valley. I radioed the DOC office in Kaikoura and we agreed to postpone the lift for 24 hours.

A wild night followed, during which neither Mike nor I got much sleep as the bivvy strained under the buffeting wind. Gust after gust swept down the valley, each made worse by the sound that preceded it. Lying in our bunks we could hear the approaching blasts ricocheting from bluff to bluff before thumping into the bivvy with a hail of small rocks and pebbles.

The next day, tired and bleary-eyed, we put out more bamboo poles to mark the route for transects through two sub-colonies. Mike struggled through the thicket of mountain ribbonwood trees in Hoheria sub-colony while I headed higher up the valley to Top sub-colony. As I finished marking the transect line, the norwester switched to a southerly and a thick mist began snaking its way up the valley. Within minutes I was in cloud, and by the time I reached the bivvy the weather had deteriorated into hail and snow. After writing up the day's notes and a late afternoon kip we cooked dinner and, following a bit of indecision on the whereabouts of the kea, set the radio aerial out early at 8pm. The radio crackled to life with its usual whine and we caught the tail end of that day's hunting tally. The signal dissolved into static and I dashed out to re-align the aerial and improve the reception. On my return we caught the tail end of a sentence: '… had a hut for the shearwater boys'.

I glanced at Mike in puzzlement. Did he say *had*? No, he can't have, we must have misheard. The radio came back to life and the hunters asked the question my brain had been refusing to contemplate. 'What do you mean *had* a hut? Over.'

In horror we heard that the hut had been moved the previous day to a large open paddock so that the air force could pick it up. During the night's storm it had been flipped by the wind and smashed to pieces. I sat open-mouthed in shock, feeling numb and hollow. Mike sat on the bottom bunk, slowly shaking his head in disbelief. I went outside to take in the aerial and spent longer than normal winding it up, alternately cursing the ill fortune we had been dealt and contemplating how we were going to cope with the changed situation. Returning to the bivvy I squeezed past Mike and crouched down, pulling out boxes stuffed under the bottom bunk until I found the one I wanted. 'There's only one thing for it,' I said, producing the bottle of single malt I had kept hidden to celebrate the hut's arrival.

'Alcohol.'

The next day might have been a bit blurry but Mike and I were out early doing the only thing we could: continuing to mark transects and burrows. The imminent start of the shearwater breeding season wasn't going to await the arrival of a research hut or anything else.

To monitor what was going on at the end of a bird's two- to three-metre-long burrow we had two options. The first was simply to dig an access hatch to the burrow, either directly above the nesting chamber or above the tunnel and in reach of the nest. Hatches were covered by large flat rocks, wooden boards and plastic trays, or, for the most frequently checked burrows, screw-top inspection hatches bought from a plumbing supplier. Choosing the location for a hatch was problematic – it could take anything from 20 minutes to a good hour to find the right spot in the burrow, and long, convoluted burrows often required three or more holes to be dug, and plugged, in order to find the nesting chamber. In subsequent seasons we would find that the shearwaters seemed programmed to extend their burrows each year; at the start of every season new hatches had to be placed over a third of the burrows.

The alternative was a 'burrowscope', a piece of equipment that allowed us to check what was happening at the end of a burrow without digging. I liked and loathed this device in equal measure. It consisted of a thick, flexible three-metre tube similar to the corrugated hose of a vacuum cleaner. An electrical cable ran the length of the tube and connected at the far end to a tiny video camera surrounded by a dozen infra-red LEDs. At the other end was a 10-centimetre-square black-and-white TV screen. The camera head could be swung from side to side by twisting a handle. Operating the burrowscope was a two-person job. One was glued to the screen, controlling the camera head by twisting the handle, a black cloth over their head to cut out the light. The other lay prostrate on the ground, one arm jammed painfully up a burrow pushing the tube as far in as possible and twisting it to right or left. The TV watcher would 'drive' the burrowscope, calling out a series of directions to the person controlling the tube at the burrow entrance: 'Right a bit, right again, and again, in four inches, stop! Turn right, and right, and back left, left again, and forward …'

It was slow and frustrating work, and the irony of sitting in one of the most spectacular settings in New Zealand staring at a grainy 10-centimetre screen with a sheet over my head was rich, to put it mildly. As well, the device required unusually acute spatial awareness. While staring at the small fuzzy TV screen your eye 'became' the camera on the end of the tube. You had to construct a mental image of the burrow, noting key features to navigate past and back, and side branches to return to and explore in case the nest was down there. Once you had found a bird you had to determine whether it was sitting on an egg, a chick or an empty nest. The bird was usually aware that something was up – the scraping progress of the tube must have sounded like a giant earthworm boring its way through the soil. Some would react by furiously pecking the camera while others calmly ignored it.

The next bit was delicate: the object was to carefully inch the tube forward and slip the camera head beneath the belly of the bird until, with a gentle upwards twist of the handle and camera head, you could make the bird stand and get a clear view of the nest. The mission was complicated by the fact that the breast feathers of Hutton's shearwaters are snowy white; it was not enough just to glimpse something white in the nest – you had to determine whether it was in fact an egg. With practice it became relatively straightforward, but the sharp confines of a burrow sometimes meant you had to approach a bird from the 'wrong' side or with an obscured view of the nest. We became expert at determining from a glimpse of feather patterns and overall size exactly which part of the bird the camera was focused on.

Mounting a delicate video camera and infra-red LEDs on the end of a tube was one thing, but securing it against the knocks, twisting and thrashing required to get it to the end of a three-metre burrow was another. Early in that first season, after one particularly hard blow, the burrowscope died. Despite a ribald cursing of the fieldwork gods and a frustrating evening spent dismembering the head into a jumble of electrical parts, it was no good. A trip to Otago University in Dunedin was required to get it working again.

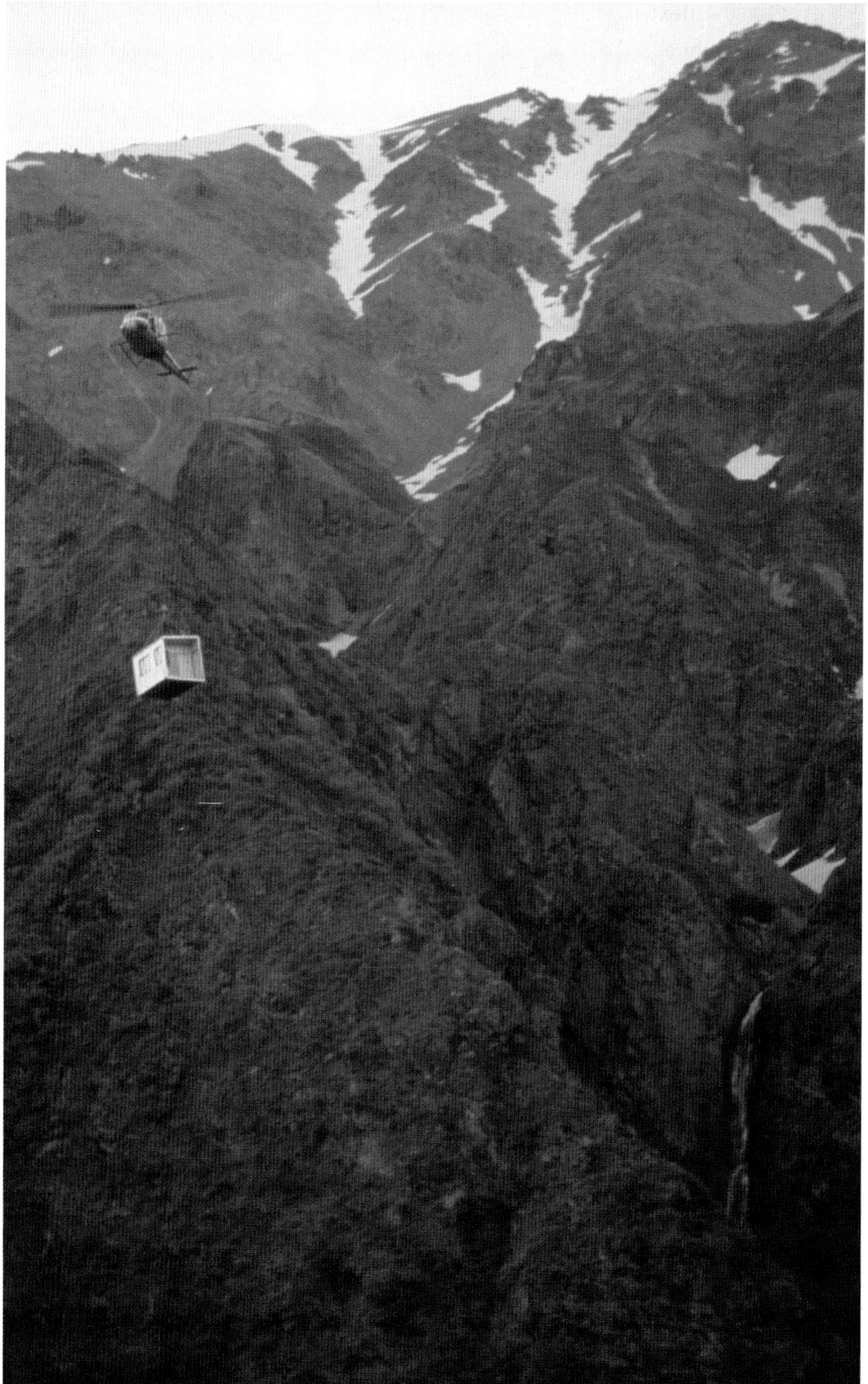

I set off the next morning, weighed down by the tube and box but otherwise travelling as light as I dared. I dropped down the thin ridge from the bivvy to the Kowhai River, scrambled carefully up the other side, then traversed a narrow deer track above the steep gorge and waterfall that fell below me. From here a hard climb up the mountainside took me to the ridge crest, which I followed, running wherever it was not too steep until I reached the final ridge above the Lower Kowhai Hut in the valley floor. The descent from here was a pig, scrambling among rock bluffs and dry waterfalls hidden by tangles of scrub, bush and briars. Once I reached the main valley the descent was straightforward, if damp, with the rivers higher than normal due to snowmelt.

In Dunedin a couple of days later I took the burrowscope in to the Zoology Department for repairs and reinforcing and set about stocking up on supplies and kit. While there I received the phone call I had been hoping for. Although weeks late the news was good: the manufacturer had rebuilt the hut in record time, and good weather and air force availability had coincided. The hut was now firmly bolted in place in the Kowhai Valley.

OPPOSITE: The hut arrives at last. Photo courtesy of Mike Dunlop

One of the very first images of an adult Hutton's shearwater taken in 1965 shortly after the discovery of the Kowhai Valley colony. Photo courtesy of Geoff Harrow

6. Discovering the nesting grounds

On Saturday 20 February 1965 Geoff Harrow set off alone with a light pack of food, ice axe, tarp and blanket, and armed with a provisional Lands & Survey map and the rough directions that motelier Ivan Hislop had given him. The day was foggy and Geoff made the first of many crossings of the Kowhai River as he followed the watercourse up its shale and gravel bed. As he progressed, the valley closed in and the river changed, falling over boulders and around tight bends and growing deeper. Opposite the Kowhai Saddle the river narrowed to an impassable gorge and Geoff was forced to climb a steep face on the river's true right. Pushing his way through mānuka and kānuka scrub and the painful hooks of bush lawyer and matagouri, he climbed higher, following deer tracks where he could, until he emerged on a narrow tussock-covered ridge that rose at an easier angle to 1600 metres above sea level.

Geoff was now in a bind: the steep, rough country was unknown to him, and because of the fog the climb had taken longer than planned. He had intended to camp at the head of the valley, as suggested by Ivan, but it was already late afternoon and he'd been walking for eight hours, so with no view available he decided to camp further along the ridge. The first priority was water – he hadn't had a drink in five hours. Dropping his pack, he descended 300 metres in search of a source, knotting snow tussocks and building rock cairns every 20 metres or so in order to find his way back to his kit in the thick fog. His thirst satisfied, he continued on for another two hours before dropping down to a flat, where he decided to stop for the night. There he hunted around unsuccessfully under tussocks looking for burrows. Nonetheless, he hoped he might be able to hear the birds, even if he wasn't near their burrows. After cooking a meal and pulling up some snow grass and koromiko scrub with his axe to serve as a mattress, he settled down with his blanket and tarp for the night.

He didn't hear a thing – or rather, didn't hear anything unusual. Like most others at the time, Geoff didn't know what he was supposed to be listening for.

Awake early the next morning, Geoff found himself in patchy fog and surrounded by a herd of feral goats. He set off again, determined to reach the area Ivan had described. Traversing the slope he came to a flat area below which a steep hillside of compacted rock descended to the gorge of the Kowhai River. A deer track dropped off the flat, and 150 metres along this he spotted a pile of feathers and bones. It wasn't that fresh, but picking up the carcass he saw the distinctive hooked beak and webbed feet of a muttonbird. He could not believe his eyes. Geoff recalls now that anyone watching would have thought he was a madman: 'I was holding a foul-smelling old shearwater carcass in both hands and dancing and wildly whooping for joy.'[1]

He carried on down the deer track and scrambled carefully down a large waterfall in the main Kowhai River before climbing over a thin vegetated ridge and descending into a narrow creek on the other side. Here he saw more feathers and some white guano among the rocks, and 300 metres further upstream he discovered the first of many burrows dug on the slope above. He stuck his arm down as many as he could locate but couldn't find or reach anything. Nearby was a fresh maggoty specimen that he dropped into a cloth bag along with two older, dried carcasses.

Climbing up from the creek onto a broad tussock ridge, Geoff found more areas of burrowed ground. From here the valley opened out before him: the slope he was standing on dropped down to the valley floor, and opposite and upstream lay further areas of tussock interspersed with scree slopes and rock bluffs. He would have carried on, but a long walk followed by a long drive to Christchurch lay ahead of him in order to be back at work on Monday morning.

It was 1965: 75 years since Henry Travers' shots had been fired from the *Hinemoa* as it lay off the Snares Islands, and more than 50 years since Gregory Mathews' description of the species. As Geoff Harrow turned to begin his descent he might well have whooped again, for he had his 'takahē': he had discovered the nesting grounds of Hutton's shearwater.

Geoff returned to Christchurch late that Sunday night and wearily took himself to work on Monday, but that evening he went to Canterbury Museum. While he was confident of his find, it was critical to have the four carcasses he had collected formally identified. However, this visit unleashed further confusion, for the museum had only one Hutton's shearwater skin at the time – labelled 'doubtful'. It was indeed doubtful and later turned out to be another shearwater species altogether.

Unable to confirm the identity of the birds, Geoff had only one option: to send the specimens to Dr Robert Falla at the Dominion Museum in Wellington, whose knowledge of New Zealand and Australian birds was second to none. The carcasses must have been pretty ripe by the time they reached Wellington, but Falla's reaction to the olfactory overload is unrecorded. Geoff was on tenterhooks for news. A few days later, on 1 March 1965, he received the telegram confirming his hopes: 'Your specimens are all *Puffinus huttoni*.'[2]

Reaction to the discovery of the nesting grounds of Hutton's shearwaters has been largely lost over time, but for the scientific community within New Zealand and abroad it was a big deal, and a brief report of the discovery even reached the pages of the *New York Times*. Geoff received congratulatory letters from ornithologists all over New Zealand, and R.S. Macarthur, the chief soil conservator for the Marlborough Catchment Board, described the find as 'of the same importance as the notornis find in Fiordland'.[3] An amateur naturalist who had ignored perceived wisdom – that the birds only bred on the coast – and instead followed clues to search the remotest areas of the Kaikoura mountains, had solved an ornithological mystery of 75 years' standing.

Geoff made many more visits to the Kaikoura region, asking hunters, musterers and farmers he encountered if they had ever seen or heard of shearwaters in the area. A few who had hunted the highest blocks or mustered sheep on the top stations had heard of muttonbirds nesting in burrows high in the mountains, and knew that young birds – conceivably shearwaters – were sometimes picked up on the coast and inland. These reports, most from the 1920s and 1930s, confirmed that shearwaters had formerly occurred at many sites in both the Seaward and Inland Kaikoura ranges.[4]

Several accounts indicated that the shearwater had been an important food resource for Māori in the area. One of Geoff's conversations was with Kaikoura resident Herbie Melville, in 1969. Despite being in his eighties Herbie still worked repairing fences on Middlehurst Station in the Awatere Valley. He recalled talking to an elderly Māori man in the early 1900s who had described annual muttonbirding expeditions up the Clarence River to the head of the Dee Stream, under Tapuae-o-Uenuku. Parties would take supplies of pāua shellfish with them for the two- to three-day journey. Pāua-shell middens have since been found at 2100 metres on the bush line on the southern flanks of Tapuae-o-Uenuku, suggesting that many such expeditions took place.[5]

A grimmer tale is recorded in Arthur Hugh Carrington's history of Ngai Tāhu, which he based on interviews with older Māori in the 1920s and 1930s.[6] Carrington's papers include an account of the long-running feud between the tribes at Kaiapoi and Kaikoura, and the people of Omihi, just south of the Kaikoura peninsula. After a series of skirmishes and minor battles in which the Omihi people prevailed, the Kaiapoi and Kaikoura tribes planned a further attack on Omihi. Carrington records:

> Kaiapoi knew of course the time at which all of the people of Omihi would be away in the mountains on their hunting grounds, catching and preserving birds, and decided to make their attack when the men, heavily laden with the result of their labours, would be returning to the pā.[7]

An attack on an unarmed group lacked the mana of a formal battle, so this was an unusual plan. But the chief of Omihi, Haumataki, foresaw the attack in a dream. 'Before the men of Omihi set out for Kaitarau, the mountain above Kaikoura … he told them he was sure that the danger of war threatened them.' But his men objected to taking their weapons, arguing, 'who would be so foolish as to belittle themselves by attacking a party engaged in the snaring and preserving of game?' They proceeded unarmed 'into the mountains and preserved their mutton-birds'.[8] The attack followed as Haumataki had foreseen, and the Omihi people were ambushed at the flat called Otāhuna as they returned heavily laden with birds.

Whether the birds referred to were Hutton's shearwaters is uncertain; however, Carrington's account is crystal clear on the presence of muttonbirds in the mountains above Kaikoura. Kaitarau, 'the mountain above Kaikoura', was the early name for Mt Uwerau, the peak above the hut in the Kowhai Valley. Otāhuna is the name for Swyncombe Station, which borders the Kowhai River at the foothills of the Kaikoura Range. Carrington's and other records provide enough evidence that muttonbirds – almost certainly Hutton's shearwaters – were plentiful throughout the Kaikoura mountains until the mid-nineteenth century.

Geoff had always loved 'finding out what was around the next corner' in the hills, and the search for the breeding grounds provided the perfect opportunity. He began a one-man mission to determine the range of Hutton's shearwaters. Each trip required a long drive from Christchurch to Kaikoura on the Friday night – a far slower trip in the 1960s than now – followed by a dawn start on Saturday, a night under a damp tarpaulin (or the stars if the weather was good), followed by an early morning exploration on Sunday before the walk out and the long drive back to Christchurch for work on Monday. Occasionally there were long weekends, but balancing his visits with family and work life was a challenge. There were many family holidays in Kaikoura with the children, during which, Geoff confessed, 'I'd whip up to the colony for a night or two on my own.'[9]

The Kaikoura mountains are not the highest peaks in New Zealand, nor are they the steepest, but the country was and remains wild and unvisited. It's not an easy landscape to get around and requires determination and a strong measure of mountaincraft to navigate safely. Over the next two years Geoff made more than 25 journeys to the area, often on his own but sometimes accompanied by fellow climbers and ornithologists. He found evidence that in the 1920s and 1930s up to eight shearwater breeding colonies had existed over a broad 30-kilometre swathe of the Seaward Kaikoura Range, 9–24 kilometres from the coast. Earlier records of Mt Tapuae-o-Uenuku indicate that the birds once bred even further inland. None of these sites were below 1200 metres in elevation, and some were as high as 1800 metres.

In the 1960s a few birds still nested in the headwaters of Snowflake Stream and others on the southeast flank of Mt Fyffe, but the areas were badly eroded, with only a few burrows remaining in what had clearly been far larger breeding sites.

After two years of searching for and uncovering the range of Hutton's shearwater, Geoff was interested in finding a study site. The Kowhai Valley, while a large and active colony, was a gruelling five- to six-hour walk and climb from the road end, making it impractical for a weekend visit. He needed somewhere more accessible. One of the local respondents to his enquiries about shearwaters was Sam Pilbrow, who ran the sheep station at Puhi Peaks, high up the Puhi Puhi Valley to the north of Kaikoura. Sam had reported that on foggy nights from September to March shearwaters would regularly crash into the lights around his homestead, and he had often heard birds calling and flying overhead. After three visits exploring the area to the west of the station, Geoff found another extensive colony of Hutton's shearwaters on steep snowgrass bluffs in the headwaters of the Wharekiri Stream below Mt Tarahaka. This colony (now known as Shearwater Stream) and the one in the Kowhai Valley were the last remnants of the former range of Hutton's shearwaters, and the only two sites in New Zealand where the birds remained.

From 1967 to 1978 Geoff focused his efforts at Shearwater Stream, which he could reach in half the time it took to walk in to the Kowhai. He averaged six visits per season over this decade, and made sure they covered at least one night each fortnight of the calendar year in order to establish the birds' return and departure dates to and from the colonies. Over time he carried in a sleeping pad, tarpaulin and spare food, and dug out a sleeping platform in the steep colony. Access to water was an issue, particularly during the dry summer months, and on successive trips he carted in several lengths of corrugated iron, a length of guttering and a jerrycan to build a makeshift water catcher and tank on the hillside. The water tank produced an unexpected bonus: during one season Geoff's son found a brand new species of mountain gecko trapped in it. Like Hutton's shearwater, it was another species endemic to the Kaikoura mountains.[10]

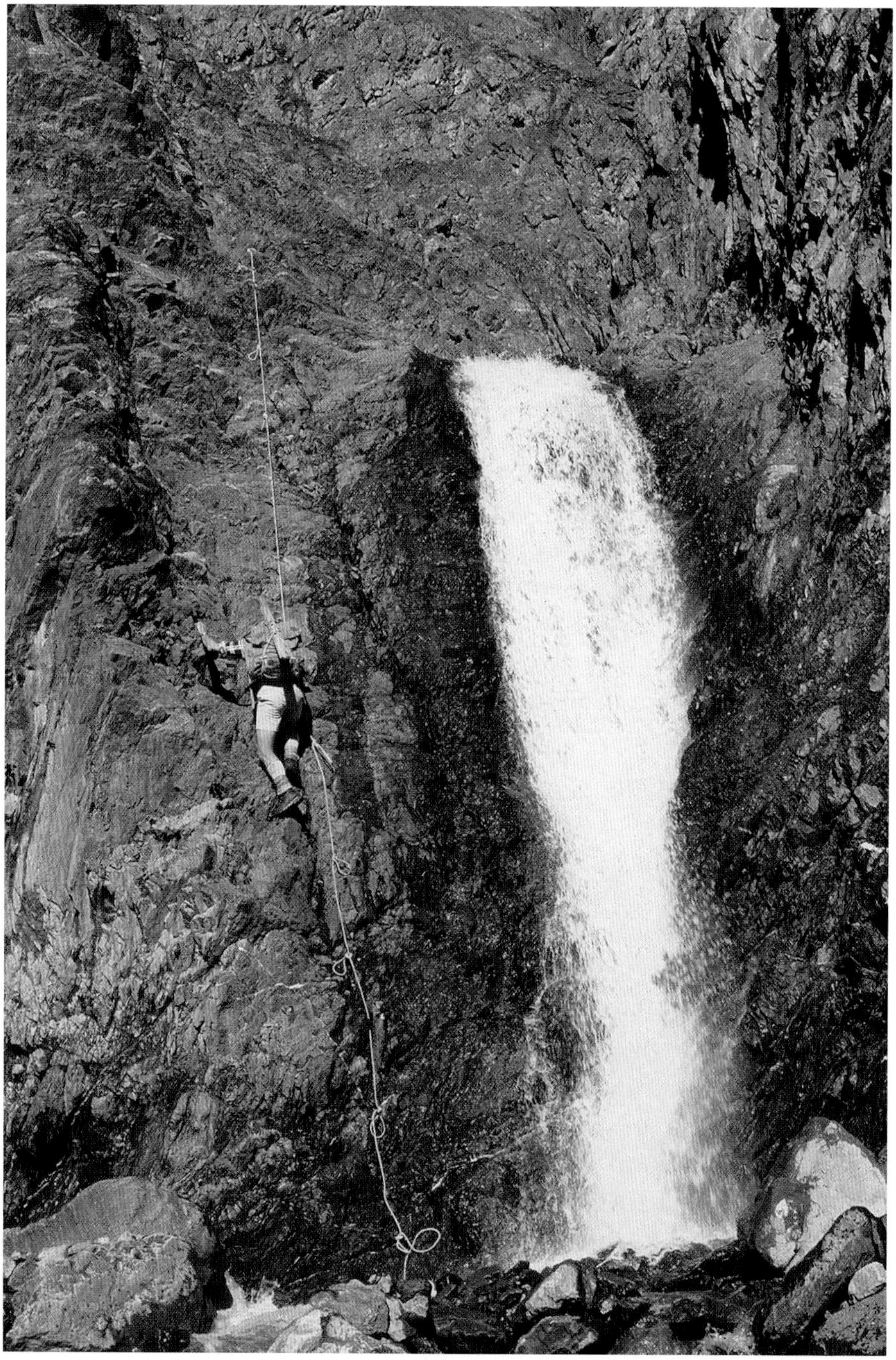

Geoff Harrow climbing the waterfall into the Shearwater Stream colony during his decade-long study of the birds in the 1960s and 1970s. Photo courtesy of Geoff Harrow

Geoff's visits throughout the area and his prolonged study at Shearwater Stream laid the foundation for subsequent research on Hutton's shearwaters. He described himself at the time as an 'amateur ornithologist and middle-aged mountaineer', but it is clear from his observations that he was far more. Geoff gathered information on the species' past and current distribution, described their nesting areas and nest sites, and noted when birds arrived and departed from the colonies and the timing of egg-laying, hatching and chick-rearing.[11] By banding adult birds and marking nests with aluminium tags, he showed that the birds returned to the same burrow each year and remained paired up with the same partner. His work also revealed that the birds could navigate their way to the colonies on even the darkest of nights, flying over 30 kilometres inland through rugged mountain gorges to land unerringly on a steep mountainside within a metre or two of their burrows.

He observed the effect of weather and the phases of the moon on bird numbers and behaviour, and noted the distribution and abundance of fledgling crashes as young birds departed the colony and made their first flight to sea. Geoff also recorded predation; he noted that the New Zealand falcon (kārearea) would pursue departing shearwaters at dawn, and discovered a falcon's feeding site below the Kowhai colony that was littered with shearwater remains. He also watched a far more insidious predator at work right within the shearwater colonies. Stoats, introduced to New Zealand in the late nineteenth century to control rabbits, had spread throughout the land and their devastating impact on New Zealand's native wildlife was well known. Stoats were present and active in both of the remaining colonies, and Geoff recorded that many dead Hutton's shearwaters had injuries to the head and neck that suggested the handiwork of a mustelid.

Concerns about the prospects for Hutton's shearwaters grew. Brian Bell from the Wildlife Division of the Department of Internal Affairs (DIA), the forerunner of DOC, accompanied Geoff into the Kowhai Valley in September 1965, just seven months after he had discovered the site. In fact he joined Geoff on six or seven early trips, along with many young and enthusiastic wildlife cadets. Brian's support was critical, for Geoff knew little about the scientific side of wildlife research. Brian taught Geoff how to band and measure the shearwaters and steered him in many other aspects. He also arranged for the DIA and the Marlborough Catchment Board to take steps to safeguard the Kowhai Valley colony. By the end of 1965 it was formally gazetted as a wildlife reserve – the highest category of legal protection available.

Brian and Geoff began to map out the Kowhai colony and swiftly realised that burrows appeared to be located in every tussock area in the basin above the gorge. The Kowhai Valley was home not to a few hundred birds: it contained tens of

Geoff Harrow with a shearwater chick, Kowhai Valley, February 1966. Photo courtesy of Geoff Harrow

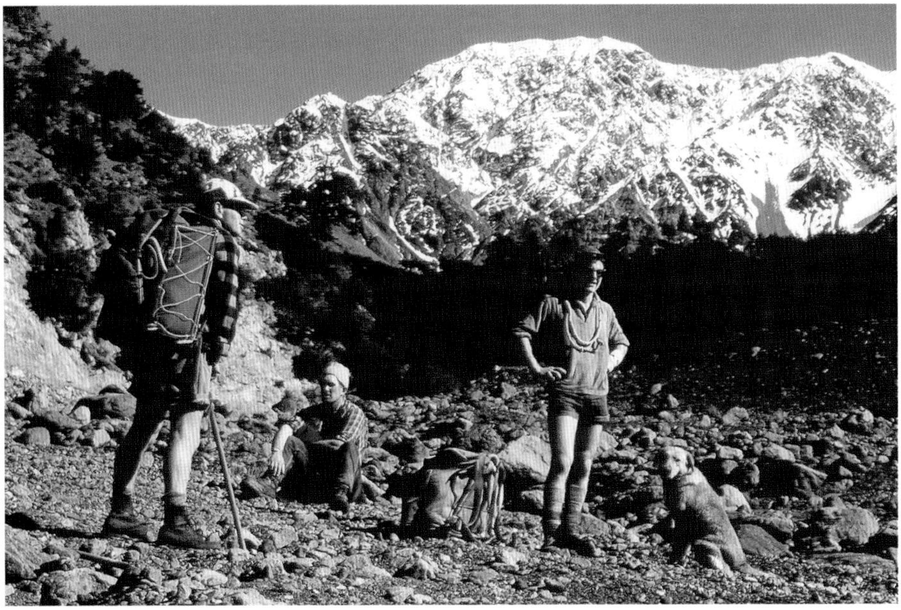

Brian Bell, Paul Woodman and unknown from the Wildlife Service on the way into Shearwater Stream, October 1967. Photo courtesy of Geoff Harrow

thousands of birds scattered across a large and often inaccessible stretch of mountain country.[12] They also found large numbers of deer and goats in the valley, as well as lesser numbers of chamois, and noted evidence of erosion and damage from these introduced mammals. The deer and goat populations were swiftly reduced through a culling programme undertaken by the Wildlife Service, but the issues posed by stoats remained. Other concerns were raised in the early 1970s: the actions of the shearwaters digging burrows in the unstable soils and scree might lead to erosion and the destruction of their own breeding colonies.[13]

Following Geoff's study in the 1960s and 70s there was a lull in the study of Hutton's shearwaters. As early as April 1967 Geoff had told a meeting of the Nelson Rotary Club that in order to develop a complete picture of the bird's activities in the mountains it would be necessary to build a hut near a colony and have a university team spend time there.[14] No research team had taken up the challenge, however.

Further short visits to the breeding colonies followed in the 1980s, to gather sound recordings of the shearwater's calls and to measure a sample of birds for a master's thesis on the comparative biology of Hutton's and the fluttering shearwater, its better known and more widespread cousin.[15]

In the mid- to late 1980s Greg Sherley from DOC established monitoring methods and estimated the combined population of the Kowhai Valley and

Shearwater Stream colonies at around 134,400 pairs,[16] with the majority in the Kowhai colony. This work found that relatively few burrows had produced fledged chicks and noted predation from stoats, falcons and harriers. Local DOC staff Brian Paton and Alison Davis visited the Kowhai colony each year from 1989 to 1995 to monitor burrows. Their work uncovered evidence of high rates of breeding failure, with overall breeding success (the proportion of laid eggs that produced a fledged chick) lower than that of other shearwater species.[17]

These years of study again turned up freshly killed shearwaters with bite marks on the head and necks, suggesting stoats were the culprits. Other damaging factors were erosion (caused by the shearwaters themselves), browsing by deer and chamois, threats to the food supply at sea, and snowfall, but there was little understanding of the relative impacts of these factors.[18]

Just a few decades after the excitement of Geoff Harrow's discovery of their breeding sites, the outlook for Hutton's shearwaters was bleak. It was clear that the historical range of the birds had shrunk dramatically over the past 50 years, but no one fully knew or understood exactly why. More work desperately needed to be done.

7. Alone in the valley

Eight days after the long-awaited arrival of the hut I got a lift from Kaikoura to the Kowhai in a helicopter: walking out was one thing, but coming back with a full load of food and kit was another. On previous occasions I had been blown away by the view, but perhaps as a consequence of the completion of the hut, or the week's break, I was calm enough this time to really take it all in. The range had received a fresh dump of snow and the mountains were covered from their peaks to below the treeline. Viewed from above, the Kowhai River became more convoluted and tumbling the further upstream we flew, jammed tighter and whiter into an ever-narrowing gorge, each side flanked by impassable cliffs and buttresses of rock. I counted three free-falling waterfalls that appeared to start like springs from the tops of cliffs, their branching sources hidden by snow. Four chamois bolted beneath us, running madly in zigzags on the scrub and snow-covered mountainside. Dave Armstrong, a local helicopter pilot, reckoned it was like Switzerland; I assured him it was far better.

The usual frenzied unloading of bags and boxes began as soon as we touched down, and four minutes later the helicopter lifted off in a crescendo of accelerating rotor blades and I waved off Mike and his visiting girlfriend, Lou Rodgerson, who were to have a well-earned break. The clattering echo of the helicopter briefly rebounded down the valley before silence fell, and I stood for the first time truly alone in the Kowhai Valley.

Tearing myself from the view I entered the hut. Although it was only around 9 x 4 metres in size it felt vast in comparison to the cramped bivvy. The effect was exaggerated by the fact that it was empty apart from a couple of Mike's bags and a box of food. The hut had been pre-fitted with cupboards, shelves and bunks, and miraculously most of these items had survived being strewn across a paddock by the storm, although several still bore a crack or split in the wood. The gas stove, fridge and water-heater had been fitted and tested, and the only remaining task was to connect the water supply.

After a few minutes enjoying the space I headed outside and began bringing in the boxes, bags and crates that lay scattered around the landing site. Three heavy-duty 12-volt batteries were awkward loads to lug over the tussocks, but in the end I had them lined up in parallel along the far wall, waiting to be connected to the solar panels. I began unpacking boxes whose contents I had last seen in Dunedin two months earlier: food, spare (clean!) clothes, books, and a pile of scientific papers on shearwaters, mustelids and predation.

A couple of hours later I was nearly finished. Work books, field kit and tools were stashed in the western end of the hut, food was in the middle, and clothes, novels and other books were in the bedroom. The last box I unpacked was prominently labelled 'soap', and from its contents I mixed myself a large gin and tonic and settled down in the chair at the desk, grinning at the unparalleled view straight up the valley to the glow of the setting sun on Manakau's peak.

Over the coming days I set to, digging more study burrows, walking the transect lines and thinking about the project and research plans. Most of all, though, I just revelled in being alone in the valley. There is always a starkness and elemental sense of self-reliance when on your own in any wild area. Gavin Maxwell, author of *Ring of Bright Water*, wrote,

> To be quite alone where there are no other human beings is sharply exhilarating; it is as though some presence has suddenly been lifted, allowing an intense awareness of one's surroundings, a sharpening of the senses, and an intimate recognition of the teeming subhuman life around one … as though life were suddenly stripped of inessentials such as worries about money and small egotistical ambitions and one was left facing an ultimate essential.[1]

'Subhuman' jarred somewhat, but otherwise Maxwell's description summed up my own feelings in better words than I could muster. Standing alone in the majesty of the Kowhai's surroundings, the ultimate essential of the valley was the ecological system it supported; the courting, breeding and continued survival of tens of thousands of Hutton's shearwaters were far more elemental and significant than my own brief presence in this place.

OPPOSITE: The snow-covered Seaward Kaikoura mountains in early spring. Author photo

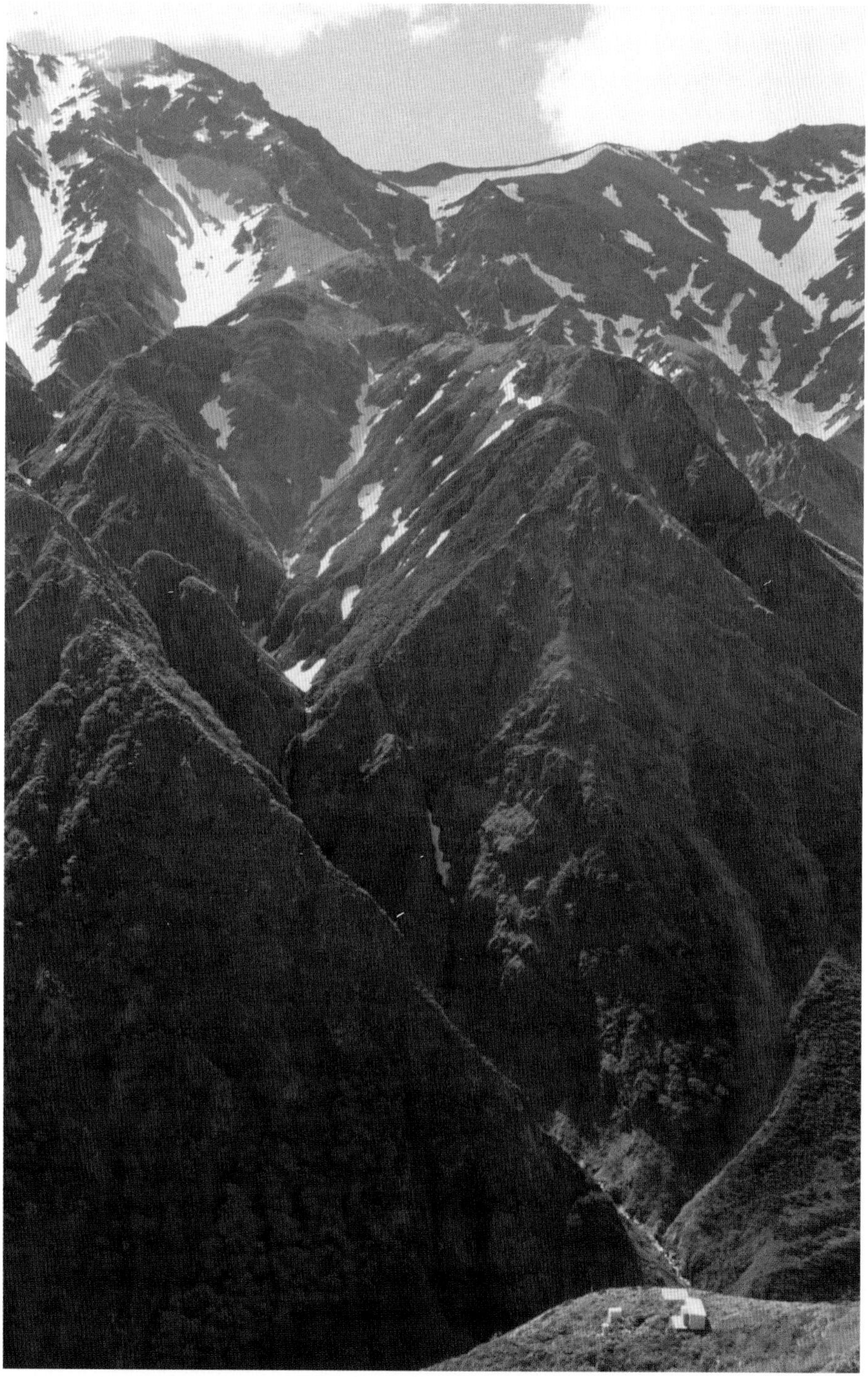

The hut and helipad dwarfed by the surrounding cliffs. Author photo

With the days now lengthening rapidly, the warmth of spring began to seep into the valley and the thick blanket of snow began to thaw. While the sun melted the snow, turning the surface to a crystalline crust pitted with shearwater guano and wind-blown specks of rock and insects, it was the more frequent northwest winds that really stripped winter's mantle from the surrounding land. The snow's retreat was far from even, for the wind, storms and avalanches of winter had drifted and piled it so that it lay thick in certain areas, choking gullies, streambeds and concave slopes in a great crust. As it melted, small patches of the underlying ground slowly emerged into view: small rock bluffs materialised within otherwise smooth surroundings, and thickets of ribbonwood trees – pinned flat by the weight of the snow – sprang upwards, catapulting tufts of snow into the air like thistledown.

The snow's slow retreat ebbed and flowed like the tide; scree and tussock would be exposed by two days of sun and a warm wind, only to be covered again by another southerly front. Drifts fractured and fell down the steep banks of Col Stream, revealing a carpet of dark-green crinkle-edged *Ranunculus* leaves, and a week later a profusion of yellow flowers burst forth along the top edge of the bank. The next day a southerly swept through and in an hour they were gone, buried under 30 centimetres of snow.

The slow uncovering and recovering of the valley was like a prolonged and teasing courtship. It made me see the valley in dozens of different ways and fully appreciate every proffered part, from the spine of a ridge that emerged from an otherwise smooth curving snow slope, to a patch of bare soil where the night's cold had frozen the ground into uplifted ice crystals like miniature skyscrapers, each capped with a tiny tuft of soil or rock, standing tall until the first sideways glance of the morning sun.

The warmth of spring brought more birds to the valley, and the wavering descent of grey warblers fluting from the dense cover of the ribbonwood trees became a common sound around the hut. The warblers were only silenced by the repeated slurring call of a shining cuckoo that occasionally ventured this high in search of a nest in which to lay its egg. Further up the valley a few New Zealand pipits scurried after insects, pausing to perch atop a boulder and proclaim their territory. Overhead two kea called, flying across the valley in their ungainly way, and swamp harriers silently drifted down the valley, wings spread in supplication to the slightest thermal, eyes ever alert for prey.

The new hut had attracted the attention of the valley's kea, who had clearly decided the roof was now a favoured meeting point. The day after my return I had the job of climbing onto the roof with tubes of silicon to seal the joints where the hut's sections had been bolted together. I completed the work over a couple of hours in the morning and knew the silicon would be well set by midday. Returning for lunch after a visit to an area of burrows, I found four excited kea peering down at me from the roof and the morning's silicon professionally stripped and scattered around the hut. After lunch I repeated the silicon seal and set to with a hand-drill, pop-rivet gun and a long roll of tin strip. After another few hours I was confident the tin strip was taut enough and sufficiently riveted to keep out the probing beak of a kea. Satisfied, I enjoyed a relaxed meal and lay down to a good night's sleep.

At four in the morning a dull metallic rolling sound penetrated my brain. It reached a crescendo that was followed by a frantic scampering of feet, then silence. A purposeful tread stomped up the roof above me to the highest point and the sound of rolling metal began again, accelerating down the pitch of the roof until, on the brink of relief, there was the same rush of skidding feet and excited squeals. A brief respite of silence and it all began again. Despite the polystyrene insulation in the roof of the hut, the two skins of metal were acting like an amplifier and the metallic clatter of the birds' claws sounded like the rattling spurs of a swaggering gaucho.

Fully awake now, I scrambled out of my sleeping bag and silently slid open the window to a cold blast of air. Quietly I placed one foot on the sill, then, gripping the top of the frame I swung myself out, and slowly, very slowly, stood up to peer over the edge of the roof. The bright eyes of three kea glinted at me in the moonlight. Although I had tidied up I must have left three or four rivet tails on the roof, or they had found them on the ground surrounding the hut. As I watched, two birds demonstrated their game, releasing a rivet tail from the roof's crest. They allowed it to roll down the roof before sprinting after it in a mad dash to grab it before it fell.

Cursing, I pulled my boots on, grabbed a broom, climbed onto the roof and swept it clean once more. The two rivet-chasing kea flew off but the third bird remained, clearly older and bolder than his co-conspirators. He was a young adult male, later to be named Aston, and I would come to know him well.

A few days later I swept out the hut and made it ship-shape in anticipation of a visitor. I had met Geoff Harrow in Christchurch a few months earlier and we had spent an afternoon discussing my plans for the coming season. Geoff was delighted about the prospects, but I detected some caution in his questions. He had heard of many such plans to study the ecology and conservation of Hutton's shearwaters and I probably looked like yet another in a long line of eager wannabe researchers. But my work had the full support of DOC, and I thought Geoff might be convinced by seeing the new research hut in the heart of the Kowhai.

Geoff was dropped off by the helicopter, along with a modest bag of clothes and the largest box of fruit and vegetables I had seen in weeks. In Hillary and Lowe's book *East of Everest* there is a photo of the 1954 expedition team at the end of the trip, all of them bearded and grinning and surrounded by their Sherpa guides and friends. On the right-hand side of the picture Geoff's face is almost hidden beneath a fur-lined hat, but a pair of twinkling eyes shine forth from the photo. In the Kowhai over 40 years later, those same bright blue eyes smiled at me as he gripped my hand and firmly shook it. Geoff was now in his mid-seventies, but still had the same fit climber's build of the young man in the photo from Baruntse.

Most of the jobs around the hut had been completed, with the exception of installing running water. Along with its passenger, the helicopter had brought in several hundred metres of plastic hose and a 1000-litre tank. Geoff revealed that he had installed the water supply at a couple of club skifields in Arthur's Pass, so together we got to work. We dug out a flat spot for the tank on the slope about 20 metres higher than the hut, and tied the tank down securely to two steel waratahs. We then started to unroll the lengths of piping, cursing and stumbling our way up through the ribbonwood trees. Geoff headed back to the hut and returned with six waratahs and a lump hammer. We attached the pipe to various trees with number-eight wire, adjusting the loops to keep the pipe at a steady angle. Where there was no tree handy we banged in a waratah and looped a length of wire off this.

We contoured around with the far end of the pipe into the stream a good hundred metres above the hut and tank. Building a small rock dam in the streambed, we wrapped a filter around the pipe's end and submerged it. The header tank started filling, and a second pipe from the tank connected it directly to the hut. All that remained was to install an overflow pipe from the tank back into the stream, and to turn on the gas-fuelled water heater. Much as I loved living in the wild, three months of hauling water to the hut and scrubbing myself in the cold stream had begun to pale. The hot water for the dishes and shower that evening was an unadulterated luxury.

Geoff and I got on well. His time in India and Nepal following his climb of Baruntse had unleashed a passion that we shared: each evening we cooked ever-hotter meals of dahl and curry accompanied by red-hot pickles that we ate with tears streaming down our faces. We shared long conversations about shearwaters, stoats, kea, mountains, climbing – not that any of the climbs I had done were on a par with his. When asked about the east face of Mt Sefton, Geoff grinned and confessed, 'It was a young man's climb. I wouldn't have gone near it after I was married.'

I also had to ask him about one aspect of his climbing in the Himalayas. Prior to the climb of Baruntse, Geoff, Charles Evans and a team of six Sherpas had headed

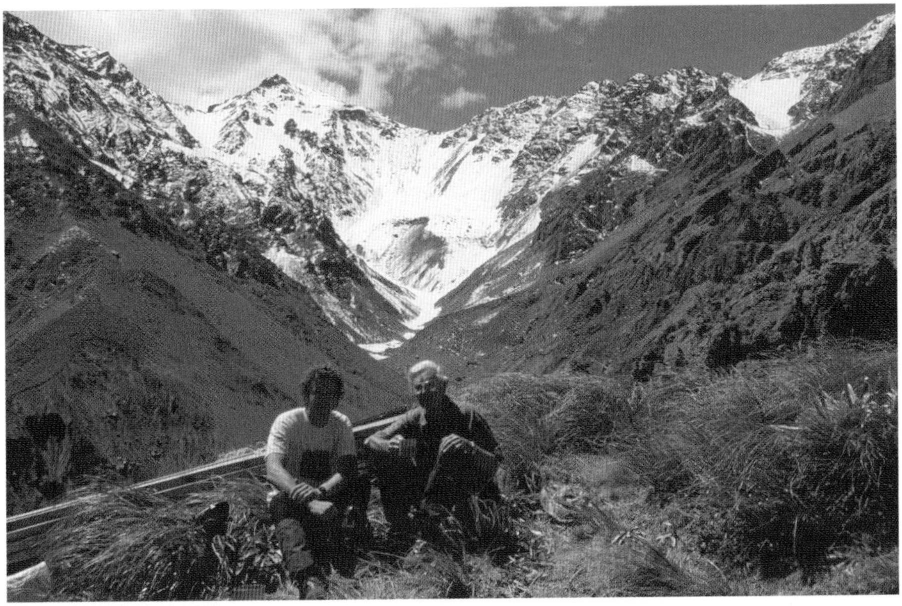

Richard Cuthbert and Geoff Harrow in the valley in 1996. Author photo

OPPOSITE: Geoff Harrow in front of the 'Harrow' colony, where he found the first active burrows in 1965. Author photo

off to explore the upper part of the remote Choyang Valley, which lay to the south of 24,000ft Mt Chamlang. Their trip had taken 20 days and Geoff described it as one of the highlights of his life, for they had the privilege of being the first people to see this terrain and made the first crossings of several mountain passes and ascents of many small peaks. The Australian *Daily Telegraph* reported on this trip and ran an article by Charles Evans describing how he, Geoff and their Sherpas had seen the fresh tracks of a yeti.[2] I respected Geoff's opinion and it was clear he was more than the amateur naturalist that he liked to portray himself as. I asked him about the yeti tracks. He laughed. 'No, they were the tracks of a bear. It was as plain as day from the claw marks and I told Charles. The Sherpas believed it was a yeti though, and Charles always liked a good story.'

After a great week in which we dug more study burrows and checked others with the burrowscope, Geoff flew out and made his way back to Christchurch, happy – I hoped – with the hut and the progress of the study. I was thankful for the chance to get to know him and count him as a friend.

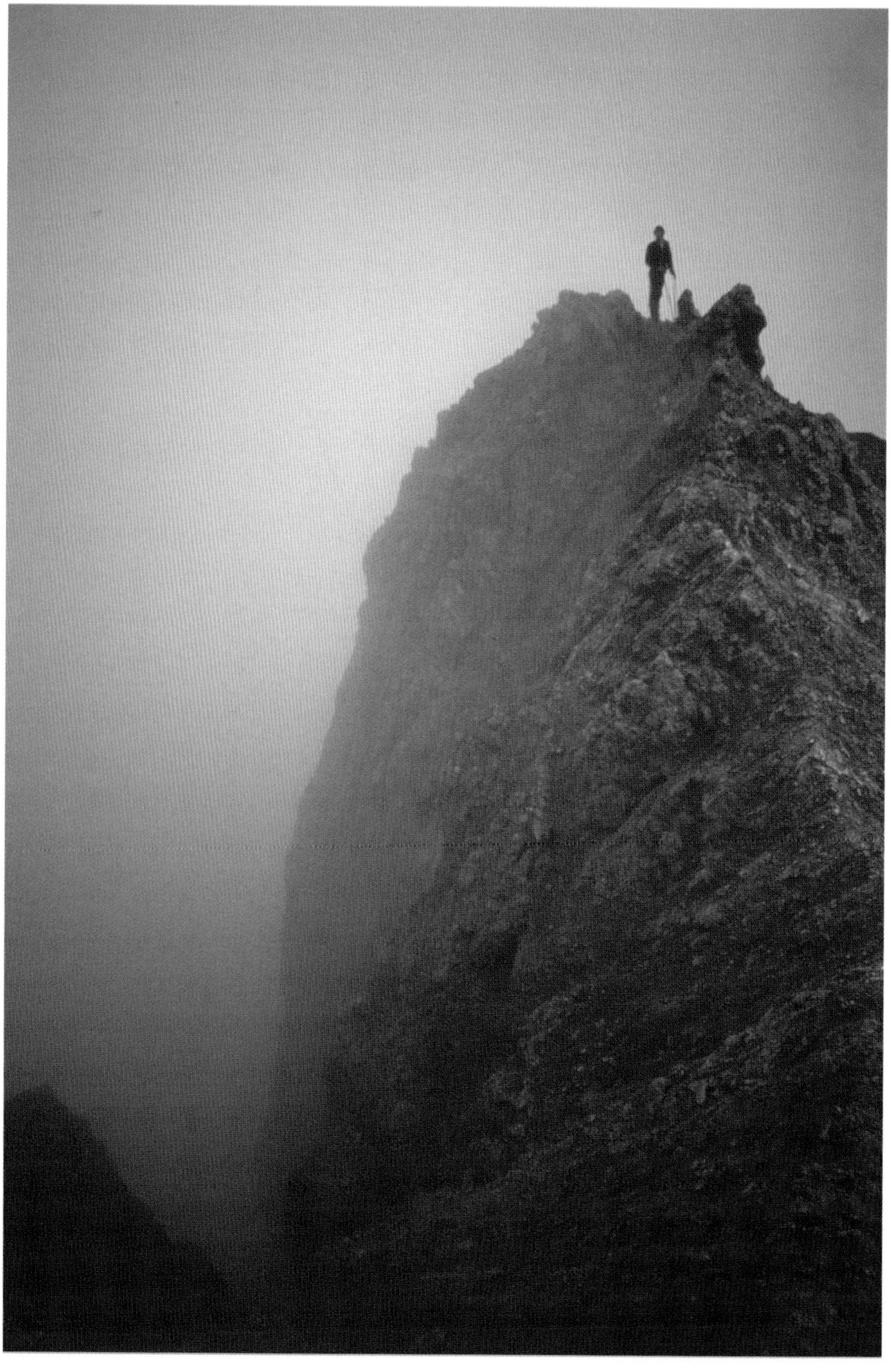

Traversing steep ground during transects through the sub-colonies within the Kowhai Valley.
Photo courtesy of Mike Dunlop

8. Searching the transect lines

With the hut completed, a good pattern of work mapped out and two great friends – Erica Sommer and Mike – helping with the research, things were going well. We settled into the routine of work: transects every two weeks through the sub-colonies to search for shearwater carcasses, study-burrow checks every month, and bursts of banding for half a dozen nights each month. In between these main tasks we continued to explore the valley and its surrounding, and kept notes on the number, age and sex of the kea around the hut. We also searched for signs and evidence of stoats and shearwater carcasses, crawling under boulders and into thickets of scrub and occasionally emerging triumphant with a depredated shearwater egg or a stoat scat. The following journal excerpt from 7–10 January 1997, written following a break for New Year's Eve, is a typical account of our fieldwork pattern:

> … excited to be back. Unpacked and sorted all kit in the remains of the day. Hut fine other than had to shake all 500 metres of the water pipe to get rid of an airlock and get it flowing again. The 8th was busy, catching up on transects with [sub-] colonies 4, 5 and Top (me), Hoheria and 15 (Mike), Col and New (Erica) … Out ringing that evening – a good night – 82 birds caught and processed, 42 of them new, the others all retraps. Carried on till 4ish and then tried to grab a few hours' sleep. Woke up with the light as usual and had a lazy breakfast out on the helipad with a book. All of us fairly sapped on the 9th, but did autopsies on all 17 birds recovered from yesterday's transects and then went for an explore down Col Stream into the main gorge and river. Don't fancy the gorge as a way out as it has severe flooding potential and it is threatened by rock fall from the loose slopes above. It felt pretty claustrophobic down there (particularly under the giant boulder on the slip) and judging by the scouring and debris the water that goes through there on occasions must be terrifying. Went downstream for a couple of hundred metres before meeting a fast section of river that had to be waded, which I decided to flag and climbed up

high instead. Came out near the bottom of the big free-falling waterfall below New colony. The falcon pair were wheeling through the air close to the waterfall. Could not see any sign of a nest and even if I had it would be in unapproachable country. Coming back up Col Stream about 500 metres below the washing spot I came across a red pudding bowl stuck between two rocks, last seen two months ago in the beak of a kea as it flew off down the valley! Out ringing again on the 9th and 10th, another 81 and 90 birds, and a good proportion of retraps. Another couple of nights like that and finish off the transect lines and I will be really happy.

I had two more transects to complete before all lines were finished for that two-week period, and had left the toughest ones until last. Each of us had picked a particular set of sub-colonies where we preferred to work; colonies 18 and 19 were mine and were situated above the huge waterfall that fell for 150 metres from the sheer rock bluffs on the far side of the main valley opposite the hut. The transects were challenging both mentally and physically and took a solid half day of walking and relentless concentration. Reaching the two colonies was the real mission, however, and in the three years that I lived in the Kowhai I made the journey over 40 times.

I travelled light: a small pack containing waterproofs, a warm hat, fleece jacket and climbing helmet, a bum bag, notebook, zip-lock plastic bags, two pencils and a permanent pen, knife and a snack, and my binoculars firmly strapped on my hip. The journey started from the corner of the helipad. Over time we had beaten a path down the tussock slopes to the south of Camp sub-colony, and I had come to know every patch of soil, rock and tussock, for I must have traversed the slope 500 times or more. With leather gloves on and a ski pole in each hand I would stand there, rather like a downhill skier, take in a couple of deep breaths and jump onto the path below. I ran downhill, my legs moving automatically over the rough ground, running faster and faster, poles out to one side jabbing into the ground as I swerved left, then right, through the tussocks.

At the bottom of the first slope I swiftly checked in the usual places for stoat scats on the boulders and on the path ahead as it crested a small rise. Running again, I traversed to the right through more tussocks, jumped onto the boulder wedged over the small dry stream, and zigzagged right, then left, through the short bushes of snow tōtara and coprosma before darting out and onto the loose scree in the main valley. I checked my watch: four minutes gone. More slowly now, I jogged down over the scree and patches of compacted ground, scanning the rocks and stoat tracking tunnels for scats, before picking my way down the large jumbled rocks beside the main river where, with a quick boulder hop, I was across with dry feet. It was all uphill now, a 700-metre vertical climb from the valley floor to the edge of sub-colony 18.

I moved off, jumping another stream at its narrowest point as it emerged roaring from the gorge below Hoheria sub-colony, then scrambling up the rocks on the far bank. I hauled myself uphill on tussock stems and the branches of young ribbonwood trees. As the scrub thickened I pushed my way through it, past springing branches that whipped across my face and the sharp stabbing spikes of speargrass that lurked menacingly among the snow tussocks. Then it was out of the vegetation and onto a narrow runnel of scree that fell vertically from the rock bluffs above, feet scrambling and sliding, ski poles thrusting, hands grabbing the occasional ribbonwood sapling for purchase. Up the scree for 150 metres before moving right onto the tussock slopes again.

There were shearwater burrows over the next 20 metres and I traversed carefully, looking for the most stable path. I sidled along the base of a vertical wall of rock, and stopped briefly to swing my pack down, grab my climbing helmet and pull it on. I moved onto a steep slope of compressed soil and rock, kicking at the hard surface, my toes stubbing painfully into my boots, and with a ski pole jabbed out a thin foothold. My rubber boots bent on the edge of the narrow hold, but the soles gripped and I moved off, traversing slowly and cautiously across the surface, not looking at the five-metre drop beneath me.

At the edge of the compressed mud I stood still, looking and listening intently. To my right stretched a broad gut, flanked on either side by a vertical wall of rock and leading upwards for 300 metres to the edge of the two colonies. It was the only way up and was the worst sort of gully, made of an unstable mix of loose and compacted scree and stacked with rocks and boulders. From the safety of the valley floor I had watched during a gusting norwester as boulders tumbled, bounced and smashed their way down the narrow confines of this gut, shattering into the ground with a visible explosion of powdered shrapnel, the crashing echo reaching me a full two seconds later. Today, however, all was still.

I took off again, moving as fast as I could across the gully, my feet alternately sliding through the deep, loose scree and skidding on the hard runnels of compacted rock that lay just under the surface. On the far side I climbed up the edge of the scree, staying close to a wall of rock that sloped up diagonally and protected me from above, until my way was blocked by a massive boulder fully half the size of the hut. I scrambled up a vertical band of rock and thin grass for eight metres, carefully brushing loose fragments of scree from the hand- and footholds, before moving onto a grassy terrace that led safely upwards for another 50 metres.

I stopped to check and listen again before crossing into the gut, for on a previous occasion I had failed to see two chamois above me and they, alarmed by my sudden appearance, had stampeded off, dislodging a small avalanche of fist-sized rocks that whistled around and past me as I crouched down low on the ground. All clear this time – I moved off, crossing the gut below another steep and loose channel. Upwards again on the edge of the gut, feet and hands seeking out holds in the relative solidity of the vertical rock flanking the gully. The gut narrowed and I scrambled up through the first sparse tussocks and onto the edge of sub-colony 18. A narrow arête led horizontally back above the left wall of the gut and I moved along this to where the ground dropped away steeply below me, falling vertically for several hundred metres to the place I had earlier traversed the first narrow runnel of scree. A flat rock beckoned – my usual seat – and I pulled a snack out of my bag and sat down to look out over the colony and across the valley to the hut, now far below me. I checked my watch: just over an hour, not the fastest time but not bad.

After a brief rest I set off again, rapidly losing some of the hard-gained height as I descended through two loose channels of scree until I reached the bottom of the colony. I was thirsty by this stage and scrambled down another slope to drink from the stream close to where it plunged over the rocks in an 80-metre fall. On occasions I would creep out to the boulders that flanked the waterfall's edge. With my body pinned flat on the rock and one hand gripping a tussock behind me, I would lie with head and shoulders leaning out into the exhilarating space, the water rushing past with a roar and spilling over the sharp rim, droplets of water briefly forming abstract shapes before they fell in a sickening arc to the void below. I would remain glued to the rock for as long as I could, hypnotised by the roaring cascade, before worming backwards with white clenched knuckles and a knotted stomach, dizzy with vertigo, to the safety of solid ground.

At the start of the transect line I began to move slowly through the colony, following the line of red-painted bamboo canes that marked the route. In contrast to the journey to the colony it was slow work: two steps and stop, scan the ground to my right below and behind, scan the tussocks and ground to my left and above, two more steps and stop – and so on. The number of shearwater carcasses was low given the size of the area we covered – on average we found one adult bird for every kilometre of transect walked. Each transect took around one to two hours to complete and required a mental effort to remain focused, concentrating on scanning the ground for the length of the line.

Spotting the telltale feathers of a bird below me, I stopped and grabbed a tape measure from my bum bag. I lined up the spot with the next marked pole and took two steps forward, measuring and noting the perpendicular distance from the line of the transect down to the bird. I noted the position of the carcass: belly down and partially under a tussock. After carefully checking the ground for any other signs I placed the bird in a zip-lock bag, jotted a number on the bag with a permanent pen, added it to my bum bag and continued with the transect.

Three hours later I traversed the last section of the upper colony and dropped down the scree and a steep ridge to my bag, which I had earlier stashed beneath a tussock. I was dry-mouthed with thirst, my brain numb from concentrating to make sure I didn't miss a single bird. Donning my leather gloves again I cautiously scanned the steep gut before setting off on the journey back to the hut. In my rucksack were the carcasses of two adult shearwaters and three grey down-covered chicks: five more data points to add to the picture.

The transect lines brought one more job with them, and unfortunately it was far from pleasant. All of the dead birds found on transect lines or down burrows had to be dissected and necropsied in order to determine the cause of death. It was vital to know whether it had been prey to a stoat, a falcon or a harrier, or was an accident or a death from natural causes. We had to find out how many were dying and what was killing them.

All corpses were measured and the pattern of any injuries or predation noted; areas with wounds were carefully plucked and skinned and the puncture wounds and bite marks measured with callipers. Rats, weasels, stoats, ferrets and cats are all predators of birds in New Zealand, and each carnivore can be distinguished by the width of the paired puncture marks left by their lower and upper canines.[1] The wounds on the shearwaters we were picking up clearly showed that stoats were killing our birds, typically with a bite to the back of the head or upper neck. Other bite marks were found on the breast, upper back, wings, legs and rump, possibly the results of a stoat's initial attempt to seize or capture the bird. Following the killing bite, stoats began feeding on the neck before proceeding to the breast, legs and upper wings, eating away the muscle and neatly rolling back the skin and feathers.

The injuries left by falcons and harriers were quite different, although distinguishing between these two avian predators proved impossible because they left similar patterns.[2] The carcass would typically be atop or alongside a tussock and surrounded by large numbers of plucked feathers. Rather than the back of the head or neck, feeding normally began with the large pectoral muscles of the breast followed by the muscles of the upper legs. In cases where most of the muscle had been consumed, the shearwaters often had triangular or long notches, particularly on the keel bone, left by a harrier or falcon as it pulled the remaining scraps of breast muscle from the carcass.

While we couldn't distinguish which bird of prey had inflicted the wounds, it was most often likely to be the work of a harrier. A single pair of falcons were present on the lower boundaries of the valley, but were only occasionally seen flying up and over the colonies and were probably hunting shearwaters further down the valley. From what I saw when walking out from the valley, any shearwater leaving the colony in the half-light of dawn would have had to run the gauntlet of two or three falcon territories on its flight to the sea.

Harriers were more numerous, however: each afternoon up to half a dozen birds could be seen slowly quartering the valley. For the most part they probably picked up and scavenged on stoat-killed shearwaters, or on birds that had misjudged their approach in thick mist or high winds and been killed flying into a rock bluff or scree slope. Quite a number of shearwaters died from such accidents and I would often pick up four or five birds lying dead beneath bluffs on a morning after a storm, some of them completely intact, others with a broken wing or bill indicating the force of their collision. While scavenging was undoubtedly important for harriers I was certain they also hunted birds, taking some on the ground as they departed in the early mornings and preying on others on bright moonlit nights.

Among the carcasses we sometimes found chicks that didn't fit any of these patterns. These birds had crushed skulls, and small patches of fat underlying the skin had been eaten away from three or four areas on the belly or back.[3] Occasionally they also had a broken wing or leg, or injuries and fractures to other large bones. They were normally next to fresh digging and holes in the ground, and had been killed by kea.

Our experiences of kea on the roof of the bivvy and the hut in the first few months were fairly typical of most people's encounters with these parrots – anyone who has spent time in the mountains of New Zealand's South Island has their own kea stories. They are a wild and spirited part of the country's mountain ecology, and among the world's most intelligent and social birds.[4] That intelligence, and their need to explore and test every potential foraging prospect, has led most people to associate kea with the hooligan-like destruction of cars parked at skifields, or damage to any items left outside huts.

As irritating as such behaviour can sometimes be, it takes up only a small part of a kea's time and energy budget. Kea spend many more hours each day foraging for berries, grubs, plant roots and any other edible items. Birds the size of a kea require intelligence, persistence and opportunism to survive within New Zealand's alpine environment, and within the Kowhai Valley the birds had a unique trick – for here they had learnt to kill and feed on Hutton's shearwater chicks. It was several months before I first observed this, for as vocal, loud and brightly coloured as kea can be, when they are foraging they quietly blend in among the snow tussocks. They also had another annoying habit that frustrated my attempts: if they noticed they were being watched, they would almost inevitably break away from what they were doing to come and check out the spy – turning the tables from observed to observer.

One afternoon when coming back around the scree above Col sub-colony, I

A kea feeding upon a recently killed shearwater chick. Author photo

stopped to scan the area with my binoculars. Near the top of the colony, where the soil was most fragile and loose, a group of five kea were silently moving across the ground. Two of the birds, an adult and sub-adult, were walking from burrow to burrow, stopping and apparently listening at each entrance. The three juveniles milled around, occasionally getting in the way of a burrow entrance but more often following the older birds. As I watched, the group halted and the adult bird began digging in the soil, stopping every 20 to 30 seconds and appearing to listen intently. After two false starts it dug a third hole, thrust its head and shoulders inside and pulled out a fat shearwater chick. Still covered with down and too fat to fight or flee back into its burrow, the squawking chick was swiftly killed, a bite to the head from the kea's strong beak crushing its skull. The five kea began to feed, delicately pulling the thick fat from under the skin.

The whole fascinating incident had taken around 20 minutes. For most of that time the two older kea were searching and listening, presumably trying to detect whether a burrow contained a chick or not. The digging took around five minutes and the killing 30 seconds. For birds who mostly forage on roots, shoots, seeds and berries, the rich nourishment provided by a fat shearwater chick would be a huge boost, building up condition and energy reserves to ensure survival through the long harsh winters. Such behaviour was likely to have been far more common among kea in the past, when Hutton's shearwaters and other seabirds were more widely distributed across New Zealand.

David Attenborough watches a kea in the colony in 1997. Author photo

9. A famous visitor

The behaviour of the kea in the valley had also attracted the interest of others and we were about to be honoured by a distinguished visitor: Sir David Attenborough was flying in to gather footage for his 1998 documentary *The Life of Birds*. I had grown up feasting on David Attenborough's programmes, his reverent hushed tones now almost a broadcasting cliché, and Sunday evening screenings of his *Life on Earth* and *The Living Planet* were the closest I came to a weekly sermon. I was excited but also slightly nervous about meeting him, for who knew what he might be like in person?

Two days later the helicopter flying in Attenborough and the film crew suddenly appeared in the valley, but rather than landing by the hut it proceeded straight to the col above the valley where they hoped to film the birds. It was a good choice – this was the very location where I had watched the kea killing the shearwater chick a few days earlier. The open nature of Col sub-colony – its sparse covering of tussock and loose, shallow soil – made it a good spot to watch from, with a high likelihood of birds.

Although the team had picked a good site they had not picked a good day, and from down the valley I could see that the helicopter had only just got them in. The clouds snaking up the valley floor meant a southerly front was on its way. Mike and I stayed in the hut and shortly afterwards the surroundings disappeared into the mist and the sky opened in torrential rain. Forty minutes later the six film crew and Attenborough, all soaking wet, appeared at the hut and politely knocked on the door. We all shook hands, Attenborough introducing himself earnestly as 'David', which was perhaps slightly superfluous.

They all crowded in and Mike and I did our best as hosts, trying to find seats for everyone and making rounds of tea. To my absolute horror, David asked for a cup of cocoa. I could see Mike laughing to himself at this request. Mike had suffered my previous attempts to make cocoa and had learned to stick to tea or coffee; my cocoa seemed to resemble either a cup of tar or scalded milk with lumps of brown powder on top. After five minutes of furious stirring I handed over a mugful that was hot and sweet with only a few small persistent lumps. David didn't seem to mind or notice. To my huge relief he turned out to be as sincere and 'normal' as he appears on screen: modest and interested, with a genuine enthusiasm for life and a real breadth and depth of knowledge.

After two more hours of heavy rain it was obvious that filming was off for the day. Fortunately the mist lifted, however, and the helicopter returned to take Attenborough, the film crew and Mike out. It was a good job they left when they did, as the rest of that day and the next were foul with torrential rain and I barely left the hut other than to complete life's necessities and to look at the river, which had burst its bank and flooded the valley floor. I stayed well clear of the river's edge, for where it funnelled into the gorge it had become a raging muddy torrent. Over the roar of the water I could hear boulders and rocks clinking and rumbling, like submerged glacial growlers, as they rolled along the riverbed.

The next day dawned clear. Thinking I had a few hours before the film crew arrived I was sitting up in my sleeping bag at 7am with a book and a mug of tea when suddenly I heard the helicopter coming up the valley. I was up in a flash and quickly jumped into my overalls before heading out to the helipad. Rod Morris, the New Zealand assistant producer on the shoot, jumped out and I helped him carry some gear from the hut to the helicopter before it flew Attenborough and the film crew up to Col sub-colony once more.

After a hasty breakfast I crept up the ridge to the col (not wanting to ruin a shot if it was occurring) and joined them. They had some footage but were still waiting for a key shot of David with a kea in frame. They were lucky – the kea were around, and in fact there were 12 of them up there, whereas I would sometimes go for days without seeing a single bird, and when I did it would rarely be in the place I expected it to be. One hour later, with Rod and me off screen quietly steering the kea into frame with the help of a few discreet crumbs of fruitcake, the crew had the desired footage. The narration was pure Attenborough, spoken in his instantly recognisable hushed tones and careful emphasis: 'This bird is a parrot, a kea. And unlike a normal parrot it's not content with nuts and fruit. This bird is a killer.'

After the shoot the crew relaxed and Rod took out his camera to capture some stills of David and the kea. I did the same, snapping a few photos of the film crew as well. I asked David if he would mind crouching down or crawling up close to the kea so I could get a better shot. 'Crawling?' he replied with a wry smile. 'I'm renowned for it.'

Ecological and zoological polymath David Attenborough beguiled by a local clown. Author photo

We chatted away for another few minutes, then Rod called through to Kaikoura for the helicopter. I excused myself and sprinted back down to the hut in order to pack up a couple of letters and parcels to be sent out, along with a few bags of rubbish. Twenty minutes had passed by the time I was finished and there was still no sign of the helicopter. I filled in the time labelling some stoat scats I'd collected over the previous two days, but after a few moments the ridiculousness of the situation struck me: Sir David Attenborough was sitting 500 metres away and here I was looking at stoat shit! I dropped the scats onto the workbench and made a 10-minute sprint back up the hill, expecting to hear the sound of a helicopter at any moment and fearing that I would miss them.

Far from it. For the next two hours while we waited for the helicopter David told story after story. The conversation roamed from armadillos to zebra-finches, from the Kalahari to Kakadu. We chatted about New Guinea, a place I had always wanted to visit and the site of one of David's first expeditions to film birds of paradise. The conversation was not one-sided, much as I would have been happy for it to be, and David quizzed me about living and working in the Kowhai. We discovered a shared passion for the mangrove swamps of South America and excitedly discussed the flatulence of manatees and the charisma of giant otters, as well as our visits to the flat-topped mountains – or tepuis – that rise magically above the surrounding rainforest on the borders of Brazil, Guyana and Venezuela.

David Attenborough is a real raconteur, and each story – and his frequently terrible jokes – was told with unbridled enthusiasm. The most enduring image I have is of him impersonating 'Sid', a Cockney chain-smoking soundman who fell tragically in love with a different woman on every overseas filming trip. Sir David Attenborough stood there, an imaginary cigarette clutched in his hand, stooped over, wheezing for breath in nicotine starvation and proclaiming, 'Guvnor, it's luv. Pure luv!' In many ways it explained his success and achievements: he is of course an ecological and zoological polymath, but his capacity as a storyteller – of making the natural world so fascinating – is his real gift.

The sound of the helicopter broke into the afternoon and, regrettably, the day had to end. David surprised me again by commenting with genuine concern that he hoped the filming had not disrupted my work too much. I assured him it had not, which was a bit of a lie but the disruption had been well worth it, for it had been a memorable few days and a rare chance to meet one of natural history's real heroes.

Rod Morris, programme producer Jo Sarsby and cameraman Mike Lemmon were to stay on in the hope of capturing behavioural shots of a kea actually killing a shearwater chick. After the departing clatter of the helicopter had ceased I wished them luck for the rest of the day and set off back to the hut as I had a full afternoon's work to catch up on. At six in the evening the three of them trooped wearily into the hut and reported rather miserably that they had not seen a single kea all afternoon. I confessed that I had been amazed at their luck in the morning, and suggested they might have to put up with a bit of a wait. How right I was.

The next morning they set off back to the colony and I packed a small bag and departed to start on a round of transects. I was late back to the hut that evening and was greeted by the same glum faces: no kea to be seen. Rod opened a bottle of wine and after a couple of glasses their spirits began to rise and we enjoyed a great evening chatting about exotic wildlife and eating a sumptuous meal. Three bottles of wine were consumed that night, all courtesy of the BBC. Fortunately it was not the time of year to catch or band birds, with chicks underground and adults coming in only every few nights. The colonies were nearly deserted after dark, so I was safely able to stagger to the bivvy happy in the knowledge that I could collapse until morning.

The next two days passed in similar fashion, with me getting on with transects and necropsies of shearwater carcasses, and Jo, Rod and Mike enduring long and frustrating hours of watching an empty tussock-covered slope. Each day was followed by a good meal, more wine and conversation. They were getting a bit desperate at this stage, however, repeatedly asking me where the kea were and when they were going to turn up. What could I say? Trying to predict the whereabouts of kea was a fool's game. But Jo was due in Indonesia in five days' time, on 15 February, so could not wait around forever. As luck would have it, I had already booked a flight on the 14th to bring Erica in: Jo would be able to go out on the same flight.

'Oh, that's sweet,' said Jo. 'How lovely.'

'What's that?' I asked, bewildered that I might have done anything 'sweet'.

'The fourteenth, Valentine's Day!' replied Jo enthusiastically, giving me a complicit smile.

I had not realised this of course, and had simply arranged the helicopter for the only day pilot Dave Armstrong had a free morning in his schedule. However, with Jo's delighted expectation beaming down at me I nodded in slightly embarrassed assent.

Over the next couple of days the 'filming' reports became, if anything, more frustrated: on the 11th Mike saw a kea, on the 12th they saw two land in the colony but leave after five minutes, and on the 13th no kea were seen at all – and we had drunk the last of the wine.

On the morning of the 14th the film team headed up to Col sub-colony once more, with Jo due to return at 11am for the helicopter. I got on the radio to Erica to report that the weather was looking good and to place an unusually profligate shopping order, as we needed our normal supplies as well as another week's food for Mike and Rod. I read out their order over the radio, which included a great number of luxurious items well outside our student budgets. Erica repeated each item to double check she had it right.

'Two camemberts, blue cheese, stuffed olives, asparagus, fruit. Over.'

'Roger that,' I replied. 'Oh yes, and lots of wine.'

'How much is lots? Over.'

'Errrr, 15 bottles should do. Over.'

'*Fifteen?*'

'Yes, 15,' I replied, glancing around to check that no one was around. 'And make sure it's good stuff – the BBC is paying.'

Jo appeared at 11am and glumly reported that there had been no sign of any kea, and shortly afterwards the helicopter appeared with Erica and the supplies. Jo wished me good luck with the project and flew off down the valley.

It just had to happen. One hour later the puffing forms of Mike and Rod appeared at the hut, burdened down with their camera gear and tripods. Four kea had turned up, headed straight into the softest part of the colony, and dug out and killed a chick within 20 minutes. Sod's law! I radioed down, and luckily Dave was still free and promised he would be back up shortly to take the men out. Twenty minutes later, as Mike and Rod finished packing their kit, I heard the sudden approach of the helicopter, a sound that was always masked by the twisting valley until the last few bends.

In the normal flurry of helicopter packing I stacked cameras, tripods, rucksacks, pelican cases and boxes of film into the hold, and placed a few bags of rubbish and a couple of boxes of stinking carcasses in the cabin. I picked up the last two boxes and hurried hopefully over to the helicopter. Mike and Rod had already said goodbye and were strapped in, and Dave was in a hurry to get down for another flight. There was no room in the hold, the spare back seat was stacked high with sleeping bags and rubbish, and Mike and Rod were already clutching camera cases on their laps. They waved me and the boxes away, happy that they had all their personal kit with them – not to mention the vital footage. I staggered back to the deck to receive Dave's customary salute as he eased the helicopter off the pad and tipped her nose down the valley.

After a hectic week of unaccustomed socialising it was good to have some space, and even better to be there with just Erica for company. I heaved a sigh of relief and glanced down at the boxes below me: one large box of luxury food and 15 bottles of excellent wine! It was not planned – my mind unconsciously prioritising the need to pack rubbish instead of the food and drink? Surely not! Suffice to say, it was a good evening.

Only a few weeks remained before the end of the first season and the birds' departure from the valley. Mike (Dunlop) came in again a week after the filming, and he, Erica and I worked long days checking all the study burrows in the monitored colonies to see if they had produced a fledged chick, and completing one last sweep of the transects and associated autopsies. Checking every burrow was laborious work and had been made more difficult by the loss of some of the marker poles and tags through the slow attrition of rain, wind and erosion, or the mischievous attention of passing kea. We had mapped and measured every burrow at the start of the season, and for every burrow we 'lost' we had to use a compass bearing and tape measure to find its location, searching on hands and knees for any evidence of a tag, entrance or rock above the nesting chamber. Each burrow was then checked, either with the burrowscope or by lying with one's face pressed to the dirt and arm extended to its furthest reach until the sudden (and painful) seizure of one's fingers confirmed the survival of a chick.

We were also out each night trying to capture, band and weigh as many fledglings as we could before they departed to sea. The last weeks before they head to sea are an important stage for young shearwaters and other petrels. After several months down a burrow, the near fledging-aged chicks emerge for the first time and spend several nights outside on the ground by the burrow entrance. As they wait, the chicks slowly absorb the landscape, sounds and smell of their colony and the position of the stars, so that in four to six years' time they will be able to return, not only to the Kowhai Valley, but to almost precisely the same burrow they were reared in.[1] I had picked up a bird earlier in the season in Camp sub-colony that was five years old and within metres of the burrow it had fledged from.

The fledglings' departure was as remarkable as their future return. On the young shearwaters' first flight ever they had to find their way through the mountains to the sea in the dark of night. Once at sea they then had to learn to fish; although many chicks departed with healthy reserves of fat, such energy stores would last only a week or two. If they were lucky they would remain at sea for three to four years before flying back to the mountains and locating the colony where they were raised in order to breed. Typically only around one-third of shearwater fledglings survive to return to the colony as natural selection whittles down their numbers.[2] Many chicks fail to leave the colony at all, picked off by passing harriers or stoats and kea, while others are killed by falcons on their way through the mountains.

The urge to depart the colony is strong even in those birds that are too weak to make the journey. On my last day in the valley I found a starving down-covered chick, too weak to fly, struggling through the tussocks in a doomed bid to reach the sea. I picked up the bird, its keel bone sharp in my hand and its wing and tail feathers matted with dirt and too short to function. It briefly struggled in my hand, seizing my fingers weakly in its bill before collapsing with exhaustion. I held the bird close and, knowing it was the kindest thing to do, quickly broke its neck with a strong twist. I placed the chick's body gently on the dried earth of the colony, there for a passing harrier or to be slowly recycled into the soil. As I moved off back to the hut to finish packing, the elegiac couplets of a song thrush sounded from the ribbonwood trees below, poignant notes in the autumnal air that signalled the end to the first season in the valley.

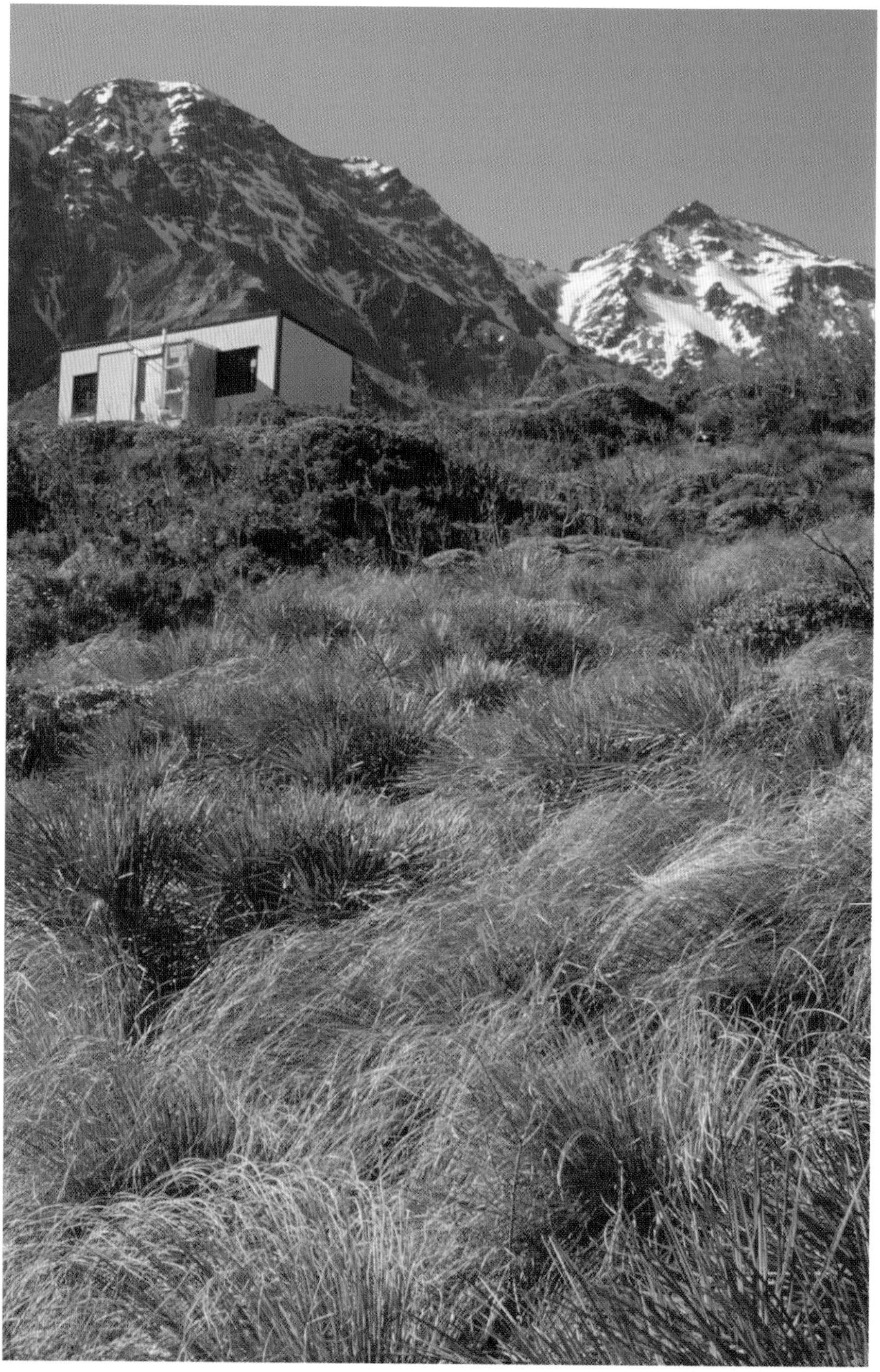

The finished hut, with snow tussock and mountains beyond. Author photo

10. A new season and new questions

The departing sound of the helicopter and piles of gear in the snow marked the start of our second field season, and our excitement at being in the valley again was palpable. It was early September and we were back in time for the shearwaters' arrival and the subsequent seven months of their breeding season. Despite my worst fears the hut had stood up to its winter battering, although we had only been able to make out the rectangular shape of the white hut against the backdrop of snow in the last moment of the flight in.

Over the course of the first field season the hut had become home, the clutter of living, working and relaxing transforming it from its original bleak shell. Blank walls had been covered in posters and photos and the shelves were a jumble of food, books and clothes. The hut had been designed in three main sections, each third broadly corresponding to areas for sleeping, eating and working. The sleeping quarters contained four bunks, some shelving, and stacks of cardboard boxes for clothes and gear that could be slid under the bunks. Windows on the north and south walls allowed a fair perusal of the weather from the warm depths of a sleeping bag, and a wooden sliding door offered a degree of privacy from the rest of the hut.

The mid-section held a gas stove, fridge, table and shelves. From here the outside door opened onto a small porch where wet clothes and boots could be removed, and where the shower was located. Dave and Keith from DOC in Kaikoura had added this porch and a large deck at the end of the first season; before this, the door had opened onto three wooden steps to the ground. With the creation of the deck the three steps were recycled into a dissection bench for shearwater autopsies.

The small central table was flanked along the north wall by a long bench piled high with spare pillows and a couple of blankets – adding, to my eyes, a certain boudoir-like elegance to the surroundings, although I was perhaps alone in this appreciation. The bench seats were hollow and the tops hinged at the wall, concealing an insulated space for storing potatoes, pumpkins, onions, garlic and other vegetables. Food supplies were limited by when flights could be arranged and what could be flown in; fresh food usually came in only about once a month, but it was rare that we had to resort to the dehydrated peas.

Despite the great temptation to grow our own supplies – the soil of the valley, enriched by thousands of years of shearwater guano, would have grown incredible vegetables – we were careful to ensure that all vegetable waste and seeds were flown out with the rubbish. Yet the shearwaters supplied us indirectly with greens, as during the summer introduced sorrel grew verdantly among the burrows and the steep streams were full of wild watercress. The bitter-iron taste of fresh watercress with the sharp lemon tang of sorrel made a great salad when other veggies had run out.

On either side of the table were shelves piled high with chutneys, hot pickles, olives, gherkins, jams and marmalade, as well as assorted books, magazines and a pile of first aid kits. The stove and cooking workbench ran the length of the south wall with shelves of herbs and spices above. The cupboards beneath were jammed with food, and had been the scene of emergency plumbing repairs when a five-day southerly caused the pipes to freeze and burst. After that experience I had crawled under the hut and added an extra join to the water pipes so the system could be drained at the start of a cold snap and at the end of the season. Heating in the hut was non-existent, other than putting the gas burners on for 10 minutes while doing star jumps on the deck outside. Baking bread or a cake warmed the hut a little and provided further reward for the effort. We frequently sat inside wearing a hat, gloves and down jackets while wrapped in our sleeping bags.

Above the stove hung four large-scale maps that covered the whole of the Inland and Seaward ranges and the meandering sweep of the Clarence River. The maps told tales of the history and nature of the Kaikoura ranges and I could happily lose myself in the contours and names. The major features had retained their original Māori names: the mountains of Manakau, Uwerau, Te Ao Whekere and Tapuae-o-Uenuku, the Kahutara, Kowhai and Hapuku rivers and Parapara Stream. Other major landmarks, such as Mt Fyffe and Jordan Stream, had been named, or renamed, by the early European settlers. The smaller features assumed names that described the character of the place: Split Rock Stream, Dead Horse Stream, Mt Snowflake and Mt Alarm. Other names just left questions. What happened along the Dubious Stream? Who waited in Fidget Stream? Could I camp in Happy Valley, sip from Whisky Stream, avoid a tryst with Roaring Meg and return along Homestead Spur to Gentle Annie? My topographic travels would usually be rudely interrupted by the smell of burning toast, my reverie broken by the mundane realities of flambéed bread and singed fingertips.

The last third of the hut was for working: shelving covered all walls. Despite periodic and severe cleaning sessions, my desk and workbench remained in a state of chaos to all but my own eyes. It was crudely centred on a laptop computer, but usually included the assorted flotsam of the previous week's work and repairs. The dismembered camera head of the burrowscope lay on one side among a scattering of screws, wires and a propane soldering iron. Empty Golden Syrup tins stuffed full of pencils and pens competed with jam jars of harrier and kea feathers. Three empty shearwater eggs awaiting measurement sat perilously close to four fist-sized concretions clustered together like a clutch of moa eggs. A sloping pile of scientific papers constantly threatened to avalanche onto the floor, their progress hampered only by a coffee plunger balanced precariously on top. Underneath, a box of watercolours waited forlornly for an afternoon of no fieldwork. Shelves on either side of the bench were stacked with nuts and bolts, tools, glue, sandpaper and paints. The SSB radio and radio-tracking gear occupied another two shelves, along with spent copies of newspapers, magazines and a catholic collection of bird and plant guides, novels, several well-thumbed textbooks and a battered statistics guide. The top shelf was lined with several bottles of gin, ginger wine and a collection of single malts – Talisker, Laphroaig, Oban and Dalmore – bottled memories of Scotland whose spirits rattled mournfully whenever a norwester shook the hut.

Postcards and pictures of family and friends were pinned around the window that framed a vista of the entire northern sweep of the Kowhai Valley. It was a view that provided distraction and inspiration in almost equal measure, for my concentration was easily broken by the silent sweep of a harrier cruising over Camp sub-colony, or a party of redpolls gamely feeding on the spent flower stems of a speargrass plant two metres from my eyes. Whenever I needed reassurance as to why I was mind-numbingly entering data into the computer or trying to solve a particularly grim statistical knot, all I had to do was look up and take in the valley.

Outside the western window two large solar panels were bolted firmly to a wooden stand, a favourite perch for kea. Often as I worked at my desk, a soft enquiring 'keeaaa' a metre to the left of my head would reveal Aston, or occasionally Motherwell, the matriarch of the group, perched on the panels with neck craned and head tilted, peering intently in, leaving me with the slightly unnerving question of just who was studying whom. The solar panels were connected to a bank of three large 12-volt batteries that met the hut's few power requirements – the computer, phone and radios, a battery charger and a couple of small fluorescent strip-lights whose output was meagre and harsh. Candles or a Tilley lamp provided more comfort and a little heating.

The rattle of a boiling billy and the prospect of coffee brought me round. Mug in hand, I told Erica I was off for a short walk: code for the fact that I was heading to one of my favourite lookout spots. I stumbled down to Col Stream, scalding coffee burning my fingers and leaving a trail in the snow. Through the snow I could feel the rocks of Geoff's old campfire under my feet, and the sharp spines of speargrass prickled my legs as I turned off the narrow path and ducked low to squeeze through the soft branches into a thicket of ribbonwood. Amid the trees an open patch of ground formed a luxuriant seat and an unsurpassed view down Col Stream to the peaks on the southwest rim of the valley. During my first season I had often disappeared to the site with my journal or a sketchpad, intent on trying to record what it was about the place that made me feel so alive. But invariably the stark grandeur of the view and the purling stream would hypnotise me and I would end up sitting still, slowly absorbing the magic of the valley.

The ability to sit silently and still seems an underwhelming skill, but doing so brought its reward, for after a few minutes any ripples of the disturbance created by my crashing through the trees would die down and the natural life of the valley would resume. I settled down to wait, my hands warmed by the hot coffee and a chunk of fruitcake balanced on my knee. After a few minutes a pair of chaffinches began to 'pink' to each other from the bushes below me, their contact calls moving through the trees. A harrier glided silently down the valley, its form lit by the late afternoon sunlight that was cresting the ridge of Mt Saunders. Through my binoculars I followed the harrier's flight as it soared effortlessly on the cool southerly breeze and weak thermals that still rose from the sun-warmed rock and scree. The bird was an old one, for its plumage was pale, hardly contrasting with the white rump that was so visible in young birds.

Out of the ribbonwood below appeared a party of six riflemen; with high-pitched squeaks they scurried noisily past in the trees two metres from my eyes. Their olive-green feathers fluffed up against the cold, they were near-spherical bundles of hyperactivity, busily probing under and over every twig, the pickings lean at this time of year. Below me a dunnock sang, hidden from sight amidst the trees. A few minutes later a movement to my left caught my eye, and glancing downwards I saw the dried stems of a tussock tremble. Breathing silently I stared at the tussock until another quiver betrayed further movement. Through the sun-bleached grass I could just make out a warmer russet-brown colour, until with another push the whiskered pink nose and black pearl eyes of a house mouse appeared, drawn to me by the crumbs of fruitcake I had inadvertently scattered. The mouse scurried forward and stopped, nose busily testing the air, before scampering forward again then leaping back, losing half of the distance it had gained towards me. I remained motionless as it dashed to within 15 centimetres of my foot, seized the largest crumb and vanished back into the tussock. The mouse was yet another introduced species in this land, and was the only rodent species present as the breeding colonies were too high up for rats, but as the light faded and the temperature dipped for the start of a sub-zero night I didn't begrudge it a few crumbs.

Levering myself up, I stretched and began to traverse back to the hut to organise my things and plan what we were to do over the next few weeks. The winter had been filled with trying to make sense of the first season's data, and analysis time in Dunedin had been intermingled with examining the body size and condition of shearwaters I had found freshly killed. The work had been monotonous and repetitive, and I realised I was a far better worker in the field than in the lab. My attempt to 'ash' some shearwater carcasses (to calculate the skeletal mass as a measure of the absolute body size) had provided the only excitement, although the ensuing fire had filled the rest of the Zoology building with acrid clouds of reeking shearwater-tainted smoke, leading to the abandonment of all lectures and seminars and a full-scale fire alert. After that, I was as relieved to be heading back to the Kaikoura ranges as the rest of the department were to see me go.

The first season of any field project always produces more questions than answers, and the Kowhai Valley research was no exception. The biggest puzzle was that stoats did not appear to be killing many shearwaters. Undoubtedly some were killed, for the studies of adults, chicks and eggs had revealed bite marks and other signs that could only have been made by stoats,[1] and every one of the stoat scats we had gathered and tediously teased apart had contained shearwater remains.[2] Yet the predicted devastation – the hundreds of carcasses I had expected to find littering the ground and the near total failure in breeding success – was not a reality. Why not? I didn't know. I needed to find out a whole lot more about stoats in order to understand their impact on the shearwaters, and a lot more about how the shearwaters coped and survived living in the high mountains. How was it they appeared able to withstand predation by stoats?

11. The breeding season begins

The caterwauling cries of shearwaters welled up around us in the darkness, the sound rising and falling as individual birds responded to a neighbour's call with their own cry in a wave of sound that ebbed and flowed across the hillside. Calling birds flew high overhead en route to one of the high-altitude sub-colonies further up the valley, while the sounds from the fluttering wingtips of low-circling birds was punctuated with sudden thumps as they crashed onto the snow's surface in Camp sub-colony.

It was early September and the shearwaters' breeding season was beginning. The birds had all departed the colonies by mid-April to spend five months at sea in waters off Australia before returning to New Zealand.[1] During this time, last season's breeding birds would have recuperated some of their energy reserves lost during the seven months spent incubating eggs and feeding chicks, and would have moulted a number of flight and body feathers. With fresh pinions, and fatter and heavier than when they departed, the birds were back and ready for the serious business of breeding.

Sitting next to Erica on a roll-mat in the snow, I rubbed my hands together to warm them. Alongside me were six cotton bird-bags, their strings looped around two short bamboo poles stuck in the snow. Occasionally one bag would twitch and the low hoots of a shearwater's call would begin and end abruptly. The noise and movement of one would set off twitching and hooting from its neighbours, like an ill-constructed set of Newton's balls. I picked up the first bag, hung it from a spring balance and waited patiently for the bird to stop moving before calling out the mass to be noted down. Carefully opening the bag, I used Vernier callipers to measure

OPPOSITE: Adult Hutton's shearwater at sea off Kaikoura. Author photo

bill length, bill depth and width, total head length and shoulder width. Then I used a stopped-rule to measure the wing chord before picking up the callipers again to measure the tarsus length. The order was well established and after each measurement I called out the number and waited as Erica repeated it before writing it down – cross-checking to ensure no error was recorded.

After taking all measurements I wrapped the bird tightly in its bag and carefully pulled a stainless steel New Zealand X-series ring off its cardboard loop. With two squeezes of the pliers the band was closed to within a millimetre around the bird's leg and carefully flattened to an oblong shape to match the leg's flat profile. I checked that the ring slid freely up and down the tarsus, then unwrapped the bird and placed it on the ground. It sat there, gaining its bearings, before shooting off down the slope with kicking feet, scattering snow over my boots and notebook. Finally I picked up the empty bag and weighed it to note the mass to be subtracted from the earlier weight.

After several months in Dunedin it was good to be back where I felt most at home. It was equally rewarding to start entering more data in the field books. The American scientist and natural history author George Schaller is quoted in Peter Matthiessen's *The Snow Leopard* as saying, 'Once the data starts coming in I don't care about much else: I feel I'm justifying my existence.'[2] Sitting on the snow in Camp sub-colony I knew that the 92 birds we had just processed would add further information to our understanding of the shearwaters' ecology and justify my presence in the valley.

As the early days of the second season progressed we returned to the usual routine in the valley: re-establishing the transect lines for shearwater carcasses in the seven sub-colonies we were monitoring, searching on the snow and under boulders for stoat scats and, after two long days setting them out, undertaking daily checks of the stoat traps. With snow still on the ground, the only job we couldn't start was rebuilding and rechecking all the study burrows. The emphasis instead was on getting out each night to capture and weigh shearwaters around Camp sub-colony, whose northwest-facing slopes were beginning to thaw. Each night we either stayed awake until near midnight then worked for two to three hours, or we set the alarm for an anti-social 3am and worked until dawn. As a definitive 'morning person', I found neither option great for my body-clock, but the magical nights among flocks of calling and courting shearwaters made up for the chronic lack of sleep.

But the reappearance of thousands of birds each night high up in the colony in early September was odd, as egg-laying was still well over a month away and the birds might have been better off feeding and building up their reserves at sea. In some areas of the valley the shearwaters' burrows were still buried under snow

– at least half a metre lay over Top sub-colony, and well over a metre had settled in some of the higher sub-colonies and more sheltered areas of burrowed ground. Nonetheless the birds were back, and not just for the odd night but returning every few nights for almost a two-month period, calling and beginning all the normal preludes to breeding as pairs reformed and individuals prospected for a partner. Despite the snow concealing any defined boundaries, they returned each night to the same patch of colony and we repeatedly caught the same individuals in the same areas.

The effort required for a seabird like Hutton's shearwater to climb from sea level to 1200–1800 metres is substantial. Like all other shearwaters and petrels, Hutton's are designed for a life at sea; on a windy day off Kaikoura in September or October they can be seen in their thousands, soaring and banking with the barest flick of a wing as they tack and jibe in the wind and are uplifted over a wave's crest. So efficient is the flight of a wandering albatross, a far larger relative of Hutton's shearwater, that a bird soaring over the waves uses no more energy than it does when sitting still on water. In contrast, the energy costs of flapping flight, such as when an albatross takes off from the water's surface in light winds, are high: flapping flight is estimated to take 15 times more energy.[3] The flying required for a Hutton's shearwater to reach its breeding group was costly, with each bird having to flap steadily for 20–40 minutes in order to gain the altitude and cover the distance.

Evidence of this cost came in this second year of the study when the snowfall was particularly heavy and lay in the highest sub-colonies until mid-November. For two months we had been out on as many nights as we could manage, catching, measuring and weighing all the shearwaters we could lay our hands on at Camp and also Top sub-colony, a site further up the valley that lay in shadow. The effort of flying in to the colonies every few nights was clearly having a similar effect on the shearwaters as someone taking up running while maintaining their normal diet: over two months, repeated measurements of the same birds indicated that they were losing weight to the point where their body mass was 30–50 grams lower at the time of egg-laying than when they had first returned from their winter migration.[4] The birds in Top sub-colony, whose breeding was delayed by an extra month due to the snow cover, lost more mass than birds in Camp sub-colony.

An adult Hutton's shearwater typically weighs 330–350 grams, so a loss of 30–50 grams was not trivial for birds about to start incubating an egg, sitting there for up to a week with no access to food. Energy reserves during incubation were critical and could mark the difference between breeding success and failure. They were also important in a bird's decision to breed[5] and the resources invested in the egg: it is known that petrels with better body condition lay larger eggs. In many bird

Shearwaters at night in the colony. Author photo

species hatching success is linked to egg size;[6] this pattern had been found in several seabirds and was likely to hold true for Hutton's shearwater. Given these patterns and the fact that females would not begin laying eggs for another six to eight weeks, what were they doing flying in to the colony every few days? As ever, we needed more data to understand the situation.

As the weeks of pre-laying activity progressed, a pattern began to emerge. Both males and females were flying in and out of the colony; the males turned up on average every second or third night while females returned on average every fourth night. This made sense because females had to retain sufficient reserves to lay an egg, whereas males were less constrained. Even more interestingly, we realised that it wasn't just a single pair of birds visiting each burrow, but up to five or six different birds. The number of visits a pair made to a burrow was a key factor in deterring other birds from visiting: the more often they were home in the burrow, the fewer visits the burrow had from strangers. For a young pair without a burrow, a smart way to acquire one was to spend as many nights as possible in a burrow in order to displace the resident pair.[7]

In the shearwaters' world, like ours, it seemed possession was nine-tenths of the law, and the only way to maintain possession of a burrow was to keep coming back from the sea in order to be present and deter others. Although the resultant weight loss could jeopardise the chances of surviving an unexpectedly long incubation shift or producing an egg with sufficient yolk to last the embryo through to hatching, the cost of not defending a burrow was even higher. Without a burrow it was not possible to breed at all, and birds that consistently failed to put in the hard yards of flying to the colony and claiming a burrow were headed for an evolutionary dead end.

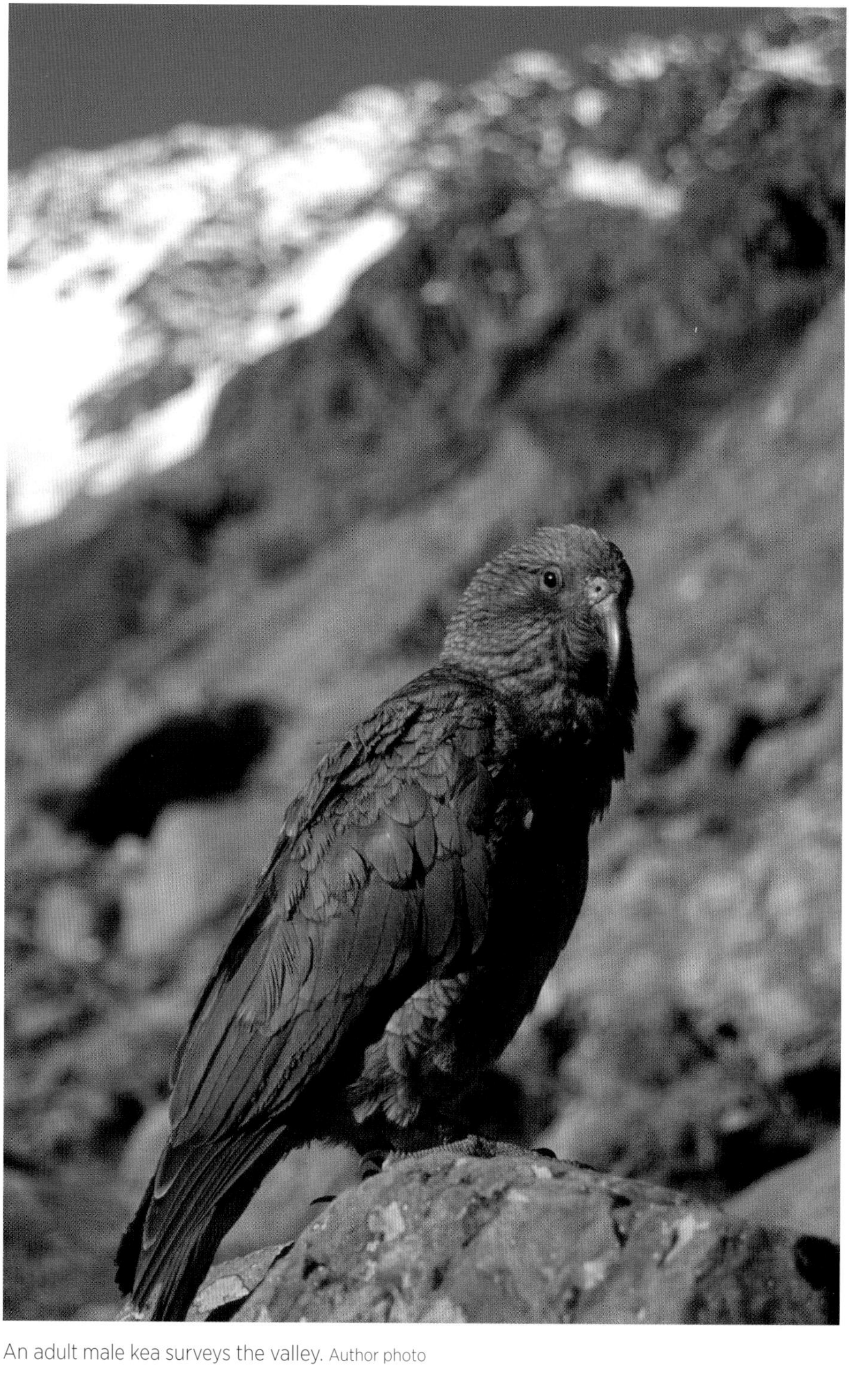

An adult male kea surveys the valley. Author photo

12. Living with kea

At five in the morning, after four hours out in the colonies, we wearily returned to the hut hoping for a couple of hours' sleep before the sun rose. I groaned, for as we reached the hut we were greeted with a chorus of screeches from three kea that bounded across the roof to peer down at us.

Two hours of fitful sleep passed, during which the kea amused themselves by trying to climb up the hut's guy-lines, galloping in unison from one end of the roof to the other, pulling out bamboo marker poles from under the hut, and a 40-minute game of tug-of-war with a scrap of nylon rope that began on the helipad, proceeded to the deck outside the bunkroom window and ended up on the hut's roof. I got up at seven and put the billy on for coffee: revenge was required.

During the first season it had become clear that kea were playing more of a role in preying upon shearwater eggs and chicks than previously thought. We could dismiss the idea that kea only opportunistically found the odd egg or took a chick: they knew exactly how to find their prey and how to kill it. The behaviour of the kea fascinated me, for they are among the most intelligent of birds. I determined to find out how they survived in the valley and the extent of their impact on Hutton's shearwaters.

Early on I had begun making behavioural and feeding observations of these birds. One such observation occurred after I had completed a check of the burrows in New sub-colony. As I scrambled around the side of the bluff I heard the peculiar and persistent squawk of an excited kea. The sound was coming from above me, but I could see nothing from where I was. I climbed a loose gut that separated the two patches of colony until I was high enough to look down onto a free-standing pillar of rock. On the very top of the pillar – a most impressive choice of location – the valley's main male and female pair were engaged in what can only be described as an enthusiastic bout of copulation. The male was hunched over the female, wings outspread and beak gripping the back of the female's neck. The female squatted down low on the rock, her tail twisted up and to one side, neck arched up and beak open, providing most of the sounds. A few minutes had passed since I had first heard them and the vigorous action and sounds continued unabated. I sat down, interested to see whether after mating they would fly off to a potential nesting site or engage in a session of mutual preening to reinforce their pair bond. Fifteen minutes later the squeals were undiminished and I quietly retreated and left them to it.

I accumulated many records, noting the plants a kea was foraging on, whether it was eating flowers or berries or digging into the ground for grubs and roots, and recording the age and sex of the individual. It quickly became apparent that kea eat, or at least pick up and manipulate, anything and everything. My observations would read 'rock', 'rock again', not to mention 'rucksack', 'boots', 'drying clothes' and 'radio aerial', as well as a lot more typical observations of plants and berries. I was often thwarted by the fact that I could not distinguish which kea was which and was forced to categorise birds simply by their age and sex. Yet from watching them around the hut it was clear that kea are most certainly individuals. We had held off catching and banding any kea for the benefit of David Attenborough and the film crew, as nothing looks more fake on a natural history film than an animal with a brightly coloured band. Now we were keen to start catching and marking the birds. Kea are smart, however – smart enough that we had to make sure whenever we caught one that there were no others looking on who would see what was happening. But they are also social animals, so the chance of finding one on its own was slim.

On this particular morning three young kea remained outside the hut, two females and one male, and were now playing on the helipad, happily gouging chunks of wood from the recently laid planks. I grabbed a fishing net and a pair of thick gloves and sauntered outside, stopping to sit on a tussock five metres away. The kea stopped and looked at me briefly before deciding I was harmless and resuming their destruction. I shifted myself to a tussock closer to the helipad, and over the next 10 minutes shuffled ever closer until I was sitting on the helipad corner with the fishing net stretched out in front of me flat on the wood.

The kea stopped to observe me again before continuing their game. All were now furiously engaged in pulling off splinters of wood along the edges of the roughly finished planking. Each bird had its feet spread wide, wood firmly grasped in its beak, back and neck jerking powerfully, head twisting from side to side like a terrier with a rat. After minutes of fierce wrestling, a splinter would suddenly break free and the kea would hurtle backwards, sometimes overbalancing completely to fall on its back with a muffled squawk of indignation. A tug-of-war would begin with all of them competing for the splinter. The young male, bigger and more powerfully built than his sisters, would usually win this rough and tumble, and would then proceed to strut in dominance around the helipad until after a few minutes he would drop the wood and seize hold of another splinter for more wrestling.

The play-fighting became more and more boisterous and the kea less and less aware of my presence until the young male, in his efforts to keep hold of a piece of wood, ran backwards into the net I had laid down. With a flip of the handle I swung the net over and down. Almost immediately the captured bird started a raucous screeching, and before I could even get to the net an adult male and female – presumably the parents of the three young birds – appeared out of the mist to land on the helipad. Although the three young birds had appeared to be foraging independently, their parents were obviously keeping a close eye on things.

Grabbing the young bird carefully around the back of his neck and shoulders I hurriedly picked up net and kea and rushed into the hut. His screeching stopped in the unfamiliarity of the surroundings and I started to untangle him from the netting, all the while keeping a careful eye on his beak and a firm grip of the back of his head, for if he seized me with that can-opener it was going to hurt badly. He was quickly weighed, measured and banded and, resplendent with a numbered metal band on one leg and a bright red band on the other, released onto the decking in front of the hut. Ruffled and indignant, he took off into the depths of the ribbonwood trees below the hut.

I sat outside again and watched the two young female kea at play with the adult pair, and waited for his return. The birds had found a stray piece of string somewhere under the hut and were now dragging this around the helipad, all four of them fighting for possession. After 10 minutes the young male reappeared, cautiously flying over the helipad four times before landing. His behaviour was subdued: there was none of his normal dominance and bossing of his sisters. Instead he sat on the edge of the helipad, feathers fluffed up and head down, to all appearances in a teenage sulk. Both sisters bounced over to check him out and in a pantomime of intrigue proceeded to stare at his bright red and metal bands, before inching closer and trying to give the offending articles a peck.

He didn't react well to this and tried to fend off their probing beaks, but their curiosity was too great and they outnumbered him, so eventually he flew off in apparent exasperation to the other side of the helipad. I sat there in hysterics, although at the same time feeling slightly guilty for his predicament. He remained subdued and submissive for another five minutes until his parents, reassured that things were pretty much back to normal, flew off down the valley. The two sisters began wrestling over a *Dracophyllum* stem, and after a few minutes of careful observation the young male bounced towards them in the peculiar sideways gait that only kea seem to use. Almost immediately he was back to his old self, leading the campaign to procure the stem and bossing the sisters around as he had done before. Relieved that he wasn't psychologically scarred for life, I watched them play for another few minutes and got down to the serious business of thinking of a name.

Naming an animal is always a quandary; in the supposedly dry world of science a name is one step towards anthropomorphising your study animal, a sin close to a hanging offence in zoological circles. Or, as one colleague put it, 'If you can name your study animals, then your sample size isn't big enough.' Despite this, I was convinced that the Kowhai kea were individuals, not just clockwork automatons blindly driven by natural selection. Among the 15 or so kea in the valley there were the shy and the bold, the naïve and the savvy, the smart and the not so smart, the beautiful and the downright scruffy. Such singular characters deserved names. Mulling possible choices I trawled though various Greek heroes, Norse gods and Himalayan mountains. But as the sun shone on the bright red band the name Hotspur sprang to mind. The noble family of Hotspur – I liked it and felt sure that it was sufficiently distinguished to grace one of the Kowhai kea clan.

A week later I captured another kea. Hotspur had been named after the late-medieval nobleman but the second kea naturally had to be called Tottenham. Hotspur's sisters were also quickly caught and, in keeping with what had now become a soccer theme, were named Hibs and Hearts. The adult female was christened Motherwell after the Edinburgh team and the fact she had successfully raised two broods in two seasons, and the alpha male of the valley became Kilmarnock for no good reason other than I liked the name.

With the valley's kea now banded and easier to identify I began watching them with further interest. Kea have a curious system of social dominance whereby adult and sub-adult birds will feign submissiveness to a younger bird in order to help it learn to forage and fend for itself. Thus while the adult male and female were both stronger than the two young females, they would generally be the ones to back off when they squared up for a tussle, the adult birds shuffling away while the young females – feathers fluffed out on their neck and breast and with arched back and wings hunched forward – strutted around in a dominant pose.

Fledgling kea are heavily dependent on older kea for finding food during much of their first year, and older birds tolerate the frequently aggressive behaviour of their offspring at this stage.[1] Juvenile kea of one to two years of age are more socially aware than fledglings and are generally submissive to adults, hunching their heads down, tucking their bills to their breasts and fluffing up their feathers. In the presence of such submissive behaviour the dominant pair in the valley, Kilmarnock and Motherwell, would share an item of food, much in the same way that the alpha male and female in a wolf pack will share with submissive wolves. That this state of dominance was all subterfuge was sometimes revealed when the adult male kea, after being pushed, bitten and battered by his over-exuberant offspring for a while, occasionally snapped. With a sharp twist of his beak he would dislodge a few feathers, to an outraged yelp and instant submission by the young bird.

Much of our understanding of the kea's ecology and behaviour was down to another mountaineer and ornithologist, J.R. Jackson. Dick or 'Kea' Jackson, as he was frequently known, worked as a teacher and then as a chemist with the Buller boot company. In his spare time in the 1960s he undertook the first in-depth study of kea in Arthur's Pass, publishing five papers that were the foundation for future studies. Dick was a legendary character and over his decade of work in Arthur's Pass he caught and banded more than 600 kea and found 36 active nests – no mean feat when kea nests are typically well hidden in a tunnel or crevice under rocks or in an old hollow tree. Jackson, along with more recent kea researchers Judy Diamond and Alan Bond, spent many hours observing the birds at a rubbish dump outside the township of Arthur's Pass, where many kea gathered for the rich pickings of food. On one occasion a National Park employee allegedly tried to kick a large burlap sack into a trench of garbage, only to discover Dick Jackson was inside and using the sack as a hide from which to watch and study kea.[2]

Given their shared interests it was inevitable that Geoff Harrow and Dick Jackson would run into each other. The pair met once or twice through the Canterbury Mountaineering Club, but really got to know each other through the New Zealand Ornithological Society. Following his discovery of the Hutton's shearwater breeding site, Geoff had continued to explore the Seaward and Inland Kaikoura ranges for other sites and to visit the colonies to find out what was happening each month. Dick accompanied him on many of these trips, particularly on the winter journeys when no one else would come. Geoff recalled, 'Dick was quite an amazing guy: absolutely obsessed with birds, very knowledgeable and superbly fit. And I never saw him ever wearing a pair of socks.'[3] Geoff was no stranger to the mountains, but in some of their winter bivouacs when his teeth were chattering with cold Dick seemed impervious to it (no socks and all), and would be leaping about saying, 'This is marvellous!' Dick was also a fine bushman as well as a mountaineer and naturalist, and according to Geoff would carry scraps of rubber from the boot factory with which to start a fire. Geoff enjoyed those trips: having a companion who was equally in his element in the mountains was a pleasure, and between them they explored many areas of the Kaikoura mountains where others wouldn't go.

Dick's sheer enthusiasm for natural history would at times frustrate Geoff, however, as getting in to the colonies took forever if there were other things about to look at. 'Anything a bit unusual and he'd be off, chasing a pipit or hedge sparrow or a falcon. Shouting "I've just got to watch this bird!" or "Got to find this nest!"'[4] Dick also undertook the first in-depth studies of the Westland petrel in the thick forests of the South Island's West Coast. Then one day in 1989 he disappeared in Westland National Park while searching for remnant breeding areas of Cook's petrel. Although his campsite and gear were found high in the Mt Hooker Range, his body was never discovered.

A few weeks after we had banded most kea in the valley, we caught one bird that was to become a near constant companion over the next two years. Aston (named after his blue band) plagued and amused us in equal measure. Like the football team I supported, he was neither stylish nor elegant, nor particularly smart, and he was certainly not one of the top birds in the valley. Instead he was a somewhat goofy and gangling adolescent whose persistence occasionally secured a modest victory, but who more often loitered mid-league with unfulfilled promise.

Aston was probably aged three or four years when we caught him. The pale yellow crown of a young bird had faded into the olive green of an adult but his eye ring was still yellow, although not the bright egg-yolk colour of a fledgling. As a sub-adult kea Aston had lost the social protection and tolerance that adults showed to fledgling and juvenile birds, and he lurked in submission whenever the patriarchal male, Kilmarnock, was around. When no adults were in sight, Aston would be forthright in bossing any first-year birds in a reversal of the normal dominance hierarchy; when Kilmarnock or Motherwell appeared he would become submissive to all.

Perhaps as a consequence of Aston's in-limbo status, he was more solitary than any of the other kea in the valley, and he chose our hut and the area around it as his base. Quite what Aston gained from this relationship was unclear, for we had a strict rule and on no occasion was Aston or any other kea given food. Nonetheless he stuck around, seeming to regard us as company or as a source of amusement. Like adult kea, sub-adults – and particularly sub-adult males – engage only rarely in the play activity of fledgling and juvenile birds.[5] Yet Aston appeared to be an exception and would play endlessly on his own or in the company of other kea if they were around. As a result, we suffered the indignity of losing boot innersoles, having clothes removed from the washing line and spread liberally around the neighbouring bushes, and watching helplessly as Aston flew around the valley clutching the red plastic bowl from which I normally drank my morning cup of tea

A young kea unhelpfully destroying study burrow markers. Author photo

– the consequence of a minute's inattention as I left my breakfast on the helipad to go and retrieve a notebook. When other kea visited the hut Aston would get down to boisterous play fighting.

The helipad and the roof of the hut, as we have seen, acted as the prime kea meeting sites; on one occasion a record 14 kea were lined up along the roof. The hut had other attractions for them too – in fact it offered an exciting array of games and challenges. The cables that ran over the hut were a favourite – kea would endlessly practise scaling the wires: with both feet wrapped around the cable and beak gripping it for balance, they would slowly haul themselves along and onto the roof of the hut. Some of the fledglings had mastered this trick, yet despite near daily practice Aston could only get halfway up when, wings flapping madly for balance, he swung upside down and suffered an ignoble drop onto his head.

The telephone antenna we had fitted to the roof was another prime target: if kea were not trying to chew through the wires (a perennial problem dogging our communication with the outside world) they would be trying to land on the shaking mast. The antenna was guarded by a row of vertical receivers and it was not the easiest landing, yet it was managed by all except Aston, who would invariably end up half-skewered in position with a couple of antenna jammed into his belly before falling amid a flurry of flapping wings.

As a species the kea (now a protected species) has suffered in New Zealand from over a century's persecution for attacking sheep in the South Island's high-country stations. The behaviour was first reported in the late 1860s when dead sheep were found with plucked wool and open wounds on their backs.[6] Kea were soon observed to be the culprits: attracted by the huge numbers of sheep and an abundant new feeding opportunity, they became a problem for many runholders. The response was swift and disproportionate, and a bounty of up to three shillings a head resulted in tens of thousands being killed across the South Island. Professional bounty hunters emerged, and as well as shooting and trapping birds, they would set out sheep carcasses containing strychnine to kill kea and anything else that fed on them. So widespread was the association of kea with sheep that the illustration of kea in the 1888 edition of Walter Buller's *A History of the Birds of New Zealand* shows kea attacking a sheep in the background. Kea still do attack sheep, landing on the animal's back and cutting through the skin to feed on the underlying fat.

Several theories have been put forward to explain how such a behaviour might have evolved, ranging from kea scavenging on moa carcasses;[7] or feeding on the carcass, maggots and other insect larvae of dead sheep; to the similarity with tearing apart 'vegetable sheep', a group of alpine plants with a superficial similarity to a sheep's fleece.[8] The kea's method of digging up and killing Hutton's shearwater chicks in order to consume the fat was analogous to the way they attacked sheep, and in the past, when Hutton's shearwaters and other petrels were more widely distributed, this behaviour must have been common.

It would be wrong, however, to suggest that kea attack sheep because of this behaviour. The main reason kea are able to survive in their alpine environment is because of their intelligence, resourcefulness and willingness to try out a dozen or more ingenious ways of finding a feeding opportunity. Kea researchers Judy Diamond and Alan Bond describe kea as an 'open-program' species,[9] a term coined by the evolutionary biologist Ernst Mayr[10] to emphasise species that display behavioural flexibility as opposed to predetermined patterns of behaviour. The constant play and social behaviour of kea allow the species to acquire new skills and seek out novel feeding opportunities. Any past habits, such as feeding on moa carcasses or even vegetable sheep, are unlikely to be relevant to their behaviour today; rather, their open-programming enables them to find and adapt to new conditions and opportunities, be it feeding on the back of a sheep or digging through burrows to pull out a shearwater chick.

The kea's confidence, resourcefulness and ingenuity remain to my mind a better national symbol for New Zealand than the nocturnal and myopic kiwi: perhaps if kiwi were the sheep killers it would have been the other way around. While I cursed

Aston and the other birds as they dragged a bamboo stick across the roof of the hut at four in the morning, living among wild kea brought rewards and pleasure, and life in the valley would have been emptier in their absence.

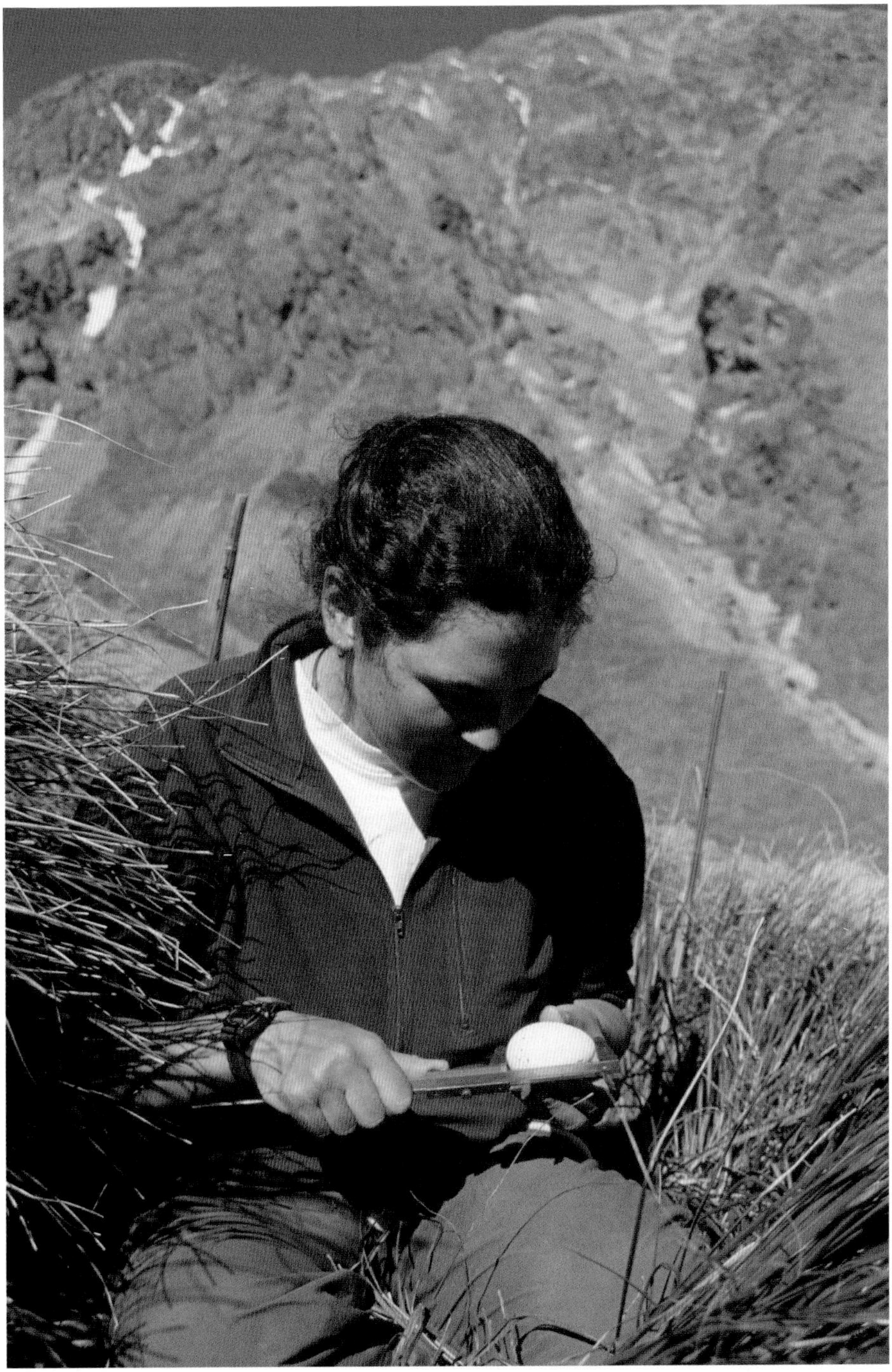

Erica Sommer measuring a shearwater's egg during the early stages of the breeding season.
Author photo

13. Egg-laying and incubation

After yet another long night I lay back in the tussock and slowly flexed my hands to get rid of the stiffness from squeezing bands for three hours. It was five in the morning and quite mild in comparison to the previous few weeks. Rather than returning to the hut for a snooze, I repositioned my roll-mat and lay down where I was to wait for dawn.

The last shearwaters were coming out of their burrows to head to sea. As the sky gradually turned from inky black to purple they were silent, vulnerable to harrier attack as the sky became light. The only sound, other than the roar of the river in the valley below – a noise I was now so used to I had to make a conscious effort to hear it – was of birds brushing through the tussock and the quiet but urgent beat of wing-tips as they took off. In still weather like this the shearwaters eased their take-off by launching themselves down the slope of the colony, and as I lay on the ground birds skimmed past a few feet overhead, wings and legs clipping the tussock tops. The last departing birds were clearly visible against the dawn sky and were running a serious risk from the pair of New Zealand falcons that held a territory downstream.

Soon the diurnal residents of the valley began to make themselves heard: two long thin 'theesssp' calls came from a yellowhammer in the shade of the valley, and first one and then a second blackbird began to sing. With the dawn chorus, the sun's rays struck the tip of Mt Saunders and the top of the snow gully opposite, reminding me of the first season when Mike and I had crested the ridge at the moment the sun rose.

All of the shearwaters in the colony had now reclaimed burrows, or established themselves as new owners of burrows, and further signs of spring were beginning to emerge in the valley. Buds on the ribbonwood scrub in the most sheltered areas were tentatively opening, not fooled by the early warmth over the previous couple of weeks; in the first season many ribbonwood leaves had already unfurled when a late cold front swept up the valley, sealing the buds and leaves in a cryogenic cast of glimmering ice. The bankside primroses were also beginning to open, although there was not yet the profusion of blooms of last year. I'd recently seen a small flock of silvereyes that had probably spent the winter down in the low-altitude forests of the Kaikoura ranges, picking their way through the ribbonwoods below the hut and gleaning a parlous living from the bark. Two blackbirds had begun to call each morning from the steep hillside opposite the hut – out-of-place voices in the mountains of New Zealand, but like the shearwaters they were responding to the stirrings of spring.

One other sign of spring was unmistakeable, for two shearwaters we had weighed the night before were uncharacteristically heavy with swollen abdomens. It was 23 October and the first eggs were about to be laid. I was relieved, as the arrival of eggs also meant we could ease off on the nocturnal banding and measuring and get back to a semblance of normal sleep.

I was interested in monitoring egg-laying for several reasons. The first was to determine what proportion of burrows actually contained incubating pairs of birds, since a colony with a low number of occupied burrows would be indicative of a population in trouble. Second, monitoring burrows with eggs was fundamental for estimating the hatching and breeding success of the birds and thereby evaluating the extent of loss of eggs and chicks to stoats or other causes. Lastly, I was also interested in the size and weight of the parents, the relative size of their eggs and the timing of laying. This was studied at a range of sub-colonies of differing altitudes, including some where snow had delayed birds' breeding. At these last sites we checked burrows every second day to record the date of egg laying.

Such monitoring had to be undertaken with a degree of caution, for shearwaters and burrowing petrels are notoriously 'twitchy' during the incubation period. We needed to make sure our work did not cause birds to abandon their eggs. Widespread desertion would be a disaster for our efforts as well as for the birds themselves. To counter this we monitored birds in four ways, with varying intensities of disturbance. One sample of burrows was monitored with the burrowscope only; a second sample of burrows, where we had previously dug study hatches, was checked by hand but only to determine if there was a bird and an egg inside. The third set we checked with study hatches and also removed the eggs to measure them, while the fourth method was the most invasive, and involved removing and weighing the adult, banding any new birds, measuring the egg, and in some instances making repeated checks to determine the length of the first incubation shift.

If Hutton's shearwaters were vulnerable to disturbance then we anticipated there would be varying degrees of abandonment related to the level of intensity of monitoring. In the end there was no measurable difference in burrow occupancy, hatching success or breeding success between the observation methods.[1] The birds were more tolerant than we had expected.

As with all fieldwork we established a routine. We checked all of our study burrows in Camp and Top sub-colonies every other day to record the day of egg-laying. Once these were complete, we set about checking samples of burrows with the burrowscope and study hatches in seven other sub-colonies to determine occupancy. The reliability of the burrowscope had improved from the first season and we spent long days crouched under the black cloth slowly inching the camera towards nesting chambers. We checked most burrows by hand, stretching an arm tentatively down a burrow until suddenly an angry shearwater would seize your finger and shake it. Ignoring the pain, we would carefully slip a hand under the bird, feeling for the smooth curve of an egg, and then get out, quickly closing up the hatch to reduce any further disturbance.

Depending on their angles, contours and bends, some burrows were definitively left- or right-armed, and we soon learnt the best arm and position for each. Checking study burrows was a pleasure on warm days, or cold, crisp days. However, lying among wet tussock after rain or snow was the surest way of becoming soaked to the skin, and the burrow checks became rounds of endurance against a creeping wet chill. On those days we welcomed the eventual relief of the walk home to dry clothes and a hot drink in the hut.

The checks of Camp and Top sub-colonies gave us an accurate picture of the timing of egg-laying, as well as detailed information on the body mass and condition of birds breeding there. The egg-laying was spread out over a month in both colonies[2] but was considerably later in Top sub-colony, where snow delayed laying by three weeks. While this delay was not particularly long, this meant the male birds in Top sub-colony had used more energy reserves flying in to secure a burrow, and consequently began the incubation period at a lower body mass than the males in Camp sub-colony.

Moreover, fewer females in the snow-affected colony actually went on to lay an egg, having lost too much mass to have the reserves to form one. Our records, and previous monitoring by DOC, indicated that over a 10-year period an average of 57% of burrows in Top sub-colony held an incubating pair; in contrast, 78% of burrows in Camp sub-colony contained eggs.[3] In the third season, when winter snowfall was light in the Kaikoura ranges and virtually no snow remained in the valley in October, the laying dates in both colonies coincided and the body mass of male birds and proportion of burrows with eggs was the same.

While recording egg-laying, we also identified the male and female birds in the study burrows in Camp and Top sub-colonies in order to be able to estimate adult survival rates. We marked the first bird we found incubating in each study burrow with a small dab of white paint on its crown. From then on, daily checks consisted of a swift glance through the study-burrow hatch to determine whether the marked bird was present or its partner. As mentioned earlier, Hutton's shearwaters and other burrowing petrels and albatrosses rely on teamwork to successfully incubate an egg and rear their single chick. After the female has spent some days at sea building up the necessary energy reserves to form an egg, she returns to the colony one night and lays her single egg.[4] Thereafter the breeding pair take about a week each sitting on the egg and foraging at sea.

The incubating bird steadily burns its energy reserves in order to keep the egg at a near constant 36°C. Typically we found these birds lost around 10 grams per day – a total of 60–70 grams (12–14% of body weight) over a week-long incubation shift.[5] Successful incubation depended on the bird's partner returning every week on average; after 10 days or more, if not replaced, the incubating bird would desert the egg in order to head off to sea and feed.

Unlike the majority of birds, burrowing petrels have been equipped by evolution with a back-up plan. Most embryos in eggs will die if the egg becomes chilled. Petrel eggs, however, if they remain safely out of harm's way in the confines of a burrow, can become completely chilled for three to four days and the embryo will remain viable.[6] Such an adaptation enables shearwaters and petrels to hatch their eggs successfully even in years when poor feeding conditions result in some gaps in continuous incubation.

Breeding success for many seabirds is generally higher when the pair have bred together previously, as such experience allows them to fine-tune the pattern of incubation shifts to maximise the likelihood of hatching. Such a pattern is clearly seen in the closely related Manx shearwater, which breeds on islands off the United Kingdom. In this species, hatching success of pairs where the birds have previously bred together is around 86%, in contrast to 55–60% for newly established pairs.[7] We had no such detailed information for Hutton's shearwaters, but our banding data showed that, like most other albatrosses and petrels, they did tend to breed with the same partner year after year. The evolutionary benefits of experienced pairs were therefore likely to apply to them as well.

14. A perfectly designed killing machine

It was now late November, and with the hard work of the egg-laying period completed we were able to relax for a while. We concentrated on the rounds of transects for a couple of weeks and caught up on data entry, running repairs to the hut and kit, and some sleep. The relaxation didn't last long, however, as the next stage of the study was about to begin. As much as we wanted to know more about the ecology of Hutton's shearwaters, we were also keen to learn about stoats in the valley. We needed a detailed understanding of both predator and prey to work out what was going on.

Our knowledge of stoat activity in the valley was limited: we knew they killed adult birds and chicks, and they obviously fed on birds and their eggs – evident in the partially consumed carcasses we were finding and the contents of stoat scats. More interesting questions remained unanswered: how many stoats were there within the valley? What was their territorial system? How did they survive the winter? The biggest puzzle of all was: why was the impact of stoats on the shearwaters apparently so limited?

At the start of the research, in fact before the first season, there had been much debate about the project's objectives and what would be done with stoats. Several staff within DOC viewed the presence of a research team in the valley as an opportunity to trap and kill as many as possible. In their minds it was a given that stoats were the key threat to Hutton's shearwaters, responsible for the range contraction to just two remote colonies. They may have been right, but to my mind simply trapping the stoats in the valley was not a long-term solution, and it did nothing to confirm our suspicions of whether stoats were in fact driving the shearwaters to extinction.

OPPOSITE: A stoat emerging from the trap. Author photo

With the support of key DOC staff, I argued that management of the species should be science-led, and suggested that this was a unique opportunity to examine the factors affecting the population. If, at the end of the study, it was clear that stoats were the culprits most people believed them to be, I'd be the first person setting traps to remove them. However, the first step was to understand their impact, and for that we needed to observe their normal behaviour.

To better understand the activity of stoats in the valley we first had to catch them and fit each animal with a radio-collar, a task that is far from easy, particularly in spring when females are pregnant. It would take a lot of effort to capture enough animals to provide a decent sample, not to mention the hard yards of radio-tracking them for long enough to build up a pattern of their behaviour. A simple map of a stoat's home range would represent many months of trapping and tracking effort. I knew it was going to be a challenge but believed it was the only way to evaluate the impact that stoats were having on the shearwaters.

We began the job of getting out the traps, checking to ensure they were working, making necessary repairs and lugging them up and around the main valley. The wooden Edgar traps were solidly built. Each weighed two to three kilograms and consisted of a wooden tunnel, on the base of which a simple treadle mechanism triggered the spring-loaded door. At the far end of the tunnel was a small nesting box stuffed with dried tussock and cotton wool and fitted with a perspex lid. Carrying the traps was awkward and I ended up tying them, four at a time, to an old external-frame rucksack before setting off up the valley. From the previous year's study we knew where stoat scats were found, and hoped that traps placed at those sites would at least enable the mustelids to encounter them.

Finding where stoats deposit scats might sound easy, but we had managed to find only 74 scats by the end of the first season. I wanted to be able to build a more convincing picture of what these animals were feeding on.

Our opportunity came after the shearwaters had departed during March. In May we had flown back to the valley to map the boundaries, to assess the habitat and vegetation within colonies, and also to determine whether stoats were still around after the shearwaters had gone. It should have been a good time of year to work in the colonies; if we did inadvertently crush a burrow by walking on the friable soil, at least there would not be a bird inside. Unfortunately the weather had other ideas: a cold southerly had swept in and coated the valley in 20 centimetres of snow, making it difficult to map the edges of the colonies and even harder to determine the vegetation and habitat beneath.

With our fieldwork plans scuppered we decided to focus on what stoats were doing, as the one advantage the snow gave us was the ability to track them. Stoats were clearly still in the valley, despite the absence of shearwaters, and over the weeks we followed their tracks to learn more about how they were surviving and what they were feeding on. The pattern of tracks in the snow gave a fascinating insight into their world but was often baffling, with paths criss-crossing and even the odd set of prints that appeared to begin or end in the middle of nowhere, as if the animal had dropped from or ascended into the sky.

While stoats and weasels have acute hearing and good eyesight, they rely on scent for hunting, and it is also their dominant means of communication with other stoats.[1] The snow provided excellent visual clues to the olfactory signals they were following, for it betrayed where an animal had stopped and pressed its rear against a rock, leaving a smear of strong musky scent from the anal glands, along with a twisted black scat or small yellow patch of urine. Each of these signals passed on important information to other stoats about the animal's sex and reproductive status and its territorial boundaries.

Criss-crossing the colonies, the darting pathways of stoats left weak and temporary scent trails, interspersed every few hundred metres with a scat or scent-marking that flashed like a bright 'keep out' sign to other stoats in the valley, or acted like an alluring perfume to indicate that a female was in season. The conditions allowed us a rare insight into their world – and the world of many mammals for whom smell is the most important of all the senses. To my mind an olfactory map of the valley resembled a view from a heat-seeking device: the areas of burrowed ground were warm with the scent of shearwaters, each burrow entrance a glowing hotspot of odours.

As well as obtaining a better understanding of how stoats made their way about and communicated within the valley, the tracks had led us to six scats on the first day, then seven, and then nine, the 3–4-centimetre-long twisted black scats easily visible on the snow. These were relatively minor rewards for the effort of pushing through the deep snow and returning with sodden feet and frozen fingers each lunchtime and evening, but the real reward came later with the thaw. Unimpeded by snow, we ran around the valley trying to get as much habitat work done as possible, and in the course of two days picked up first 16 and then 22 scats – over half the total we had found in the previous seven months. Our minds had become tuned into where stoats were likely to deposit scats, and over the next two seasons we collected a further 700 samples.

Now in the spring of the second season, with knowledge – but still little understanding – of where stoats were travelling, we set out the traps, carefully ensuring each one was level and on solid ground before piling large rocks around and on top to secure it against the strong winds that racked the valley. While stoats and weasels are practically hard-wired to enter tunnels, they are also cautious and difficult to trap, and any wobble might put them off. We baited each trap with a fresh piece of rabbit meat and wiped the entrance of the traps and the rocks around with a dribble of blood and a smear of rabbit guts. It wasn't a job for the squeamish, but in a valley with nearly 100,000 shearwater burrows we had to do everything we could to make the stoat traps as attractive as possible. Setting the traps was fiddly and best achieved lying flat on the ground with one arm thrust into the device, carefully adjusting the wire pin until it was balanced on the very edge of the trigger. The only way to test them was to set them off, after which we had to reset them all over again. We tested each trap four or five times until confident that the slightest pressure on the treadle would trigger it.

Now the really hard work began, for it was a twice-daily job – first thing in the morning and as late as possible in the afternoon – to check every trap. It didn't matter what the weather was doing, or whether we had spent the whole previous night banding birds or a long day doing transects – the traps still had to be checked. Stoats run on such a high metabolism that even with the insulation in the trap's nest box and a chunk of rabbit meat, leaving an animal incarcerated overnight was a likely death sentence.

Six weeks on we hadn't caught a single stoat. Justine Ragg, an experienced hand at ferret catching and tagging who had come to the valley to help with this work, had to leave to resume her own research. Two days later I was checking the last trap underneath Top sub-colony, keen to get the round finished and return to the hut for breakfast. The trap's door was down, which wasn't unusual – they were hair-triggered (even capturing a giant wētā on two occasions) and after a windy night we might reset a dozen or more – but as I placed my hand on the trap to slide back the wooden cover on the nest box I heard a sharp hiss: we had got one at last.

I radioed down and half an hour later Erica appeared, having run down the slopes from the hut and up the valley. Stopping to grab a breath, she thrust at me the stoat kit and a welcome muesli bar from her pocket. Catching a stoat in the trap was one thing; getting it out and radio-collared was another, and while we had run through the protocol with Justine on several occasions it was different in practice. Donning thick leather gloves I wrapped the trap in a pillowcase and, feeling through the cloth, carefully released the trigger and lifted the door of the trap. Nothing happened. I glanced at Erica and she shrugged in puzzlement, before moving around to the nest box and giving it a tap. Still nothing. Another tap. Nothing again. Erica crouched down and looked along the tunnel through the narrow gap between the nest box and the main tunnel. The stoat was clinging on determinedly in the central tunnel.

Tilting the trap upwards we gave it a sharper rap. Suddenly, like a torpedo, the stoat launched itself into the pillowcase, ricocheting around inside like a pinball.

Squeezing the bag tight until the stoat was trapped in one corner, I felt through the material to locate the animal's head and then find the larger muscles of its hindquarters. Taking care to insert the needle into muscle I injected an anaesthetic. It was a few minutes before the stoat stopped moving. Now we had 10–15 minutes to fit the radio-collar, making sure it was tight enough not to slip over the stoat's slim head but not so tight as to constrict movement or feeding. The brass collar, which acted as the aerial, was secured by a tiny brass nut and bolt, and I fumbled with chilled fingers to align the thread, cursing the manufacturers as I did so. After securing the nut we slid a piece of black heat-shrink tubing over the join and, with the animal's fur and neck protected by a piece of cardboard, heated the plastic with a cigarette lighter until the brass nut was tightly encased. After 10 minutes we were done and I quickly measured the stoat's body mass and length and confirmed that it was a mature adult male, a fact already apparent from the strong musky odour in the trap and pillowcase.

Most conservationists in New Zealand rightly detest stoats and weasels, for the damage they do to the country's native wildlife is profound. Yet the beauty and grace and predatory skill of these animals was clearly apparent up close, from the point of the male's nose to the tip of its black tail. Weighing in at 340 grams and with a body length of just over 30 centimetres, this male stoat was a perfectly designed killing machine. With short legs adapted for hunting small mammals in tunnels and under the winter snow in North America and Eurasia,[2] and a long sinuous body, the stoat is a sublime blend of electric energy, speed, intelligence and ferocity. Watching a stoat bounding up a near-vertical slope in the valley, or porpoising through soft snow in a sinusoidal wave of motion, I always found a breath-taking sight, but it was equally amazing to be holding the animal, to see in close detail the textured foot pads and rounded ears, and to feel the sharp white canines and the musculature in its haunches.

How stoats came to be in New Zealand is a sorry example of settler short-sightedness and a case study of why the introduction of species to a foreign land is generally a bad idea. Rabbits, introduced in the 1830s for sport and food, had quickly became established, their populations reaching such proportions that their grazing threatened the very soil the grass grew on in the sheep pastures and high-country stations. In some years their rapid breeding causing rabbit 'plagues' in the South Island,[3] particularly in the 1870s, 1920s and 1940s.

Rabbits introduced near Kaikoura in the early 1860s had quickly spread inland. Herbie Melville, the octogenarian Geoff Harrow had spoken to in 1969 about the

A sedated adult male stoat. Author photo

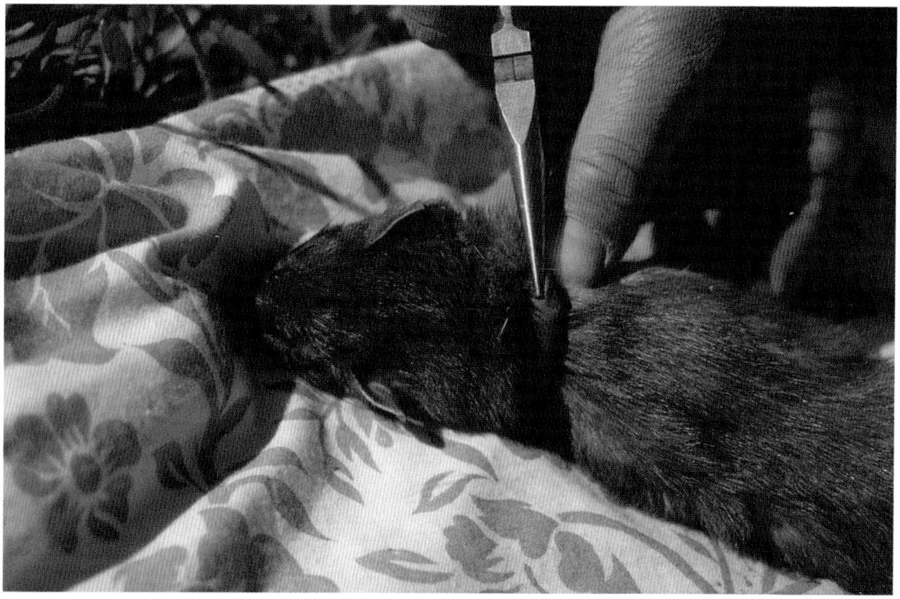

Fitting a radio-collar to a stoat. Author photo

historical Hutton's records, had recounted the scale of the 1920s rabbit plague in the Awatere Valley, where tens of thousands of rabbits had consumed all the grasses and other vegetation in the valley and begun gnawing through the bark of cabbage trees. Herbie recalled hundreds of rabbits being smothered in the stampede to consume a tree's green leaves when it fell.[4]

Following the logic that predators kept rabbit numbers under control in Britain, settlers decided to introduce stoats, common weasels and ferrets into New Zealand. From the mid-1880s mustelids captured by gamekeepers in Britain were shipped across the world. The survivors of these long journeys were released into an environment that was quite different to Britain's. Deprived of voles and other small mammals that were common in the northern hemisphere, the animals' preferred source of prey became the large range of generally naïve and often ground-nesting birds, lizards, frogs and giant insects. Stoats killed some rabbits, but New Zealand's native species in the large areas of forest and alpine environments were easier meat. Rabbit numbers remained at high levels while an ecological disaster unfolded for the native wildlife.

Our captive stoat began to twitch, front legs paddling and jaw flexing open and closed, and I hurriedly placed it back in the nest box; as beautiful as it was I didn't want it coming round in my hands. Leaving the animal to recover in the trap with another chunk of rabbit meat, Erica and I each completed a transect that was a few days overdue. After two hours I returned. The stoat hissed several times from the trap. Slipping on a glove, I propped up the door with a handy stone and retreated 10 metres with my camera. After a minute's inactivity a pink nose tip cautiously appeared in the trap's entrance and remained still, sniffing the air for 20 seconds or more. Then in a stream of movement and two bounding leaps the stoat was gone, hidden among the tussocks once more. I switched on the radio transmitter, plugged in the antenna and listened in satisfaction to the healthy beep of the tag slowly receding as the stoat made its way off through the colony.

15. Encounters with chamois, falcons and harriers

Our regular transects provided a good sample of the whole valley, with sub-colonies ranging from the lowest-altitude sites – where burrows were under a thick cover of mountain ribbonwoods and other scrub – to the highest sites, where the uppermost burrows were situated between dwarf grasses and sedges and bare scree at the edge of the vegetation line. Yet I still had an itch to explore every aspect of the landscape. If the day's tasks were complete and there was nothing pressing in the hut, I frequently took off into a new patch of colony or a new area of the valley. Although each sub-colony was much like its neighbours – which in its way reassured me that the areas we were monitoring were representative of the valley – the vegetation, soil and surrounding scree varied with altitude and aspect. As I explored I slowly absorbed the rhythms of life and learned some of the Kowhai's secrets. Chief among these were the activities of the other wildlife present in the area. While shearwaters, stoats and kea dominated my waking hours, they were not the only species about; nor were we the only large mammals.

The early European colonists introduced species for food, sport and pleasure. They apparently decided they needed creatures to enliven New Zealand's landscape, as if the unique local ornithological assemblage of species was somehow insufficient. Cages full of blackbirds, song thrushes, European robins, meadow pipits, skylarks and various finches were carefully shipped from England and the survivors released in the South and North Islands for the purpose of providing familiar songs, sights and game. Attempted introductions were made of 144 bird species, of which 33 survived and thrived.[1] In the Kaikoura ranges our dawn chorus consisted of

OPPOSITE: One of the valley's other inhabitants: a young chamois. Author photo

European songbirds as well as the muted hoots of shearwaters racing the morning light and falcons on their way to the coast.

As a conservationist I have mixed feelings about such introductions. While I am vehemently opposed to introducing any non-native species to a new location, I cannot negate my own background of growing up in the English countryside where the sighting of a brown hare was a red-letter day, and where the melodic song of a blackbird was a quintessential part of a summer evening. It gave me an almost guilty pleasure in the Kowhai Valley to see a flock of redpolls flushing from the tussock seed-heads, or to hear a blackbird singing from below the hut, or the repetitive 'little bit of bread and no cheese' song of a yellowhammer as it perched on a boulder-top among the tussocks.

I kept such feelings firmly hidden from my New Zealand colleagues: they were mostly made of firmer stuff, and most of them didn't share my own English background. In Geoff I found a soul mate, however, for although New Zealand born and bred, he appreciated wildlife in all its forms. Geoff was almost as excited to tell me about glimpsing a rare cirl bunting, an introduced European species, as he was in reporting any native wildlife.

Among the species brought to New Zealand for food were pigs and goats, introduced by Captain Cook and other early explorers. Later colonists introduced red deer, Sambar deer, Sika deer, European chamois, Himalayan thar and even moose. All of these species quickly became widespread and established apart from the moose (although tales of moose sightings in the darkest depths of Fiordland continue to surface). Within the Kaikoura ranges, feral pigs, feral goats, red deer and chamois could all be found, their numbers varying with altitude and habitat. Feral goats could be seen in small groups in most places: on some of the higher slopes in summer I saw large mobs of 30 or 40 animals, but I never saw them actually within the shearwater colonies. When Geoff Harrow first found the Kowhai colony in the 1960s he observed large numbers of goats present throughout the valley, with heavy browsing of the snow tussock and obvious trampling damage to the shearwaters' nesting habitat.[2]

Geoff's discovery of the colonies inspired a lot of subsequent work; perhaps one of the earliest and most important jobs, overseen by Brian Bell of the New Zealand Wildlife Service, was to cull goats from the area. Subsequent efforts by DOC throughout the Seaward and Inland Kaikoura ranges had kept goat numbers in check and prevented their reinvasion of the shearwater colonies.

Red deer were present in the foothills, although only in low numbers and in the lower margins of the valley. I sometimes heard the challenging roar of stags in their autumn rut. Deer would also occasionally venture high enough to reach the colonies, although when they did enter the Kowhai they remained in the lower forested reaches. I rarely ventured into these areas, as most of the work was higher in the valley where the shearwaters nested. However, on occasion I would wander down to sit quietly and watch silvereyes and riflemen gleaning a living among the leaves, or to simply lie back and observe the infinity of different greens against the clear sky. The deer would rest among these glades and I could usually smell their presence before I arrived. Tucked among the trees, fresh black deer droppings lay like plump brandy-soaked raisins, and often a flattened patch of grass marked where a buck or hind had lain for the night.

Also resident in the valley was the European chamois or 'chammy'. The first of these, a gift from the emperor of Austria,[3] were released on Aoraki Mt Cook in 1907 and rapidly spread throughout the alpine region of the South Island.[4] They have never been abundant, however; the keen interest of New Zealand's hunting community kept them in check – and also made them wary. Chamois were present in the Kowhai, and although Keith and Dave from the Kaikoura DOC office took out one or two animals a year (often to the benefit of our diet in the hut), for the most part they were left undisturbed.[5] At the start of each season, when snow still lay on the ground, I would watch chammy through my binoculars, high in the colonies opposite the hut or on the steep slopes of Death and Double Death sub-colonies. At the higher sites lone females would take themselves away from the herd to calve, and in November, if I was lucky I sometimes spotted an isolated female with her single kid. As spring and summer progressed these females came down and integrated with other females to form small herds of four to six animals, each with a dependent youngster.

Lone males were seen throughout the valley and would give a snorting downward whistle when alarmed or disturbed by my presence, sometimes standing their ground and rapping a single foot on the dirt like a bull preparing to charge. Young males were occasionally seen with the small herds of females, but often they remained solitary and high up, crossing elevated slopes of the valley's surrounding ridges and sometimes leaving a narrow track across the steep rock scree. The resident adult males browsed on the abundant snow tussock, fattening themselves throughout the summer before the serious business of rounding up and holding a harem began in the autumn rut. With the first snows the creatures moved below the scrub and treeline, where the cover provided some browsing opportunities throughout the cold winter months.

Moving through the colonies to monitor burrows and transects, or to follow the radio signals of tagged stoats, gave me plenty of opportunities to see and interact with chammy. I learned to steal silently to the crest of a ridge or bluff and cautiously peer over to watch an undisturbed animal below. Some encounters were unexpected – and perhaps all the better for it. One day late in the second season was particularly memorable:

> 11/3/98 – Had the most incredible day yesterday. It was bright and dry, cool with patches of sun and skidding cloud. I went up to [sub-]Colonies 18 and 19 to complete the fortnightly transects and stopped at the usual point on the ridge after the long steep gut for a breather and to scan the areas of colony. I ended up having a breather for 40 minutes, as I got engrossed watching harriers tack and soar over the slopes below me. The transect was going well, with two carcasses found, and I was on the penultimate leg which would take me back underneath the ridge where I had earlier sat. Just as I was turning a movement caught my eye and I stopped as a buck chammy stood up 15 metres away on the ridge crest in front of me. We stood, transfixed, like a snapshot from our respective evolutions – hunter and hunted in the eternal moment of recognition. I saw the dilation of the pupil, the snort of fear and my mind saw the chammy spring from view, yet it did not happen: he stood there watching me as I watched him. Moments passed into time and as I remained motionless I slowly watched the tension pass out of the taut muscles in his shoulders and haunches, until still carefully watching me, he sat down in the tussock.
>
> Hardly daring to move, I also slowly sat down and carefully pulled out my binoculars. The chammy's body was hidden behind the ridge and tussock and his head and shoulders filled the view. The detail was incredible: I could count the eyelashes underscoring the amber bronze of his eyes. I cursed my decision to travel light and leave my camera, yet at the same time I was not upset: moments like this are not to be lost fiddling with a camera and the image is fixed in my cortex, if not on film. We watched each other for 20 minutes and we both grew more relaxed until he was looking down the valley chewing the cud with only the occasional glance in my direction. Gently I stood up and without a backward glance I stole off on the next leg of the transect line. A hundred metres later, and before I moved out of sight around the next ridge, I looked back and he was still there, undisturbed. I felt elated. Whether his boldness was because he was on his own, or because he had seen me moving though the colony and decided I was not a threat, I don't know. The fact was that I had been in full view 15 metres from a wild animal and he had accepted me and continued with his own natural behaviour.

The next day I set off with my camera for another transect through sub-colony 15, rather unrealistically hoping there might be a further chamois encounter and I would get photos to match the images in my mind from the previous day. Sub-colony 15 was one of the high areas that we surveyed for breeding success and predation, and while I had watched chamois from there it was not an area where I regularly saw them. Midway through the transect I heard the sudden snorting whistle of an alarmed chamois and looked up. To my amazement there was an animal 20 metres above me, and this time it was a female with a young kid. The female whistled again and nervously retreated a little, but the fawn stayed still in confused indecision. The mother whistled once more, then took off up the slope and over the ridge. The kid remained and then advanced curiously towards me. I stood still, slowly slid my rucksack off my shoulders and took out my camera. Soon the kid was just eight metres from me, the distance measured out clearly by the focus ring on my camera lens. The light was low and I was forced to use a wide aperture and slower shutter than I wanted, but with the camera braced against my eye and my left arm locked as solidly as I could hold it I took photo after photo. I heard another urgent whistle and this time the young chamois responded, taking off in bounding leaps across the scree slope to join its mother. They ran off, kicking up dust in small explosions of energy as hoof struck scree, the late afternoon sun illuminating it like cigarette smoke in a black and white photograph, the roiling particles hanging in the still air like visual echoes long after the pair had vanished from sight.

Chamois sightings were definite highlights. Others were provided by two other species, both native and both predators of the shearwaters we were studying. The New Zealand falcon (kārearea) and the swamp harrier (kāhu) were present in the valley, the first in the form of a resident pair in the gorge below the foot of the colony, and the latter seen in varying numbers, from lone individuals to half a dozen birds. Both were attracted by the opportunities to scavenge and hunt Hutton's shearwaters. I didn't often see the falcons, although when walking out I was almost certain to encounter one just below the valley or further down the Kowhai River, where I presumed another pair held a territory.

In our first year the falcons' nest was a few hundred yards below the hut and we frequently heard the high-pitched incessant 'kek, kek, kek, kek' of a bird calling high overhead. If we were lucky we might catch the arching arrowhead of a falcon stooping from the sky. Most of these calls and stoops were for display, as there were no other falcons around to challenge the resident pair. Apart from the shearwaters, which falcons likely took at night or dawn,[6] the only birds that seemed to attract the falcons' attention were the kea, and on several occasions I watched a falcon swoop inches away from an unwary kea – to the latter's obvious alarm. On one memorable occasion during my the second field season the falcon seemed to mean business, either to drive the kea away or turn it into lunch:

> 14/11/97 – Saw my first falcon of the season, high above the hut and trying to take a kea out. The falcon was above and made at least five stoops at the kea as the kea

> flapped rapidly in panic towards the cover of the colonies opposite. They locked twice in mid air, and fell tumbling together, the kea kicking and screaming at the falcon before breaking loose, the falcon casually using the momentum of the fall to loop up higher into the sky and then close its wings and stoop down again at the kea. After the fifth stoop the falcon broke off and drifted slowly and almost arrogantly down the valley, while the kea – still bitterly calling in alarm – flew rapidly to crash into the safety of the ribbonwood trees of Double Death colony. Through my binoculars I could see the kea crouching cautiously amongst the branches, unwilling to venture forth from the cover and still calling in alarm.

Falcons were territorial and aggressive with it, and when walking out from the valley on several occasions I was 'buzzed' by a tercel or male swooping at speed at eye level, forcing me to rapidly drop my head as he skimmed by a few centimetres overhead. I had likely come close to the pair's nest, probably high on a ledge overlooking the valley floor, and I always picked up my pace to escape their aggressive intent. Geoff told me a similar story about walking into the Kowhai Valley, although he had actually wanted to climb up to their nest to see if it contained shearwater remains. He had clearly got too close, and suddenly he felt a 'slight tap' on the crown of his head as the male bird swooped past. Moments later Geoff had blood soaking through his hair and dripping past his eyes, the tap from the falcon's rear claw having opened a neat razor-like incision in his scalp, which began to bleed copiously. On another occasion, when the tercel and female falcon were absent, Geoff had climbed up to their nest and counted the remains of 14 shearwaters.

While I never saw a falcon kill a shearwater, I did see another rare sight. Like all other resident birds, the falcons at the foot of the colony and further down the Kowhai were intent on one task: breeding and producing a chick to carry on their genes. Unlike the shearwaters, New Zealand falcons continue their parental care after the chick has fledged, and the one or two fledglings typically stick around for several months as they learn the intricacies of hunting. As I headed down the river one day in my third year I heard a falcon calling, and spotted two flying high over the valley floor. As I watched, one bird dropped something from above. The second bird took three powerful flaps to position its body before stooping and hitting the object, from which a puff of feathers could be seen falling. I couldn't make out the species of the prey, but from its size I guessed it to be a blackbird, song thrush or tūī. As I watched, the spectacle was repeated: the dead prey was dropped and stooped upon several times – the adult female was teaching her young the art of hunting.

The other bird of prey within the valley was the harrier. We saw them every day, sweeping low over the colonies searching for prey and effortlessly circling on the crest of a thermal. Harriers seem to be highly underrated birds in New Zealand, perhaps as a consequence of their relatively new and highly efficient habit of feeding on road-kill. Yet the tumbling aerobatics of a pair of courting harriers framed by a backdrop of the Kaikoura mountains is a glorious memory for me, and as exciting a scene as can be provided by many of New Zealand's rare and more 'glamorous' species.

New Zealand's harriers also offer a classic example of niche expansion.[7] Within Australia and New Guinea the swamp harrier is specialised for life in the marshes in much the same way as the European marsh harrier. In New Zealand, however, harriers can be found from the mountains of the South Island to the pasturelands of the north. They are equally able to make a living in the beech and mixed podocarp forests, over rolling tussock-covered hill country and braided alpine riverbeds, and in the marshes and wetlands along the coast. Harriers in New Zealand are also more catholic in the food they take and the ways they hunt. In Australia they mainly prey or scavenge on rabbits, small rodents, and ground- and water-birds that live in the marshland areas where the harriers are mainly found. In New Zealand they scavenge like vultures on dead sheep and road-kill, and are perfectly capable of stooping like an eagle to kill an unwary rabbit or pūkeko.

The difference between New Zealand and Australia and New Guinea is the level of competition the birds face. In Australia and New Guinea harriers fly with over 40 other birds of prey, each species occupying a specialised feeding niche or habitat, forcing swamp harriers in these countries to remain in the marshes where they specialised. Harriers in New Zealand compete only with the native falcon and the rare vagrant Nankeen kestrel, enabling the harrier to expand into other areas where it can successfully take enough prey. Indeed, on one bright moonlit night I flushed a harrier from the ground right among the Hutton's burrows, suggesting that harriers are even expanding into the niche that normally belongs to owls. I only saw that once, but the fresh remains of several shearwaters in the colonies at dawn with tell-tale raptor feeding signs suggested that harriers could and would take birds on the ground at night.[8]

More often, harriers within the Kowhai were to be seen flying over the ground in search of adult shearwaters that had struck a rock bluff after a windy night, or for the remains of a chick killed and dragged out onto open ground by a stoat or kea. Even at first light there would always be one or two birds, wings spread wide, silently combing the mountain slopes for carcasses. But despite the frequency with which I saw harriers in the valley, my efforts to secure a decent photo had come to nothing, for harriers are extremely wary.

I had the perfect photo already exposed in my mind's eye: a harrier lit by the warm light of the evening sun, holding a dead shearwater with one talon, head raised, light glinting from its eye, plucked shearwater feathers falling from its beak – and all framed against a panorama of snow and dark mountains. Poetic indeed! But getting such a shot was going to take far more than luck, and the only realistic chance I had was to build a hide and get close to a harrier feeding on the ground. On Erica's next trip to Dunedin I asked her to visit the army surplus store and buy me some camouflage netting. This duly appeared, although there was a bit more than I had anticipated: when folded out the huge roll would have safely covered a tank. I cut a manageable-sized strip, stuffed it into my pack along with a load of stout bamboo poles, tie-wire and string, and headed to the top of Col sub-colony. I had just the spot in mind: the hide would sit close to the tussocks where the film crew had crouched, overlooking the level ridge at the top of the sub-colony with the snow-covered peak of Manakau as a backdrop.

I set to work with pliers and wire, tying the bamboo into a tight square frame. Unravelling the camouflage netting, which was surprisingly heavy, I threw it over the frame – which immediately skewed alarmingly to one side under the weight. More wire was needed, as well as guy-ropes for the four corners and another few bamboo poles to keep the roof up. After a couple of hours I stood back to admire my efforts. I had constructed a monstrosity: it squatted above the ground like a giant green breeze-block, netting flapping limply in the breeze. Squeezing myself inside I found that the hole I had carefully cut for the camera was too high; the only way I could get my eye to the viewfinder was to crane my neck at an impossible right-angle.

I decided to leave the hide there for a couple of days – perhaps a bit of time would help it to blend in and become part of the landscape. Four days later I set off back to the hide with my camera, tripod, some snacks and a fairly fresh dead shearwater chick for bait. As I crested the col I was confused to see a bare patch of ground where the hide should have been, and I stopped and stood in puzzlement. Even for the kea this level of destruction was going a bit far. The gusting norwester that had blown up the previous evening seemed a more likely suspect. Either way, it was gone.

It was a few weeks before I found the time to try again, and I set out once more with more netting stuffed into my pack. This time I planned to build a less ambitious structure, and would look more carefully for a site that gave me some natural cover and protection from the wind. After searching for over an hour I found a good spot a few hundred metres downstream from where I had put the last hide. Two medium-sized boulders embedded in the slope formed a sharp step that I had stumbled over. Soil had piled up on top of them and several tussocks grew around them, their long stems overhanging the rock-step and merging with the tussocks below. By crawling in next to the rocks on my belly I was already well hidden, and from where I lay I had a good view across the stream to a clear patch of ground on the opposite hillside some 20 metres distant. I embedded five bamboo canes into the ground at an angle to the hillside so that they leaned up against the boulders, then laid the camouflage netting on top of the canes but beneath the falling tussock fronds. Crawling inside, I set up my camera and tripod and cut a small hole for the lens. I was learning.

The next day I returned with a dead chick and placed it on the bare ground opposite the hide. From where I stood the hide was invisible – it took me a few minutes to locate it even though I knew it had to be there. Squeezing myself inside I settled in for the wait. It was a warm afternoon, and with the sun hitting the hillside and my hiding place well insulated by the thick walls of tussocks I found myself fighting to keep my eyes open. Unused to having such a restricted view of the valley I concentrated on the sounds and smells around me to force myself to stay awake. The ground simmered in the heat, rich with the aroma of baked earth, dust, pollen and grass, overlaid with the 'musty museum' scent unique to all shearwaters. Grasshoppers, which proliferated in the summer in their tens of thousands, ricocheted through the tussock stems and bounced off the top of the hide with a sound like exploding popcorn. A small stream, fed from the tall banks of scree, percolated quietly down through the rocks to its own harmony and rhythm. Half a dozen redpolls flew overhead, porpoising through the air to a tango of notes, 'cha-cha-chaa, cha-cha-chaa'. On the rocks above, gun-metal grey cicadas mechanically ticked the passing of the day and a New Zealand pipit scurried after them, uttering its short 'tssks', tail bobbing at rest, before a short flicking flight and a dash on fast legs after another morsel. Above them all a skylark hung from a gossamer of song.

A shadow of movement passed overhead. Glancing up I saw the silent form of a harrier drop softly onto the carcass. It stood with the talons of one leg curled into the soft white breast feathers of the dead chick, its head up, alert, eyes ablaze for any threat. My index finger curled slowly onto the shutter release and I moved forward to press my eye to the viewfinder. As the image tightened into focus the harrier launched smoothly into the air and swept down the hillside, gripping the chick firmly. A takeaway meal was not a contingency I had planned for and I banged my head against the tripod before ruefully crawling out of the hide and setting off back down to the hut.

I returned three days later with another dead chick and two short lengths of number 8 wire. Setting the body down on the same patch of soil, I bent the wire into two loops and sank them into the ground around the wings of the chick, pinning it down firmly. I retreated to the hide and settled in to wait once more. Three hours passed and I was on the verge of leaving when a harrier dropped into view. The bird

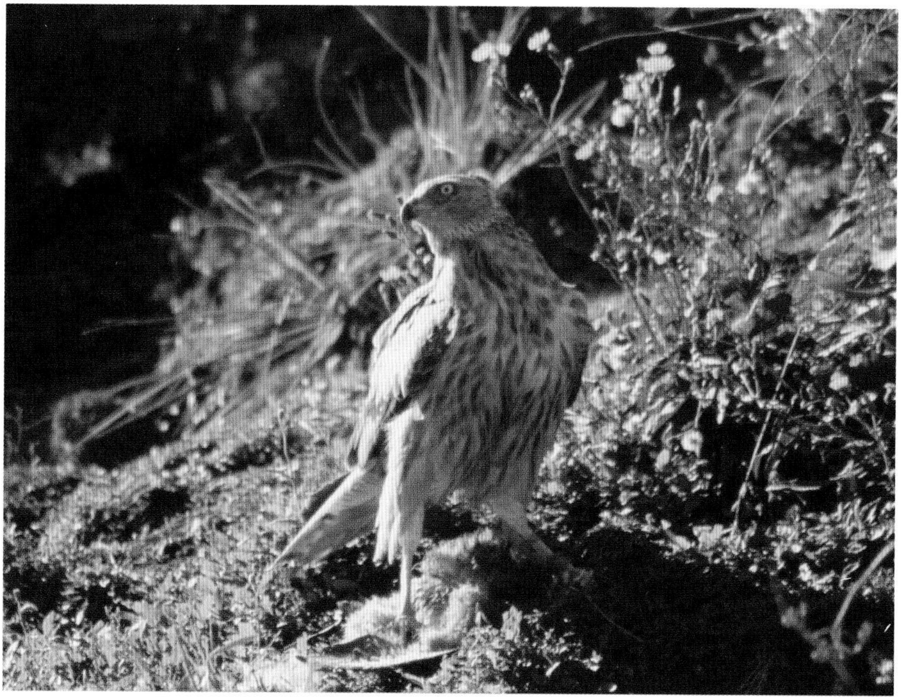

A swamp harrier feeding on a shearwater chick in the Kowhai Valley. Author photo

was an old one, its back a tawny buff brown and the long primary feathers visibly worn. The harrier scanned for danger before stepping forward and seizing the shearwater chick. This time, however, the chick stayed firmly in place, and after two aborted take-offs the harrier stopped and once more scanned the sky and hillside. I held my breath lest a sound betray my presence, until the harrier turned its head and with one foot on the chick started to feed. The shutter on my camera whirred quietly and at last I had the shots I wanted. I felt I'd earned them.

16. Hatching and growth of the shearwater chicks

The hatching of the shearwater chicks marked another turning point in the cycle of life within the Kowhai Valley. The first eggs hatched in early December, with a peak just around Christmas in the lower-altitude colonies, and continued over a month-long period, reflecting the spread of egg-laying dates. Incubation took 46–56 days with an average of 50.[1] The eggs with longer incubation periods were most likely those that had been abandoned for several days by parents both at sea, for embryo development would pause during these periods. An egg that has been cold for five days requires five further days of incubation at 36°C in order to develop to the point of hatching.[2]

Newly hatched chicks weighed just 30–40 grams and emerged from the egg with wet and spiky grey down like aged punk rockers. As its down dried it fluffed up until the chick became a near spherical ball with eyes and wings completely hidden by fluff, the only visible reference points a pair of small grey feet and a stubby bill. Unsurprisingly, the size at hatching correlated with egg size: the largest eggs produced the heaviest chicks.[3] In the higher-altitude and snow-delayed sub-colonies where the birds were in poorer body condition at the time of laying, eggs on average were smaller and lighter. In good years with plenty of food at sea, these differences in hatching weight were unlikely to matter, as each parent would return every night or two with food for the newly hatched chick. In poor years, however, the variation could be crucial: a higher hatching mass and a larger lipid-rich yolk sack within its guts enabled a larger chick to survive for three or four nights without food, whereas smaller and lighter chicks had a greater chance of starvation. Natural selection acts on the finest of margins, and small differences could mark out the survivors who would pass on their genes to the next generation. In the third year of the study no such altitudinal variation was seen but, as noted earlier, in that year

A shearwater chick within the safety of its burrow. Author photo

the snow melted early and birds at both high- and low-altitude sub-colonies began breeding at the same time.[4]

For the first week after hatching the parent birds alternated their visits to the colony, with one bird present at all times to keep the chick warm until its own metabolism was sufficient to provide heat to survive through the day and night. Thereafter the chick was on its own; both adults would fly out to sea and return every few nights to feed their ever-growing and voracious offspring. In the first two weeks after hatching chicks would spontaneously 'peep' when disturbed by us for weighing and measuring, their soft call and cross-billed nibbling of our fingers an urgent demand for food that we were unable to satisfy. As they grew they learned that we were not there to feed them, and the gentle nibbling was replaced by a few violent pecks aimed to discourage our activity.

Petrel and albatross chicks undergo an unusual pattern of development, with their growth and rearing period among the longest in the avian world. The most extreme examples are the royal and wandering albatrosses: adult birds spend nearly

A well-fed shearwater chick. Author photo

10 months rearing their single chicks from hatching to fledging point, and their breeding cycle lasts a year.[5] Being smaller, Hutton's shearwaters are not so extreme, but it still takes almost three months for a chick to reach the point of fledging. In contrast, the New Zealand pigeon or kererū, which at around 630 grams is twice the mass of an adult Hutton's shearwater, fledges its single chick in 35–40 days.[6]

The slow development of Hutton's shearwaters and other petrels is matched by another unusual feature: the chicks are renowned for getting fat – not just small amounts of puppy fat, but serious obesity. At its heaviest, a shearwater chick can weigh a third more than its parents[7] and be so fat it can only shuffle slowly in the confines of the burrow. After reaching their peak mass ('peak oil' might be an appropriate term, given the lipids involved), chicks continue to be fed but at a reduced rate, and slowly lose weight as they start to grow their flight and contour feathers. After slimming down for over a month to a weight where flight is possible, a healthy chick fledges from the colony, flying out to sea with a crucial reserve of abdominal fat that will serve as an energy source in the first weeks at sea as it starts to forage for itself.

Natural selection will favour a breeding pair that can fledge a chick with a minimum of effort and, as a consequence, produce more chicks in the long term. This pattern of growth in petrels has been much studied – numerous academic careers have been forged over the bloated barrel of a petrel's belly. While there were bigger ecological questions to answer in the Kowhai (such as the impact of stoats on the species) we were still interested to understand how Hutton's shearwaters provisioned their chicks.

To determine the pattern of feeding we would need to measure the bodyweight of chicks, not daily or every few days, but *every couple of hours* throughout the night for several weeks. Adult birds landed silently, entered the burrow, fed and departed within 10 to 30 minutes; regular weighing would enable us to work out the frequency of feeding and how much food was being delivered.

We found that meals weighed on average around 50 grams with a maximum of 90 grams.[8] The parents did not coordinate their trips; sometimes a chick was fed by both parents on the same night. The results were often spectacular: a plump but well-proportioned chick of 150 grams could, one hour later, be panting like an overstuffed Christmas turkey and have nearly doubled in mass from two parental feeds. On occasions I feared a chick would burst, so swollen did its belly become with the puree of fish and crustaceans its parent had delivered.

Theories behind the extreme obesity of petrel chicks range from a non-adaptive fixed rate of feeding – where adult birds feed to a set routine oblivious to the needs and demands of the chick[9] – to more adaptive explanations, such as the need for insurance against fluctuating future food supplies,[10] or the unpredictable feeding frequency of parents.[11]

Many more studies will be undertaken before this is conclusively resolved; however, our evidence from Hutton's shearwaters did not favour the first or last hypotheses, for Hutton's adults did regulate their feeds by returning more frequently to chicks whose mass was below average for their age and size, and less often to those with a higher-than-average mass.[12] However, while the adults could regulate how often they returned – on average every other night once the chick had reached seven weeks of age – they did not regulate the amount of food they brought in; the average meal size of 50 grams persisted over the season regardless of the chick's body mass.

Another significant factor determining how often Hutton's shearwaters would return to the colony to feed was the adult's own body condition. Adults with a low body mass for their size would spend longer at sea before returning to the colony to feed the chick, their first priority being to feed themselves and maintain their own condition.[13] In years of poor at-sea food availability, chicks could starve or fledge at a low rate as their parents prioritised their own survival. This strategy makes evolutionary sense for a long-lived species: a Hutton's shearwater has on average around 14 breeding years.[14] In contrast, short-lived passerines such as riflemen or redpolls are lucky to survive from one winter to the next. Their evolutionary strategy is to produce as many broods as they can in a breeding season, even if the effort of doing so puts their own survival at risk.

We followed a sample of 20 chicks for three weeks, weighing each chick every two hours from dusk to dawn, through wind, rain and moonlight. Each round took roughly an hour, leaving us just under an hour back at the hut for coffee, tea, a bowl of cereal or a short nap before morning. After a week my legs began to follow the round on their own, dragging a reluctant mind and body with them, the long nights disappearing in a hallucinogenic blur of downy grey chicks, spring balances and the night-time sounds and smells of the colony.

Over the seasons a team of field assistants, volunteers and friends visited the Kowhai to assist with the work. Chief among these was Erica, who was present in all three seasons, and Mike, Sheryl Hamilton, Al Wiltshire, Caren Genery and Justine Ragg, who also came for long periods. Others, including Keith, Dave and Faith Barber from DOC, came for several week-long stretches. Their help and enthusiasm was unstinting, and it was a privilege to share the magic of the place with people who appreciated it.

Among the regular visitors was Geoff Harrow. Following his visit to the colony in the first season we had kept in touch and become firm friends, and I would stay with Geoff and his wife each time I passed through Christchurch. Geoff visited each year and in the second year brought his brother-in-law and fellow mountaineer Deryck Morse. Together they lent a welcome hand in banding several hundred shearwaters at night. Deryck had accompanied Geoff on many of his earliest explorations in the Kaikoura mountains, searching new areas for remaining colonies as well as visiting the Kowhai colony. He had been badly injured in World War II and could stick a pin into the left side of his body without feeling a thing, but remained an active climber and had climbed Aoraki Mt Cook with Geoff in 1956. He had no problem walking in and scrambling around the Kowhai Valley in the 1960s, and was still active 30 years later when he and Geoff joined us at the hut.

In the third season Geoff was accompanied by his wife Lyndsey. Despite almost 20 years of visits to the Kaikoura ranges and many weekends spent at Puhi Puhi Station she had never visited the colonies; the attentions of two children, the walk and steep climb in and, later in life, a worn hip, had denied her the opportunity. With the availability of a helicopter and the comfort of a hut the situation was

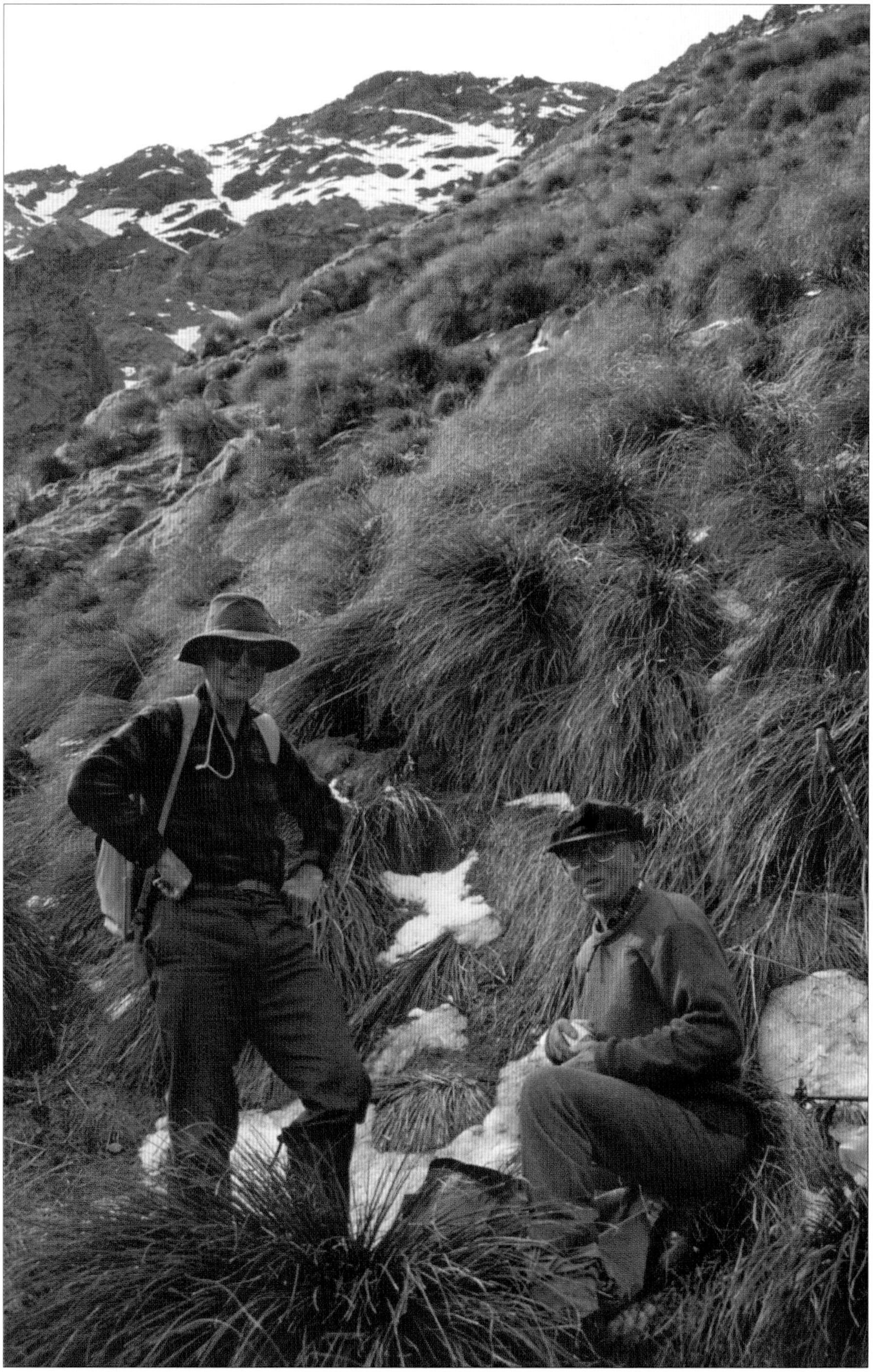

Geoff Harrow and Deryck Morse assisting with work in the colony in 1998. Author photo

different, and 30 years after Geoff had first visited the shearwaters Lyndsey finally came to have a look.

Geoff's visits were always great fun, and knowing our love of fresh fruit and vegetables and the infrequency of helicopter supply runs he would always arrive laden with enough to feed an army, including fresh fish carefully wrapped in damp newspaper to keep it cool. Geoff and I would talk endlessly of mountains and climbing, wildlife, the Himalaya and Antarctica. Whenever our tales of climbing exploits became too enthusiastic we would be brought to heel by Lyndsey, who would peer over her glasses and tell us we were 'silly men, the pair of you'. Not that she was unadventurous: she had accompanied Geoff around India in the 1960s, when Western travellers were far from common, and was the only grandmother I knew who owned and regularly used a boogie board in the surf off Christchurch.

Most of the time, however, Geoff and I talked about Hutton's shearwaters and their behaviour, and the possible factors that could have caused the shearwaters to retreat to two alpine valleys in the heart of the Kaikoura ranges. Chief among the topics we discussed was the role of stoats.

Erica Sommer fitting a radio-tag to a stoat. Author photo

17. Tracking the valley's stoats – and an unusual grass

As the chicks began to hatch and grow we continued the regular transects and burrow monitoring, the obsessive measurement and weighing of shearwater chicks and the trapping of stoats. Pregnant and nursing female stoats are notoriously difficult to trap: over two seasons we failed to catch a single female during the late winter and spring months, but as soon as their kits were out of the den we began to get females in the traps.[1] The number of captured stoats grew until we had 16 animals with collars on. But that was just the start: once they were equipped with a collar we began to spend our time radio-tracking them.

We initially tried to track the stoats via triangulation – taking three directional readings of the animal from spread-out locations in the valley and then plotting the resulting triangle to estimate where the animal was located. This method works well in a fairly flat and even landscape, but among the Kowhai's cliffs and bluffs the accuracy was poor. Moreover, the hard rocks and scree made it difficult to get an accurate signal, as the radio signals reflected and bounced from one steep-sided gut to another, leaving us listening to echoes and obtaining false directions for the animals. We abandoned triangulation, and instead began to track each stoat individually, walking for hours up, down and across the valley following a signal until we could locate the animal on the ground to within a few square metres. It was painstaking and time-consuming but was the only method that worked with any degree of accuracy.

As well as mapping the movements and range of the stoats in the valley, we were searching for evidence of shearwater kills and of stoats caching multiple bodies. When we had located a stoat we then searched the nearby ground and burrows closely, often marking the site with a ribbon of tape and returning the next day with the burrowscope to investigate the contents of all burrows in the area. Our estimates of predation, particularly for shearwater adults killed in the colonies at night, depended critically on the transects revealing an accurate representation of the mortality, which in turn depended on dead adult birds being randomly distributed in the colonies. If stoats were storing most of their kills in one or two burrows or underneath a boulder, then our estimates of mortality from the transect lines could have been very inaccurate. As the data started to come in I was relieved to see there was no evidence of widespread caching behaviour by stoats. Instead, we were simply finding individual depredated shearwater adults and chicks, down burrows or on the ground among the tussocks.

To supplement the radio tracking and confirm the fate of dead birds, we decided to track freshly killed shearwaters as well, using spools of cotton thread. This is an old but effective method for revealing the fine-scale movements of animals. The unwinding spool leaves an exact trail, tracing an animal's path from tussock to tussock and in and out of burrows. We found that stoats returned to their kills for up to four nights to feed, and on occasion would also move dead shearwater adults and chicks, but still we found no evidence of caching.

Tracking stoats took us into areas we had never found a reason to visit. We followed them from the highest, most inaccessible patches of colony to thickly vegetated areas in the lower confines of the valley. It was a good excuse to indulge my urge to explore, and when time allowed I would head off to visit another remote patch of colony and look on the valley from a new aspect. Some spots I returned to repeatedly just to sit and watch. These sites were usually distinguished by a good viewpoint, or a well-formed rock to sit or lie back on, or because they elicited memories of an encounter with a stoat, chamois, falcon or other species.

One such location at the top of sub-colony 15. The transect line ended at the sub-colony's highest point where the burrowed ground and vegetation thinned and turned to bare rock. Here the colony was bounded on one side by a sheer drop that fell into a gorge, on the far side of which was 'Impossible' sub-colony (so named for its inaccessibility – I ventured there once on a hair-raising afternoon and never returned). This was a favourite spot from which to savour the surroundings and chew a last muesli bar if one remained in my bag. As I sat I would scan the tussock slopes opposite through my binoculars, waiting until I had spotted at least one member of the small herd of chamois that always seemed to be present in this area. This herd seemed to prefer the security of Impossible sub-colony, where as far as I was aware I had made the sole human visit.

From this vantage point it was only a quick sidle to the head of the loose scree that ran to the valley floor, and even in poor weather with an approaching southerly front I knew I had time to sit and watch before an fast and exhilarating run to the valley floor, followed by a short section of the main valley and the short slope up through Camp sub-colony to the hut.

In midsummer my scree runs took me through small flocks of looping black mountain ringlet butterflies that were drawn to the sun-infused warmth of the dark greywacke rock. Uniquely in New Zealand, and following the same rare behaviour as a few other mountain-dwelling butterflies in the Himalaya and European Alps, the black mountain ringlet lays its eggs on the rocks, relying on the sun-warmed surface to speed up development within the short summer season.[2] Once the egg hatches, the caterpillar's life is far from straightforward; it feeds on only one species of grass, and its slow growth rate means it may have to survive through one or even two winters before pupating and emerging as an adult. Mountain ringlets were one of the few day-flying insects in the valley, and along with large numbers of grasshoppers were the most common insect present during the day.

Large numbers of stoneflies and caddis flies were also seen on warm summer days, emerging from their stream-bound larval stages for a brief mating cycle before dying, their life purpose fulfilled. In midsummer, after several warm nights of hatching and mating, their dead adult forms would lie like confetti along the edges of small pools in the valley's streams.

At night the insect life changed dramatically. When banding birds by the light of a head torch we would be surrounded by a profusion of moths attracted to the glow of our lamps, while Kaikoura giant wētā and ground wētā crawled over our legs and

A Kaikoura giant wētā. Author photo

arms. With the assistance of Brian Patrick from the Otago Museum, we borrowed a lightweight moth trap and began trapping around the hut and nearby streams at night. New Zealand has many night-time specialties and the relative absence of diurnal butterflies and moths is made up for by an abundance of nocturnal forms. Over the three seasons the trapping revealed 90 species of native moths and butterflies; 12 species of caddis and stoneflies; 14 species of beetles and weevils; and giant, cave and ground wētā.[3]

As well as common species, among the catch were many range-restricted endemic species – ones that occurred only in the Kaikoura mountains. These included at least three new and as yet undescribed species of moth, rare and alpine-specialist species of caddis fly and, perhaps most interesting, a new species of ground wētā that seemed to be restricted to living in the shearwaters' burrows. Such an apparently close relationship meant that this wētā's range had in all likelihood contracted with that of the shearwaters, making this ground wētā as vulnerable to extinction as the Hutton's shearwaters upon whose burrows it depended.

The presence of several new and undescribed species of insect, as well as range-restricted and alpine-specialist species, highlights the biodiversity of the Seaward and Inland Kaikoura ranges, and the importance of these mountains as a centre of endemism. Hutton's shearwater is the most obvious example of such a species: it breeds nowhere else in New Zealand or the world. Other such species in the Kaikoura ranges include three species of giant wētā[4] (the Kaikoura giant wētā, the bluff wētā and the scree wētā) as well as the new ground wētā found in the shearwaters' burrows.

After persistent rain, large grey leaf-veined slugs appeared on the valley floor before retreating slowly to the stream banks and rocks to avoid the sun. These slugs were another new and undescribed species from within the *Pseudaneitea* genus,[5] which is native to New Zealand. The rare and distinctive black-eyed gecko, discovered by Geoff Harrow's son Paul, was first found at Shearwater Stream[6] and is now known to occur in the Seaward Kaikoura mountains as well as on Mt Arthur in Kahurangi National Park in the northwest of the South Island.[7] Species of Marlborough rock daisy, pink tree broom and weeping broom are also restricted to the Inland and Seaward ranges.

The vegetation within the colonies was superficially simple. Two species of snow tussock, *Chionochloa flavescens* and *C. pallens*, were the main vegetation type in the mid- to high-altitude sub-colonies, and stands of mountain ribbonwood trees (*Hoheria lyalli*) were dominant in the lower-altitude sub-colonies. While these three species largely made up the two principal habitats in the valley, many other species were also present. In the lower reaches of the valley, where the soil thinned and was too exposed for ribbonwood trees, snow tōtara, mountain toatoa, hebe, *Coprosma* and *Dracophyllum* shrubs covered the ground, forming a layer of vegetation under which the shearwaters burrowed among the roots. In autumn the waxy red fruits of snow tōtara and *Coprosma* would colour the slopes like miniature Christmas decorations, providing valuable food for kea through the colder months.

Two species of speargrass, also known as Spaniard plants, dotted the tussock slopes like crown-of-thorns starfish among a bed of sea-grass. Somewhat oddly, the speargrasses belong within the carrot family, with the genus name *Aciphylla*, accurately meaning 'sharp-leaved'. In the colonies large speargrass plants, *Aciphylla ferox*, were easily spotted – and avoided – but young plants lurked low between the snow tussocks and would catch me unawares, stabbing me painfully in the shins and calves and frequently drawing blood and curses. Along with the largest speargrass species, the golden-leafed and mercifully softer *Aciphylla montana* also occurred in the valley. In midsummer the tussock slopes were brightened by the white flowers of *Celmisia* daisies, sweet-smelling *Anisotome* herbs and yellow *Ranunculus* buttercups.

The tussock slopes and valley floor also hosted introduced species; cocksfoot and sweet vernal grasses occurred among the burrows, along with the tongue-shaped leaves of sheep sorrel that supplemented our diet in the summer. The fantastically named 'mouse ear' and 'king devil hawkweeds' were common too and covered the tussock slopes with their yellow flowers; in late summer, along with a native dandelion, their seed-heads provided a near constant spindrift as we pushed through the tussocks. Small bellflowers and white-flowered, purple-stemmed violets grew on the valley floor, and two species of grey-leafed penwiper plants, both endemic to New Zealand, were common on the screes, where they clung to the ever-moving slopes with long roots trailing like sea anchors. From January onwards their creamy white inflorescences dotted the scree slopes like field mushrooms, their sweet scent a miracle of chemical alchemy from the uncompromising rock. Higher up, vegetable sheep and other cushion plants hugged the alpine ridges among the lichens and mosses.

I am far from being a botanist, but Janice Lord, a lecturer in the Botany Department at the University of Otago, identified more than 100 species in the valley and confirmed the floristic interest of the shearwater colonies. Their isolation, the absence of habitat modification from burning or grazing and the accumulated fertiliser from thousands of years of shearwater guano had created a rich and varied habitat, which included many rare and range-restricted species now absent from similar ranges in North Canterbury and Marlborough, where they would once have been abundant.

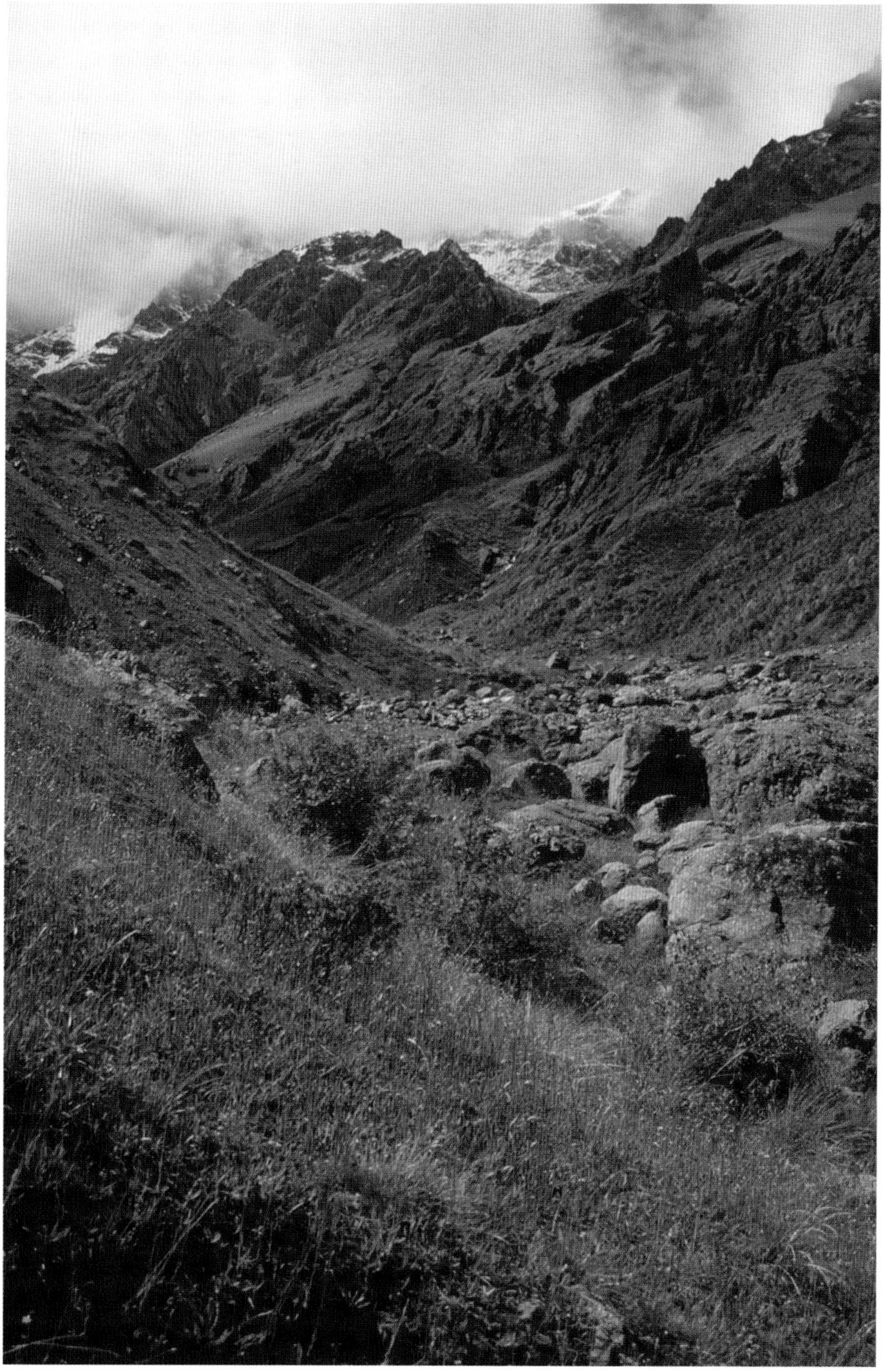

The valley floor at the end of summer. Author photo

Among the range of plants found by Janice, a small and dark green *Carex* sedge stood out for me. Unlike any other plant in the valley, this sedge was confined to areas with shearwater burrows. Neither Janice nor I knew the reason for this restriction, although the higher nitrates and phosphates within the burrowed areas seemed a likely cause. However, while the reason for its fidelity to shearwater areas was unclear, its presence provided an important clue to the past location of Hutton's shearwater colonies, and for understanding why the shearwaters had retracted to two steep valleys high in the Kaikoura ranges.

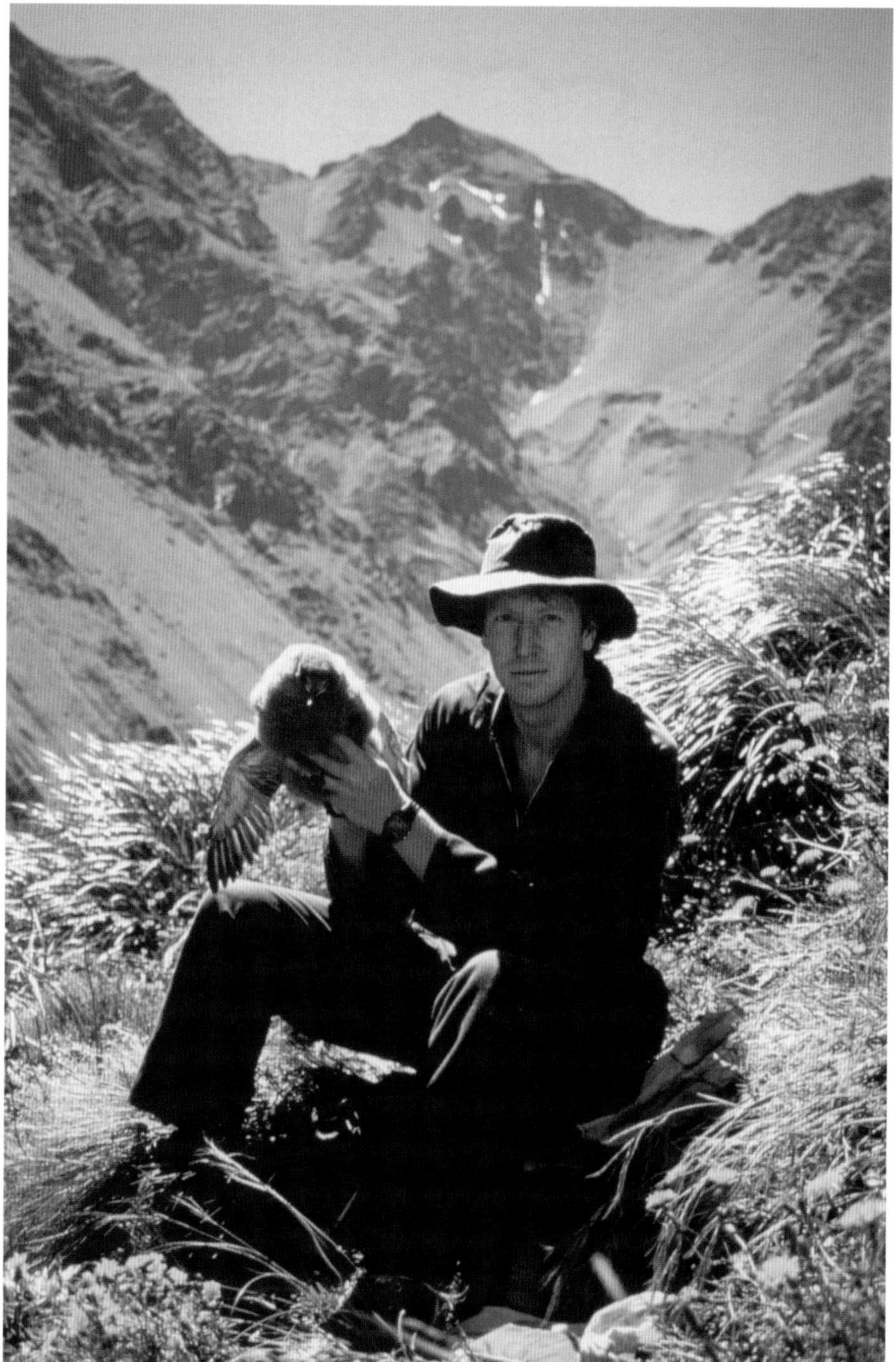

Richard Cuthbert holding a large shearwater chick. Author photo

18. Piecing together the data

Radio-tracking stoats, monitoring the transect lines and burrows, and measuring and weighing the fattening shearwater chicks continued until the end of each season. From December onwards the valley had a more mellow character than in the pre-breeding and incubation periods, when the area was still cloaked in snow and southerly fronts swept in regularly. The days were often clear and bright, and in midsummer the greywacke and argillite rocks and scree radiated the heat of the sun until the valley became an oven. Long days spent in the heat, crawling and lying among the prickly tussocks checking burrows or using the burrowscope, were a test of endurance. The streams and river in the valley floor provided relief, and at the end of a hot day we often stripped off and submerged ourselves in a shallow pool, washing away the dust and dirt and reinvigorating the soul.

In the final month of the season the near-morbidly obese chicks started to slim down and their barrel-round bodies of grey down gradually morphed into adult forms as their contour and flight feathers developed. During these final weeks the chicks spent hours preening in their burrows, and a cloud of grey down would puff out of each burrow whenever we removed a chick for weighing. In the last few weeks before fledging, many chicks sported a single ridiculous tuft of down on the crown of their head or around their neck, the only areas they were unable to reach. Young shearwaters that crashed in the glare of street-lights in Kaikoura were easily distinguished by traces of grey down clinging to their heads and backs.

Through the regular measuring and weighing of chicks we had come to know the characters and quirks of some individuals: those that would hide in the same alcove of their burrow, those that remained docile when moved, and those that would wait silently out of reach then suddenly seize your fingers. Each chick's departure left a poignant sense of loss when suddenly and overnight their burrow became empty, but also brought a feeling of relief that they had successfully made it through the long breeding season. We recorded losses to stoats throughout the year, but coming across the partially eaten corpse of a study-burrow chick was always a bitter blow, especially in the last few weeks before it was due to fledge. All populations suffer losses, but these ones made me seethe for revenge.

Cheering us up on such days was the never-ending entertainment provided by the resident kea population, and in particular by Aston. Following his capture at the start of the second season Aston had kept his distance from the hut for a week or two – the experience of being held and banded had clearly not been to his liking. But the hut's allure was strong, and soon he was back on the roof each morning and evening, continuing his endless battle to climb the metal guy-lines and picking up any stray pen, book, cap or other item that we had inadvertently left unattended and not bolted down. Aston was such a fixture that, like an over-anxious parent, after a few days' absence I would grow worried for his whereabouts until I heard the rattling clatter on a roof and his soft 'kaa' – and cursed because once again it was four in the morning.

Aston didn't confine himself to the hut; often when we were checking nests or returning to our bags at the foot of a colony we would hear a gentle call and he would bound away in sideward leaps or an ungainly flurry of wingbeats. Rucksack pockets would have been unzipped and notebooks, pens and clothes removed and scattered. We reached the point of hiding our bags under tussocks or carrying them all the time to prevent him from emptying the contents. He also routinely pulled up and shifted the bamboo poles and metal tags marking the routes of transect lines or study burrows.

On occasion Aston followed us as we checked burrows, trying his utmost to pull out the metal tag from the preceding study burrow before moving on with us to the next, always staying one burrow behind us and out of arm's reach. There was nothing we could do but laugh and engage in an arms race of thicker and more deeply planted poles and tags. Aston always had time and persistence on his side, though, and the loss of some of the markers was part and parcel of living in the hall of the mountain king. What Aston or the other kea got out of pulling up the tags and poles was a mystery, but they have an innate curiosity to explore, poke, pull and dismantle any and every object. These behaviours enable them to glean a living in the mountain environment, and are the very traits that would have led them to discover the rich feeding opportunities provided by a Hutton's shearwater chick deep in its burrow.

OPPOSITE: One of the valley's young kea. Author photo

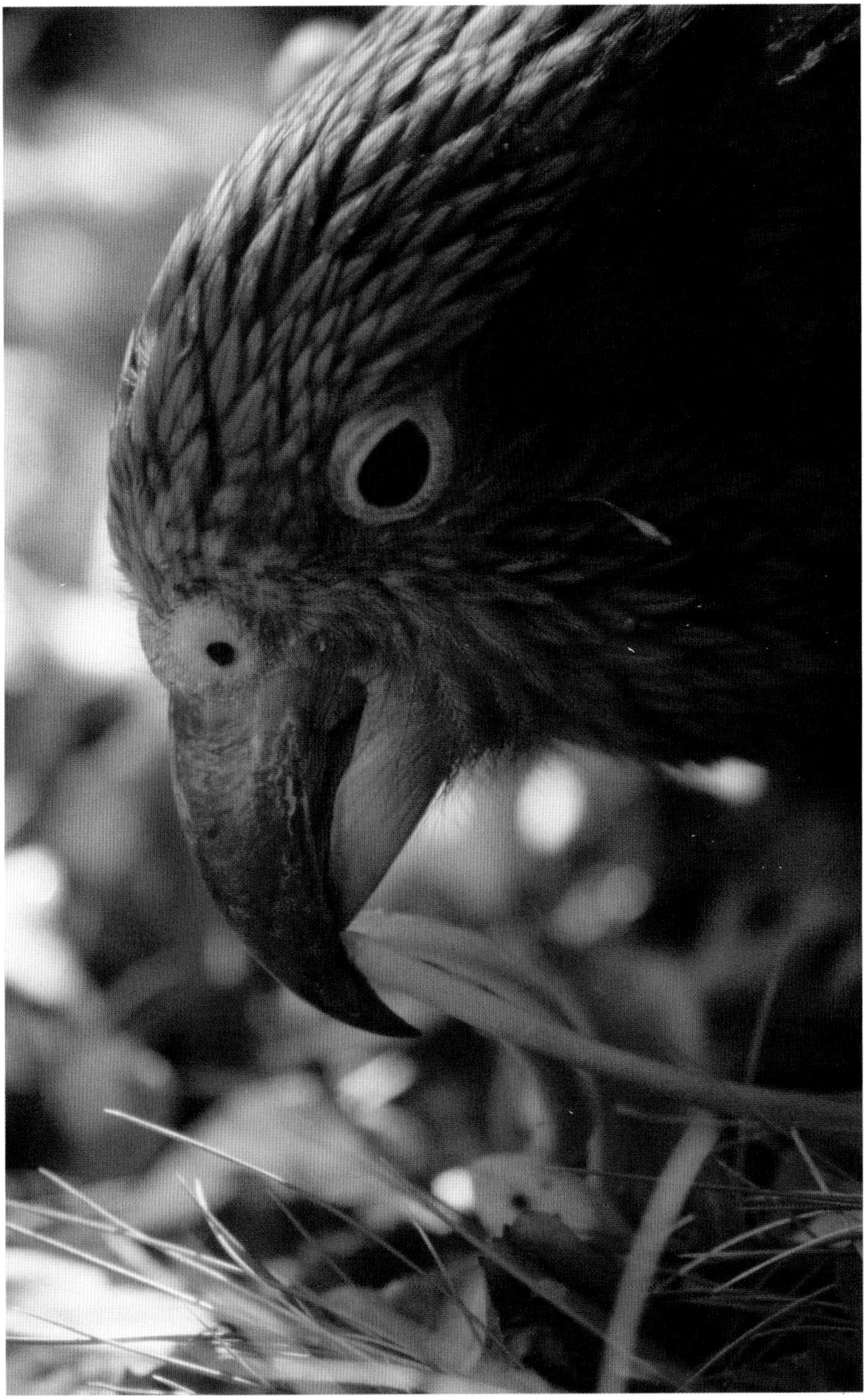

Some kea antics left me dumbfounded as a scientist and convinced me that many kea just want company and most definitely possess a sense of humour. On one occasion I was traversing around a small bluff, descending via a steep shortcut to the hut below. A small rock rattled past. I stopped and scanned around quickly, as such a sound was often caused by a chamois above me and larger rocks could follow. A second stone rolled down and clipped my cap: there was definitely something around. Looking up I could see nothing, but I did hear a small series of muffled and excited squeals from above. Climbing up, I peered over the lip of rock the stones appeared to have come from. There was Aston – who else? – and he was in the process of bulldozing another stone towards the edge with his beak, but now stopped in mid-act and started innocently preening his tail feathers.

Climbing back down, I continued to traverse the bluff. Suddenly I heard several muffled squawks. I turned to see Aston roll off the bluff, fall a full four metres and land on the sloping rocks below with a loud hollow thump. His body continued to tumble, bouncing head over tail onto the scree below, before coming to a final silent stop. Horrified, I scrambled down as quickly as I could to his still form. When I was just metres away he staged a miraculous recovery; the valley echoed to one loud 'Keeeaaaaaa!' as, in a flashing arc of orange, blue and green feathers, Aston swooped off down the mountainside. I shouted and waved a fist at his departing form, with tears of laughter rolling down my face.

I was beginning to experience the satisfaction of having answers to many of the questions we had set out with. I had an intuitive feel for the ecology of the valley and – most important – the hard data to back me up. After three years in the Kowhai Valley we had information on the diet of stoats, their home range and territorial behaviour, and the knowledge that they did not cache large numbers of shearwaters. We had estimates of egg and chick losses and adult predation rates from the monitored burrows and colony transects. We also had estimates of shearwater breeding success and adult survival during our time, supported by the earlier work of Kaikoura DOC staff, which provided a time series of breeding and survival data that stretched back to 1989.

The data from the 10 years was telling, for while the first four years of monitoring had revealed a worrying situation with low levels of breeding success, in the next five years breeding success was high. The reasons for the change were not clear, but we knew from radio-tracking work and the behaviour of stoats that some animals would concentrate their hunting in relatively small patches of colony, so the poor breeding success of a particular sub-colony could be down to one stoat having targeted the majority of burrows within a small monitored patch. Alternatively, and perhaps more likely, the number of birds breeding and their success depended critically on the marine environment, which could vary greatly from year to year.

For a long-lived seabird like a shearwater, with an adult lifespan of 20–30 years, some years of poor breeding success were to be expected; from a population perspective the odd poor year did not matter as long there were enough good years. In the poor years few birds would attempt to breed, and those that did had a low chance of rearing a chick through to fledging. Over the 10 years, overall breeding success – the proportion of eggs that went on to produce a fledged chick – averaged 47%.[1] The figure may sound low, but it is equivalent to each breeding pair successfully producing a fledgling every other year; over the 10–20 years that most pairs will breed for, that is sufficient to replace the population. Comparison of that figure with other shearwater species is also telling: a 32-year study of short-tailed shearwaters on a predator-free island off Australia revealed an almost identical value (48%) of breeding success for this species.[2] Breeding success for three other shearwaters, again in predator-free areas, indicated a range of 43–63%, which encompasses the average figure found within the Kowhai Valley.[3]

Despite most stoat predation of Hutton's shearwaters occurring on chicks, the Kowhai study indicated that the majority of breeding failures occurred during the egg stage, with hatching success averaging 57%. This is similar to the pattern of most petrels and albatrosses, with the vagaries of weather, foraging trips and the coordination of incubation shifts the causes of most failures.[4] In contrast, fledging success for the Hutton's shearwater – the proportion of hatched chicks that fledge successfully – was high and averaged 85%. Comparison with other shearwater species is again instructive: fledging success of the sooty shearwater and Manx shearwater averaged 83% and 87% respectively in two other studies.[5] Despite the attention of the valley's stoats, the majority of Hutton's shearwater survived, and hatching, fledging and overall breeding success matched the range of values found for other shearwaters breeding in areas free from introduced predators.

The other – even more crucial – statistic to estimate was annual adult survival. For a long-lived seabird like Hutton's shearwater, a 3–4% decrease in average adult survival rates would have a major impact on the population, whereas a similar or even greater drop in breeding success was less critical.[6] Established adult breeders were worth more to the population because of the chicks and fledglings they would produce over their reproductive life span. In contrast, a fledgling chick had only a relatively small chance of surviving its first few years at sea, finding its way back to the colony and then finding a mate, a burrow and becoming a breeding bird. Consequently, while the survival of chicks and young birds at sea is important, their net worth to the population as a whole is less than that of an established breeder.

We were measuring adult survival in the colony through the banding and recapture of adult breeding birds. Thanks to the work of the Kaikoura DOC staff we already had a sample of birds marked from three sub-colonies, and during our years in the Kowhai many hundreds more birds were banded. The banding records indicated the presence or absence of each bird over every year of the study, and from this information we could estimate the likelihood of recapture and survival in each year. Not all birds were captured: in some years birds might have a 'sabbatical' and not return to breed; or we might have continuously missed catching a bird down its burrow or on the colony's surface, even though it was present. And obviously some birds were not recaptured because they failed to survive their winter migration or had been killed by a stoat or falcon in the colony.

The combination of the recapture frequency and true mortality figure allowed us to estimate annual adult survival, which was the average survival rate of all birds across the sub-colonies where they were being banded and recaptured. For the Kowhai Valley this estimate came in at 93%, with 7% of breeding adults failing to survive from one season to the next.[7] Comparison with other shearwater species breeding in areas free from introduced predators indicates that this value for Hutton's shearwaters was particularly healthy, with annual survival in Manx shearwaters and short-tailed shearwaters estimated at 90.5% and 90–92%, respectively.[8] As for breeding success, the Kowhai shearwaters seemed to be coping with the impact of stoats in the valley, despite the fact that we knew stoats were killing some adult birds.

These high estimates of breeding success and adult survival were strong evidence that Hutton's shearwaters could withstand the levels of predation they experienced. A population model using these estimates, and utilising values of at-sea survival of young shearwaters from other studies, predicted that in the majority of cases the population should be stable or increasing. While these results were very positive I knew it wasn't enough: the case needed to be water-tight to convince people that stoats – which were such a devastating predator to most native birds in New Zealand – were not driving the species towards extinction.

The estimates of predation that were independently derived from the repeated transects through colonies and the necropsy of dead birds, and from the monitoring for dead chicks and adults in burrows, added a set of braces to the belt already established by the estimates of chick and adult survival. The transect lines, autopsies and burrow checks indicated that predation by stoats accounted for annual losses of 1% of adult shearwaters and around 7% of eggs and chicks.[9] These small rates

OPPOSITE: Adult Hutton's shearwater in the Kowhai colony. Author photo

of loss corroborated the high values of breeding success and survival found in the shearwaters themselves, and provided further strong evidence of the relatively small impact that stoats were having on the population.

19. The true impact of stoats

If the shearwaters were enjoying high adult survival and adequate levels of egg and chick survival, then what was limiting the impact of the stoats on the population? It had taken a while, but the data on the stoats in the valley finally helped to answer the question.

Over three seasons we had collected more than 800 stoat scats in the valley, which provided us with a picture of their diet from early spring, when adult shearwaters were turning up to breed, through to late autumn and early winter, after the last fledglings and adults had departed the colony. Finding the scats was one part of the job; the other was far more tedious, as each scat had to be soaked in a solution of warm water and detergent, carefully teased apart with tweezers, and the prey items carefully sorted into appropriate categories and identified. It was a mammoth task but with the help of Justine, who assisted with the stoat trapping, and Erica, who dedicated many rainy days to scat sorting, we had got there.

On the surface the results were unsurprising. Of 788 scats where prey remains could be identified, nearly all (785 to be precise) contained remains of shearwaters in some shape or form.[1] We already knew that stoats killed and consumed shearwaters and the scats confirmed their almost total reliance on this source of food. We found lesser evidence of other prey: skinks and invertebrate remains were found in 8% of scats, with the latter group mainly consisting of Kaikoura giant wētā as well as beetles, moths, flies, woodlice and spiders. Hairs from house mice were present in just 12 scats and from brown hares in seven, proportions of 1.5% and 0.9% respectively.

The results also indicated significant seasonal variation in the stoats' diet and provided evidence of a lean period during the early winter months when shearwaters were absent from the valley. Stoats consumed almost exclusively adult shearwaters from September through to late November; however, once the first eggs hatched they exclusively ate chicks to the end of the breeding season. Such a prey switch mattered because of the higher value (from a population perspective) of a breeding adult compared to a chick. The fact that stoats were targeting only chicks from December onwards was therefore good news, particularly as the peak population of stoats in the valley occurred from January, when each resident female's litter of kits became independent and started to hunt. From a stoat's perspective the prey switch made sense: why attempt to subdue and kill 330 grams of sharp-billed and truculent adult bird, when every other burrow contains a fat, sessile and near defenceless chick?

The results were also interesting for the months of April and May, two months after the shearwaters' departure from the colonies when snow was beginning to lie in the valley. Numbers of invertebrates, skinks and mice all increased in the stoats' diet during these two months, but still were found in only 10–25% of scats. Shearwater remains made up the rest of the scats and still dominated the diet, including eggs, chicks and adults. How could this be, when no there were no shearwaters around? It made no sense until we started following stoat tracks in the snow and discovered that they were retrieving the decayed remains of prey from burrows and beneath the snow. Old and desiccated shearwater carcasses were being scavenged, and even the papery dry webbing between the bird's toes and the scaled skin of the tarsus were being stripped off and gnawed to the bone.

A number of studies have demonstrated that populations of stoats and other mustelid carnivores are limited by their prey availability in the winter months, and at least half of all stoat mortality will occur in this period.[2] These studies were mainly undertaken in New Zealand's forests, or in northern Europe where the vole population is an important but limited food source under the snow. In the Kaikoura mountains there was no such alternative prey. While the Kowhai Valley's stoats were fat, well-fed animals for seven months a year, their numbers crashed each winter, effectively limiting their impact on the shearwaters the following spring. But what stopped stoats from the surrounding valleys and lowland hills from moving into the shearwater colonies to exploit the rich food opportunities during the season?

Over the second and third seasons we had managed to catch 16 stoats from more than 2500 nights of trapping effort, and our long days and nights of radio-tracking had obtained good information on where and how they were moving. This data indicated that adult males and females were both highly territorial from December onwards.[3] However, males were only territorial when it came to other males and, similarly, females were only territorial in relation to females.

This intra-sexual territoriality is common in mustelids, with members of the same sex defending their own home range, but with a male's range overlapping with one or two females and thereby allowing mating opportunities.[4] The only territories in the Kowhai that overlapped with animals of the same sex were those of two young stoats. One was a young female, whose range almost completely overlapped an adult female's range, probably indicative that this young female was one of the kits from the adult female whose range she was sharing.

The other overlapping territory was that of a young male, whose home range overlapped the corners of three adult males' ranges; however, most of this young male's range was in the main valley floor away from the shearwater burrows. In contrast, while adult male and female ranges included three or four shearwater sub-colonies and the areas of rock and scree between them, we knew they were spending almost all of their time where there were burrows. The young male was between a rock and a hard place. He had a range in the valley floor where shearwaters and prey were scarce, and ran the high risk of trespassing onto an adult male's territory in order to access birds and prey opportunities. Socially subordinate stoats tend to use different habitats to adult animals;[5] if this young stoat survived the harsh winter he may have moved to establish a territory in another area of the valley that contained burrows.

The strong intra-sexual territorial behaviour also limited the number of stoats present; the whole area of the Kowhai Valley where shearwaters occurred held 20–30 adult stoats at most.[6] It was a fair number, but placed in the context of there being over 200,000 shearwaters in the valley it meant that these stoats could only kill a tiny proportion of the birds' population. Even if the 20–30 stoats each killed one shearwater every day for the seven months of the breeding season, it would still only account for 2–3% of the total population of shearwaters present. Our study indicated, however, that stoats returned to feed on the same carcass for up to four days. If this reflected the killing frequency of stoats, then with a bird killed every two to four days the impact of such losses over the season against the 200,000 shearwaters present would be even less.

These numbers made ecological sense and helped explain the minor impact of stoats on the shearwater population. Yet it wasn't enough. I wanted some hard data to demonstrate that this pattern of 'safety in numbers' was a reality. If the theory was correct, any small colonies would rapidly become extinct due to the high rates of predation. Ideally I needed estimates of predation rates from a number of small to mid-sized Hutton's shearwater colonies, but in the Kaikoura mountains there were only two remaining colonies, both of which were large.

While Hutton's shearwaters could no longer provide such data, another shearwater species could. The sooty shearwater, or tītī, was still abundant in New

Zealand's southern islands, with millions of pairs breeding on the Snares Islands and hundreds of thousands of birds breeding on the Muttonbird Islands off the south coast of the South Island. The sooty shearwater is the traditional New Zealand muttonbird and provides an important cultural harvest for Māori in the South Island. While sooty shearwaters remain abundant on islands, their numbers have been nearly wiped out from the mainland and only a few tiny remnant colonies remain, mostly clustered around the Otago Peninsula where the famous mainland colony of northern royal albatross is also located.

A major study led by Henrik Moller from Otago University had been running for several years to investigate the cultural aspects of the tītī harvest and the ecology of this species in the south of New Zealand, and the remnant Otago Peninsula colonies had been monitored for several years. These colonies ranged from 36 to around 2000 burrows and, like the Hutton's colonies, were subject to predation. We compared rates of hatching, fledging and breeding success as well as predation rates from the proportion of burrows containing dead adult birds and chicks.[7] The results were beautiful – that is, unless you were a sooty shearwater breeding in the smallest colonies, where hatching, fledging and breeding success were all close to zero, and where there was a high chance of mortality for both adults and chicks. As the colony size grew, however, breeding success increased and predation rates dropped. The tītī colony of around 2000 burrows had similar high breeding success and low predation rates to Hutton's shearwaters in the Kowhai Valley.

This pattern, known as inverse density-dependent predation, is predicted to occur in situations where predator numbers are limited by factors other than prey density.[8] The pattern exactly mirrored the case of stoats and Hutton's shearwaters where, despite almost unlimited food opportunities, stoat numbers were limited in summer by their territorial behaviour and in winter by elevated rates of mortality.

If stoats were not a significant factor for the Hutton's shearwater colonies, then what had caused the loss of historical colonies and the retraction in range to just two surviving colonies high in the Seaward Kaikoura Range? I knew I had to look beyond the horizons of the Kowhai Valley to determine what was different about the extinct colonies that Geoff Harrow had uncovered in his explorations of the Kaikoura ranges in the late 1960s.

20. Beyond the valley's horizon

When Mike and I had climbed Manakau, the highest peak in the Seaward Kaikoura Range, in the early months of the first season, we had stood on the summit in a customary mix of exhilaration and exhaustion. Despite the nagging knowledge that we still had to get down safely, we had sat on the peak for a good 20 minutes enjoying a last energy bar and just taking in the view. The snow-covered Seaward and Inland Kaikoura ranges and the Clarence Valley lay before us; beyond them the northern extent of the Southern Alps hung in the haze of the horizon. I knew I was looking over much of the former range of Hutton's shearwater, and I made a silent vow to explore as much of this land as was physically possible.

Over our three years in the Kaikoura ranges we carved out time to ensure we visited all nine of the known extinct colonies, as well as making regular visits to the birds in Shearwater Stream where Geoff had undertaken most of his studies. Getting to these sites was far from easy for they were all high in the mountains, and the soft rocks of the Kaikoura ranges and the rapid geological uplift meant they were often guarded by deep-cut river gorges and shattered and crumbling rock ridges. Access was made even harder by the topographic maps. While these painted an accurate enough picture of the ranges, I found from experience that once within the confines of a river's gorge or pushing up a thickly forested ridge, the apparent detail of the contour lines merged into a more impressionistic form.

The lower-altitude slopes of the ridges were generally easier to move through and still harboured some large trees and good forest. Here we would pause in our walk to watch fantails among the branches, unafraid of our bush-bashing presence and noisily scolding us like squeaking children's toys. Other forest birds were also present, including the always comically large-headed tomtit and the occasional

South Island robin flicking through the leaf litter for food. Overhead, bellbirds, brown creepers and kererū called.

At higher altitudes the forest changed and the steep hillsides, thick with mānuka, kānuka, matagouri and spikey bush lawyer, hid rock bluffs, waterfalls and stands of bush so dense that the only approach was to crawl or find another route. The best option, if possible, was to pick up a deer or pig trail and follow the narrow track, keeping low and pushing under the shoulder-high vegetation. Eventually, with a bit of luck, the bush would thin until we broke free onto slopes of snow tussock and low-growing snow tōtara and hebe scrub. From here the broad contours of the landscape were easier to follow, although the terrain remained steep and incoming weather could suddenly cloak a sunny ridge in the thickest cloud and mist.

We accessed some of the extinct colonies from river valleys to the west of Kaikoura township, and approached others from the Kowhai, climbing up to 1200 metres or more and following a ridge line before picking a route to drop into a neighbouring valley. Erica had accompanied me on many of these trips, but on occasions I took off with only myself for company. Fit as a chamois after more than two years in the Kaikoura ranges, I travelled with a light rucksack and the minimum of food, relying on speed, knowledge of the terrain and my own capabilities. My only equipment was a map, compass, waterproofs and bivvy bag, notebook and binoculars, and two telescopic ski poles that were my ever-present tools on the crumbling greywacke.

I have had long arguments with friends on the ethics and responsibility of solo trips in the mountains. To me, the feeling of isolation and independence of being on my own was thoroughly exhilarating; all senses were intensified and sharpened, as a single slip or sprained ankle was potentially fatal, and the sheer focus and concentration required to move safely was cathartic and energising. Those feelings were matched by the self-reliance that such trips required, and the knowledge that the consequences of any mistakes were entirely my own responsibility.

My biggest fear when high in the Kaikoura ranges was a weather change, such as the arrival of mist or cloud to cloak the surrounding mountains or, worse, the appearance of long cirrus clouds above Manakau that heralded the start of a northwest storm. On one occasion I had set off for a two-day walk to an extinct colony, intent on climbing to the main ridge of the Seaward Kaikoura Range for an overnight bivouac before tramping over Manakau and back to the hut the following day. After half a day of walking to find the old colony areas and collect the data that I needed, I filled a two-litre water bottle from a nearby stream and set off for the ridge crest, picking my way up the easiest line and skirting through bluffs and scree slopes.

After three hours of climbing I reached the skyline and stood on the main ridge crest of the Seaward Kaikoura Range. I looked out over the Clarence Valley, baked dry at the end of summer. Above the Inland Kaikoura Range tell-tale cirrus cloud indicated the start of a norwester building. I continued south along the ridge in the direction of Manakau, keeping a weather eye on the approaching cirrus in the west and conscious of the first tentative gusts beginning to buffet me. The summit ridge of the Kaikoura ranges was no place to be in a northwest storm, but there was no easy way off the ridge other than forward or back. In 1964, in a similar storm, Canterbury Mountaineering and New Zealand Alpine Club member Derek Winter had been blown from the summit of Mt Uwerau, falling several thousand feet to his death.

With this knowledge in the back of my mind, high on the ridge crest with three hours of light remaining and the wind picking up, I made my decision. I drank long and deeply, then dumped all but two mouthfuls of my remaining water, turned and began to run, betting a lighter load and my fitness against the incoming storm. I crested the summit of Manakau nearly two hours later, pausing for a minute to draw breath and gaze at the surrounding mountains, then carefully scrambled down keeping myself low to the ridge to avoid the growing gusts. I reached the hut safely two hours later in the dark, near to exhaustion and happy to be home.

The purpose of our visits to the extinct colonies was to determine whether and how these differed from the existing colonies at Shearwater Stream and the Kowhai. Our knowledge of the sites' locations in the valleys was limited; all we had to go on was a valley's name, an approximate description, or an old sketch map from Geoff's day. But as we traversed the hillsides at the same altitude as the two extant colonies, we would encounter the same aspect and snow tussocks as within the Kowhai – and there, nestling between the tall grasses, was the dark green sedge that only occurred in burrowed areas in the Kowhai and Shearwater Stream colonies, confirming that we were standing in an old colony. At each site we measured the slope angle, the aspect and altitude of tussock areas and the depth of the topsoil. We also searched for evidence of stoats, rats and mice or the presence of goats, deer, chamois and pigs.

These trips were a highlight, not just for the challenge of reaching the sites, but also because they always revealed new aspects of the ranges that helped build a fuller picture of the Kowhai and Shearwater Stream and the wildlife within them. As I stood among the snow tussocks of the extinct colonies, however, I always experienced a sense of loss. Like the forlorn castles or stone circles in the UK, slowly crumbling into disuse, the valley before me was an empty shell of tussock and ridges. No kea squabbled above me, no harriers quartered the ground in the morning light, and the screaming 'kek-kek-kek' of a New Zealand falcon high overhead was missing.

The burrows that would have supported populations of ground wētā and skinks had long since collapsed to nothing. At night as I sat next to a small campfire, the screaming calls of tens of thousands of courting shearwaters were only amplified by their absence. Just the bare bones of a landscape remained, the skeletal remnants of a living system and a forlorn echo of a former vibrant and functioning ecosystem.

The abundance of life on many islands is driven by the fertilising nutrients from seabirds, which influence plant species composition, invertebrate abundance and the overall primary productivity of the island.[1] For tens of thousands of years Hutton's shearwaters had been bringing the rich nutrients of the oceans onto the land, the birds' guano and their decomposing carcasses depositing nitrates, phosphates and other trace elements along the flight paths and in the colonies. This nutrient enrichment was not confined to the Kaikoura mountains: fossil records from 2400 to 3000 years before present, from caves in North Canterbury, indicate that mottled petrels, Cook's petrels, diving petrels, storm petrels and shearwaters (most likely Hutton's) occurred across a wider range of the South Island and at lower altitudes than the current disribution of Hutton's shearwater.[2] Elsewhere the remains of petrels are prominent in caves and dune deposits,[3] and prior to the arrival of humans (and the rats and other species they brought with them) it is likely that tens of millions of seabirds would have been enriching the landscape across the mainland of New Zealand. Today, the two remaining Hutton's shearwater colonies, sooty shearwater colonies on headlands of the Otago coast, Westland petrels in the steep forests near Punakaiki, and small colonies of grey-faced petrels in northern parts of the North Island are the last traces of the vast mainland seabird colonies that would have acted as ecosystem drivers for wide areas of the country.

While most of the known extinct sites were in the Seaward Kaikoura Range and therefore relatively close to the Kowhai Valley or Kaikoura township, one extinct colony was in the Inland Kaikoura Range at Branch Stream, close to the highest peak, Tapuae-o-Uenuku. Notes from the first recorded Pākehā ascent of the peak in 1849 state that 'the Titi (muttonbird) breeds in large numbers on the Mountain (Tapuaenuku), and … many persons have been killed hunting for them'.[4] This was not the only historical record of shearwaters from near this peak; the *Marlborough Express* on 19 January 1883 featured an article entitled 'A Trip to Tapaeanuku. By One of the Party', in which an unnamed climber gave a detailed account of his climbing trip, including the presence of muttonbirds and burrows.[5]

These days anyone making an ascent of Tapuae-o-Uenuku usually approaches by vehicle along the Awatere Valley to the west of the Inland Range. However, the 1883 party approached from the eastern or seaward side of the range, and we wanted to follow the same route to make sure we encountered the same terrain and colonies. We could have taken a helicopter, but the sight of the Clarence River from the summit of Manakau during my first climb of that peak had sowed the germ of an idea, and despite our lack of river knowledge or rafting skills we talked a rafting company in Hanmer Springs into renting us a raft. Four of us set off, and delightful thoughts of languidly sipping gin and tonics while floating down the river were soon replaced by a harsher reality. It was midsummer and the river was low; a persistent and strong northerly wind blew up the Clarence Valley and met the blunt prow of the raft head on. We paddled remorselessly for hours each day over long stretches of flat water interrupted by brief sections of rapids, made rockier and more difficult by the low water levels. Each evening we hauled the raft out and camped by the river.

The landscape was stark and beautiful but not untouched, and the sometimes bare or thinly grassed hills bore the mark of decades of overgrazing by sheep and cattle. After five days of paddling we secured the raft and our river kit among a glade of trees and struck out west to tramp in to Tapuae-o-Uenuku. Our walk picked up the same route described in the *Marlborough Express* article and we followed 'over spurs, gullies, and mountain streams, [that] gave us a foretaste of what we were to expect further on'. The 1883 writer had noted 'a brood of Blue Mountain Ducks, seven in number … one may safely say that they are not becoming scarce among the mountains'. Blue ducks are now lost from the Clarence Valley and the Kaikoura ranges, cats, ferrets and stoats having taken too many nests and broods.

After a long day's walk and a difficult descent through a gorge we reached Branch Stream below the eastern flank of Tapuae-o-Uenuku, where we camped in snow tussock that would once have been shearwater ground, just above a glade of mountain ribbonwoods. I had no doubt we were in the right location. The 1883 account is revealing:

> At the bottom of this gorge were mountain birch trees, and under these, with the 'canopy of Heaven' above us, we camped for the night. Notwithstanding our exposure to the keen air, to say nothing of an occasional howl of a wild dog, or various other noises made by birds or pigs, we snatched a few hours' sleep, and at 3.15 a.m. on Monday were up and busily engaged preparing breakfast for it was this day that the ascent of 'Tapey' had to be made. Starting away at 4.30 a.m., we made up a long spur, and it was on this spur of rich loamy soil that we came across the breeding places of the mutton birds. They burrow in the ground like a rabbit, remaining out of sight all day, but at night venture out and set up a terrible row. One or two of the birds only were to be seen, but numerous feathers around the burrows gave evidence of a great many more. From these holes we had a straight climb of nearly 3000 feet to the top of the ridge adjoining the mountain itself.

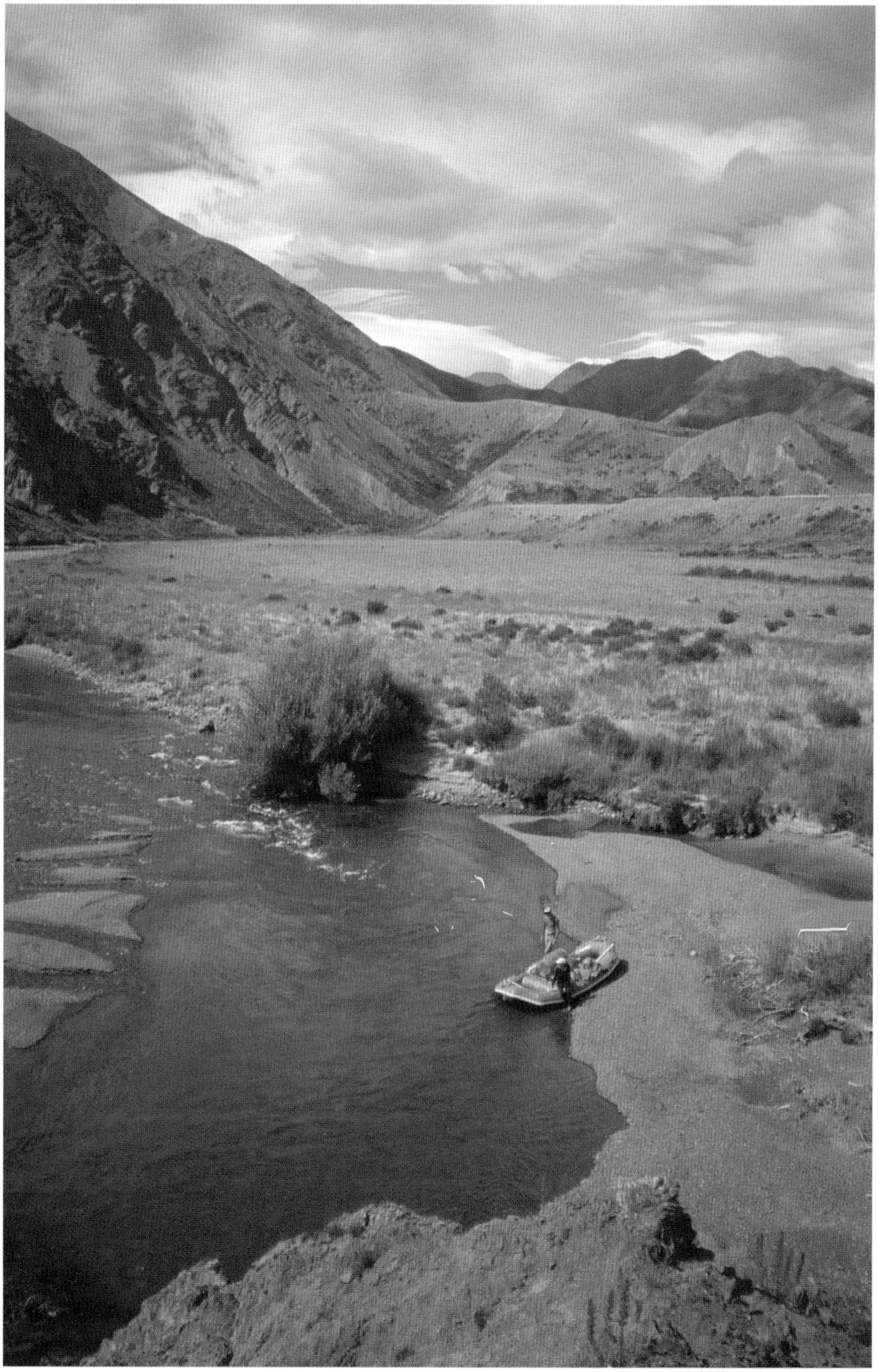

Rafting down the Clarence River to survey extinct colonies. Author photo

It is a clear description of a shearwater colony – from the 'terrible row' of calls, their nocturnal behaviour, the rabbit-like burrows and the numerous feathers – and the only such species present in the Kaikoura ranges would have been Hutton's shearwaters.

Also mentioned in the 1883 article was the unknown harbinger of the species' demise: pigs were heard at night from the campsite among the 'mountain birch'. From my visits throughout the Seaward and Inland Kaikoura ranges I knew that the two factors that distinguished the extinct colonies from the two remaining colonies were their relative accessibility and the presence of pigs. Evidence of other mammals, such as rats or deer and goats, was either absent from all of the sites (in the case of rats, which only occur at lower altitudes) or was present at some sites but with no consistent pattern. Similarly, there was nothing to distinguish the extinct colonies from the remaining two colonies in terms of their altitude, aspect, steepness or general vegetation. In contrast, at six of the eight extinct colonies, we saw either pigs or evidence of their rooting up of the ground. At the remaining two extinct sites there was no sign of them, but access to these two areas was relatively straightforward and the tussock was contiguous with areas of forest and bush where wild pigs undoubtedly occurred.[6]

On the contrary, access to both the Kowhai Valley and Shearwater Stream colonies is far from straightforward. The Kowhai is surrounded on three sides by the high ridges of Uwerau, Saunders and Manakau. To the south, steep vertical bluffs guard the flanks, and as the river exits the valley it narrows to a steep gorge with a 20-metre waterfall. Our route out involved wading across the river above this waterfall then climbing a steep and unstable bluff, following a thin deer and chamois trail and pulling on tussocks to scramble up short vertical rock steps. After this, the deer track sidled along, crossing two more steep, narrow streambeds before the country eased. A few hundred metres further on another steep stream descended from high up the scree slopes, cutting a precipitous path through the valley's flanks to the Kowhai River far below, and this necessitated another scramble down and a climb out before the terrain flattened off once more.

Access to Shearwater Stream was, if anything, even more difficult, and involved a long, steep scramble up bluffs. Geoff Harrow and subsequent DOC fieldworkers had hammered iron stakes and pitons into the rock at intervals and installed knotted ropes to haul on through the steepest sections. The other flanks of Shearwater Stream were guarded by vertical cliffs and bluffs, and above the highest section lay the peak of Te Ao Whekere, the second-highest mountain in the Seaward Kaikoura Range. So although pigs were present throughout the forests, bush and accessible valleys of the Kaikoura ranges, they could not get to the Kowhai and Shearwater Stream colonies.

Pigs were present on the boundaries of both colonies, however. On one occasion when I was walking out from the Kowhai I reached the flat area beyond the second gorge, around one kilometre from the hut, home to a sheltered glade of ribbonwoods with lush grass underneath. I pushed my way up fast from the steam and stopped briefly on the flat. Lungs heaving and blood pounding in my ears, I spent a few moments taking in the huge areas of grass rooted up to a depth of 20 centimetres or more. At the same time I heard a rustling and crashing in the bushes 10 metres away, and a large sow broke cover with three piglets at her heels. Fortunately she bolted away from me, and continued to run as I chased after, pushing them away from the colony until they crashed into a deep patch of scrub where I was unable to follow.

This and other sightings caused me to begin mapping all the observations I made of pigs on my trips through the Kaikoura ranges, whether glimpses of animals, signs of rooting or simply droppings. I joined up these map records on the basis of altitude and contiguous areas of tussock or forest cover where pigs could move freely. The results were telling: pigs were present in all of the extinct colonies and in the areas adjacent to and bordering the Kowhai Valley and Shearwater Stream. They were only absent from the two remaining colonies of Hutton's shearwaters.[7]

Pigs have been present in the South Island since 1773, when Captain Cook released a number of animals in the Marlborough Sounds.[8] Whether these survived is debatable, but subsequent introductions by Cook and other sailors, as well as semi-feral populations kept by Māori and transported by canoe to other settlements, soon led to an established wild population. Pigs spread throughout the forests of New Zealand and by the mid-1800s were widely established.[9] By then they had largely reverted to the behaviour and hairy black appearance of their forebear, the wild boar. Their range and numbers soared with the increased conversion to agricultural land and were thought to be at their highest in the 1940s.[10] Pigs became a major agricultural pest, damaging pastures and crops and killing livestock, and as a result were targeted by hunters and farmers, who killed tens of thousands in the late nineteenth century. The shortage of hunters, ammunition and fuel during both world wars led to further rises in pig numbers, and these periods of increase coincide with the time that many of the remaining Hutton's shearwater colonies appear to have been abandoned.

Although hunted and controlled in most areas, in the Molesworth Station, which lies to the west of the Inland Kaikoura Range, pigs were protected in the

1930s 'because they killed numerous rabbits in the same way they destroyed ground birds – rooting out burrows and preying on the young'.[11] If pigs were destroying rabbit burrows in this area of New Zealand it's likely they were doing the same to Hutton's shearwater burrows in the neighbouring Kaikoura ranges. Pigs have been observed preying upon seabirds and other ground-nesting birds, and the introduction of pigs to New Zealand's subantarctic Auckland Islands has caused the almost complete loss of this island's formerly huge colonies of burrowing petrels. As early as 1909 one commentator wrote, '[T]he introduction of pigs ... has already resulted in considerable havoc among the ground-nesting birds, by destroying both eggs and young.'[12] A similar report in the 1920s came from New Zealand's Poor Knights Islands, where pigs were described as 'by far the most destructive to plant and animal life of the animals introduced by human[s]':

> The effect of pigs on the fauna is best seen in the wiping-out of the breeding-grounds of burrowing petrels, a process which involves the killing of many birds. The rare Buller's shearwater and other petrels are practically extinct on the southern islet, but abundant on other islets of the group.[13]

Despite these early warnings, and more recent records of pigs destroying petrel colonies in the Galapagos Islands[14] and actively preying upon lambs in Australia,[15] the message that pigs are a destructive predator had been largely lost. A book on introduced predators and bird conservation published in the mid-1980s stated, 'It is probably stretching the point rather too far to include mice and pigs among the list of immigrant killers brought to New Zealand.'[16]

The evidence was pointing to a conclusion that had not previously been drawn in explaining the contraction in breeding range of Hutton's shearwaters. Of course pigs would not have been the only cause. A partially destroyed colony reduced to isolated patches of burrows with a few hundred scattered pairs of birds had lost the 'safety in numbers' protection of a large colony. Stoats preying on the few remaining birds would have extinguished any last population,[17] but they could not have done so without the large-scale habitat destruction and predation initiated by feral pigs.

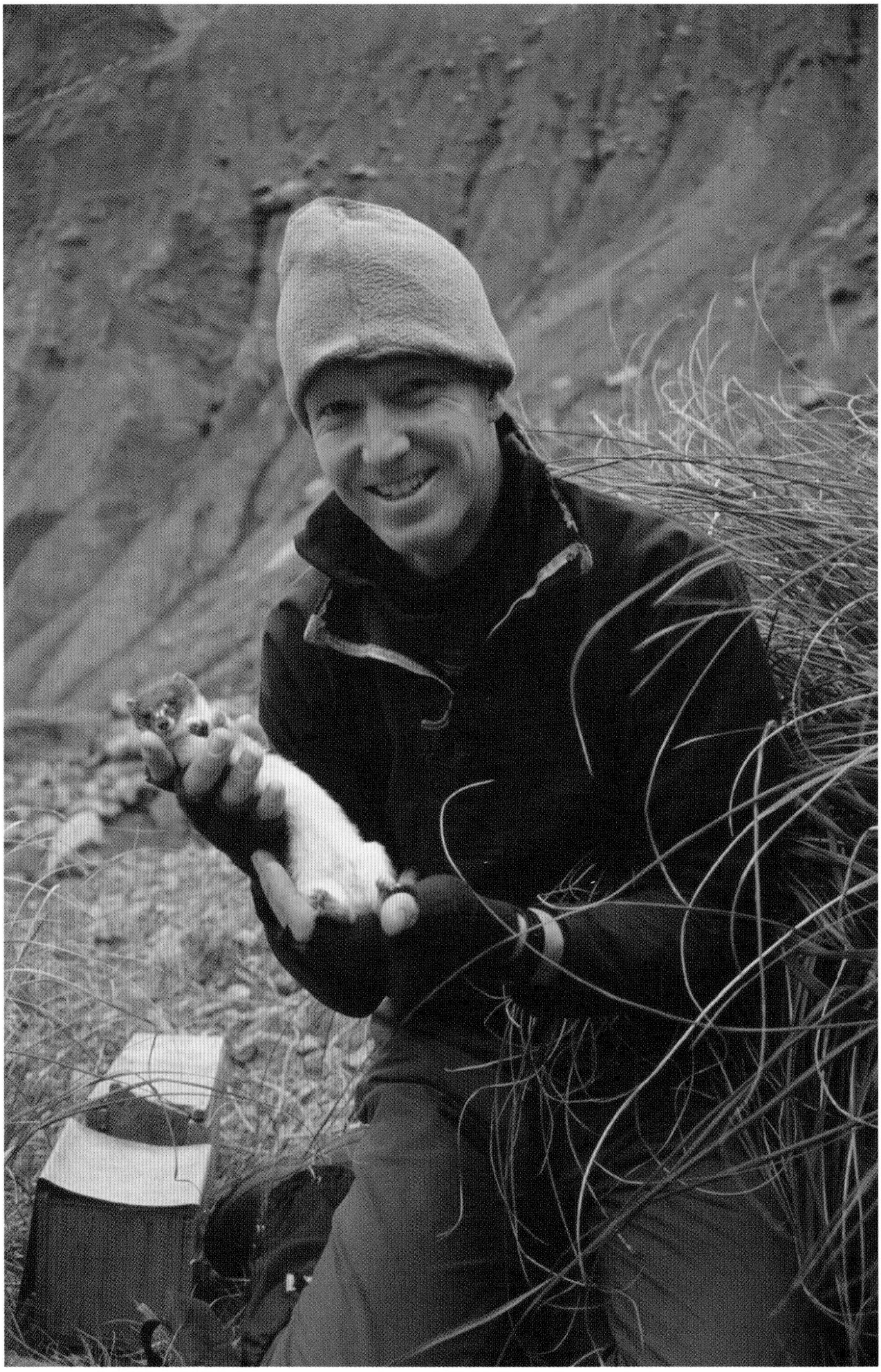

Richard Cuthbert with a trapped (and sedated) stoat. Author photo

21. Ongoing conservation efforts and a new beginning

I no longer live in the Kowhai Valley; a career in conservation has taken me to other species, projects and continents. Yet reminders of the Kaikoura ranges are an almost daily event, my time there having inspired, infused and infected my mind with ceaseless wonder for these mountains. Odd noises, pieces of music, certain foods and the scent of a particular brand of soap can pull me back, until I can smell the powerful musk of a male stoat and taste the sweet juniper-like flavour of a ripe snow tōtara berry; feel the painful nip of a shearwater's bill cutting the edge of a fingernail and the indescribably soft down of a newly hatched chick; hear the continuous rattle of rocks slowly eroding from the valley sides, the clockwork rasp of an angry wētā, and the harsh yet evocative call of a kea.

Random memories of the valley crowd back into my mind: giant wētā slowly crawling over our legs and down the sleeves of our overalls as we measured chicks, their mechanical progress and clawed feet pricking our flesh. A female stoat disturbed from her kill repeatedly darting out of sight and reappearing between the tussocks five metres from where I knelt to examine the dead shearwater, hissing fiercely until I moved off. A party of redpolls feeding on speargrass flower-stems two metres from the hut window, twisting seeds from between the wicked spines. An exhilarating scree-run from high on the valley's west flank, alert to the subtle changes in texture, legs working as fast as possible, ears popping with the rapid descent to the valley floor before a sudden stop among mountain ringlet butterflies looping around in the heat of the sun. Two stoats furiously chasing each other as I stood stock still on the gravel floodplain of the lower Kowhai River, so oblivious to my presence that they cut behind my legs and between my ski poles until, in a sudden moment of realisation, they stopped and stared at me and with one bound were off and hidden in the scrub. The repetitive call of the yellowhammer with its prison-stripe plumage, dandelion-yellow head and chestnut back and rump, long tail extended in bouncing flight, alighting on a boulder-top with a quick flick of the white outer tail feathers. The explosive sprint of a hare flushed from dense tussocks, darting out beneath my feet and running straight, all purpose, bounding forwards on pumping hind legs. Picking a line to a new patch of colony within the valley, glancing downwards as the rubber soles of my boots flexed and gripped the compacted scree, calculating which way I would jump and land if the physics of friction and the solidity of the rock proved different to my experience; or just sitting, watching and enjoying the valley from a new vantage point. And the exultant symphony of thousands of courting shearwaters framed against a backdrop of snow and ice.

For a short while I had the privilege of becoming part of the Kowhai Valley. In turn, the Kowhai Valley became part of me.

The work on Hutton's shearwaters has not ceased, and efforts and interest to secure the continued survival of this species are ongoing and growing. Following the realisation of the threat that pigs posed, the Kaikoura DOC team began hunting around the boundaries of the colonies to ensure that any local animals were rounded up and culled. Because hunting couldn't take place regularly, Mike Morrissey and other DOC staff constructed a walk-in pig trap in 2009 on a flat area of land near the entry point to the Kowhai Valley. The trap remained empty for several years, but in April 2013 it captured 11 pigs.[1] It is vital that numbers are kept low in the vicinity of the colonies to minimise the chances of a pig ever accessing the breeding grounds.

Monitoring work has continued in order to verify that the main conclusion of the research in the shearwater colonies – that stoats, while they are present, are not greatly impacting the shearwater population – remains true. Visits to the Kowhai Valley and Shearwater Stream are ongoing to measure the density of burrows and to establish that the number of burrows (and therefore breeding birds) is not declining. Results of burrow counts from 1987 to 2007 confirmed that burrow numbers had not decreased; if anything, the data suggests that numbers of breeding birds have actually increased in both colonies over this period.[2] Visits during 2007 also found that the number of dead adults and chicks on transect lines and down burrows were similar to the previous study, suggesting no major change in stoat predation rates.

Annual monitoring of breeding success in both the Kowhai Valley and Shearwater Stream colonies is undertaken at the start and end of each season, led by DOC and the Hutton's Shearwater Charitable Trust. A sample of burrows is examined with the burrowscope to record whether they contain a near-fledging chick. After three nerve-wracking early seasons from 2006 to 2008, when breeding success was low in both colonies, raising the spectre that stoats were having an increased impact, the levels returned to normal. Breeding success in both colonies from the 2006–15 seasons averaged 60%,[3] higher than the average value of 47% that was recorded in the Kowhai Valley from 1989–98, and as good as, if not better than, the levels of success recorded for other shearwater species breeding in areas without introduced predators.[4]

Stoat-trapping was initiated in the smaller Shearwater Stream colony in 2008 following two poor years at this site: in 2006 and 2007 just 4% and 6% of eggs produced fledged chicks. The absence of trapping in the Kowhai Valley in the same seasons offered the best possible test of the impact of stoat predation on Hutton's shearwaters; if stoats were having a major detrimental effect then breeding success at the Kowhai colony should be markedly lower in comparison. Over the recent years of trapping at Shearwater Stream, breeding success in the two colonies has been almost exactly the same, with a colony average of 58% in the Kowhai Valley and 62% at Shearwater Stream.[5] These results confirm once more that stoats are having a limited impact.

The ongoing monitoring also shows that breeding success in each year is strongly correlated between the two sites, with good and bad years in the Kowhai Valley corresponding with the same level of success at Shearwater Stream.[6] This suggests that the breeding success of Hutton's shearwater is most strongly influenced today by factors outside of the colonies. The high variability is likely to be a consequence of at-sea feeding conditions, which can vary greatly from year to year. A similar result is found for the red-billed gull, whose large population on the Kaikoura Peninsula has been studied for more than 40 years. This species forages closer to shore than Hutton's shearwater and its diet throughout the breeding season mainly consists of shrimp-like euphausiids. Over a 21-year period the variation in abundance of euphausiids had major effects on the breeding performance of the gulls, with years of high prey availability being positively related to the timing of breeding, the number of pairs, clutch size, egg size and breeding success.[7] Numbers of euphausiids themselves were correlated with the Southern Oscillation Index (an indicator of the El Niño/La Niña conditions), as well as the frequency of northeasterly winds associated with upwelling nutrient-rich waters off the Kaikoura coast. Because Hutton's shearwaters are likely to forage over a far greater distance and consume a broader range of prey than the red-billed gull, their situation is less clear cut. However, it is likely that similar at-sea processes are affecting the numbers of birds attempting to breed and the breeding success of Hutton's shearwater.

While the two colonies remain healthy, Hutton's shearwaters will always be threatened if they are restricted to just two breeding sites. Other species have become similarly vulnerable, such as the kākāpō and takahē, both of which became restricted to remote and small areas within Fiordland. Conservationists translocated birds to multiple offshore and onshore 'islands' in order to safeguard them against ongoing threats and to minimise the impact of any major environmental event, such as a fire or earthquake, which could otherwise have wiped out the species if they had remained at just a single site.

Following this approach, a community initiative was born in Kaikoura in 2005 to establish a third breeding ground for Hutton's shearwater on the Kaikoura Peninsula. Collaborators in the project are the Hutton's Shearwater Charitable Trust, DOC, the Tukete Charitable Trust, Te Rūnanga o Kaikōura, Whale Watch Kaikoura, Forest & Bird and the Kaikoura District Council.

Starting a new colony is far from simple. You have to find the right area of land and protect it, and then the birds have to be taken there and encouraged to breed. Simply transferring some adult birds to the site will not work; they will head out to sea the next night and return to their burrows in the Kowhai Valley or Shearwater Stream. For shearwaters and other burrowing petrels there is one window when translocation is possible: when near-fledging-age chicks are beginning to emerge from their burrows and fix their location against the stars, sounds, scents and night-time noises.[8]

In March 2005 a helicopter lifted off from the Kowhai Valley colony with five cardboard boxes on board, each containing two large, healthy Hutton's shearwater chicks judged to be around two to three weeks from fledging. These 10 chicks were transported to a small number of burrows dug on the Kaikoura Peninsula, for a trial translocation. Following this attempt more than 100 burrows were dug on the peninsula site, and in 2006, 2007, 2008, 2012 and 2013 around 100 chicks were transported each year from the mountain colonies to the new site. For two to three weeks the chicks received a daily sardine smoothie, carefully syringed via a gastric tube straight into their crop, and at night they would come out of their burrow entrances to absorb and learn the location of their new colony. The task required a large and well-organised team, and DOC and the Hutton's Shearwater Charitable Trust arranged and coordinated a pool of volunteers from the Kaikoura community.

The survival of these fledglings was far from assured, for each chick faces three to four hazardous years of life at sea with the immediate requirement of learning how to dive and forage. During this period young Hutton's shearwaters may well follow the adult birds and migrate to Australia or to waters all around New Zealand. Small parties of birds have occasionally been seen as far south as the Snares Islands,[9] in the same vicinity as the first bird shot by Henry Travers in January 1890.

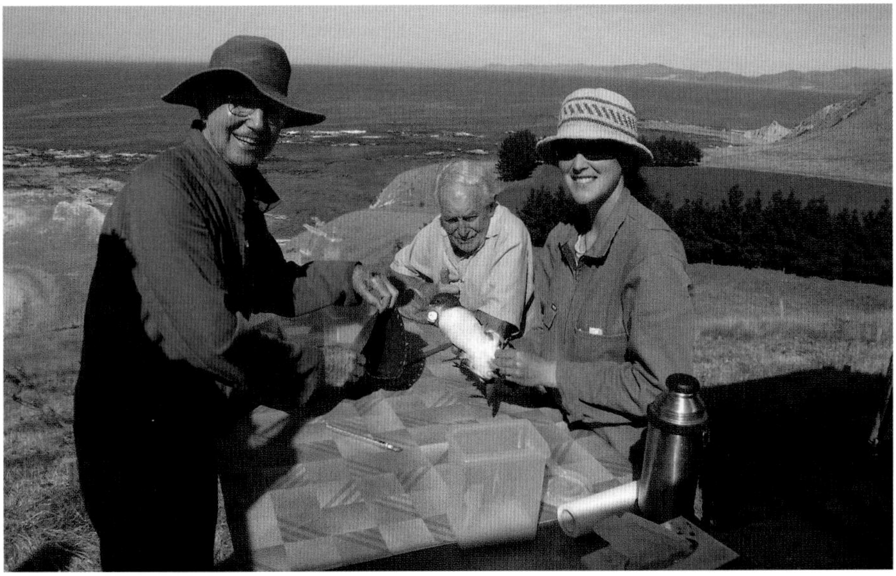

Geoff Harrow, Sam Pilbrow (the former landowner of Shearwater Stream who assisted Geoff in the 1960s) and Erica Sommer feeding shearwater chicks during the 2007 translocation on the Kaikoura Peninsula. Photo courtesy of Erica Sommer

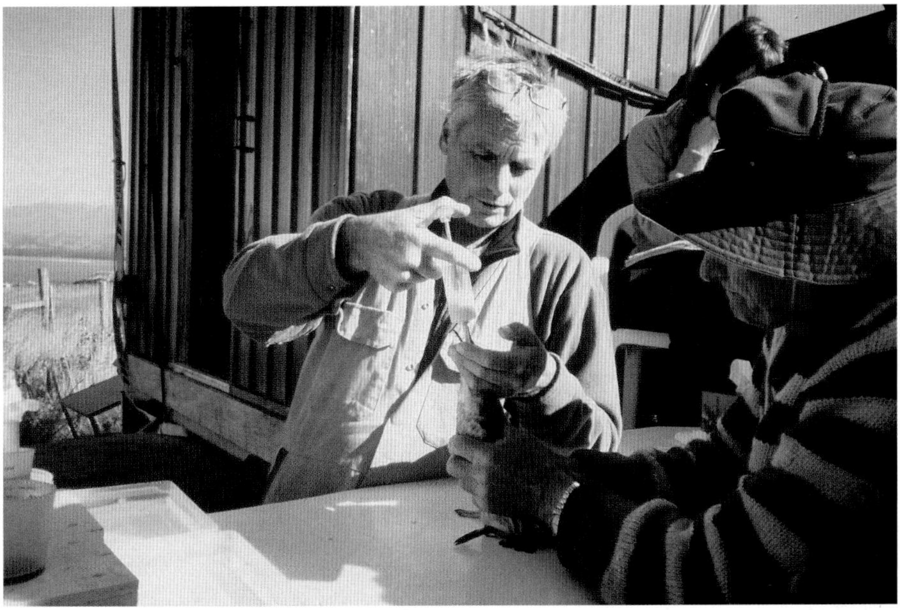

Paul McGahan from the Hutton's Shearwater Charitable Trust feeding a shearwater chick during the 2008 translocation. Photo courtesy of Geoff Harrow

In December 2008, three years after the first pilot translocation, a long-lost sound was heard on the Kaikoura Peninsula: the hooting, braying call of an adult Hutton's shearwater returning to land at the new breeding site – the first in at least 100 years. Over subsequent years more and more translocated birds have returned to the peninsula, in some cases bringing other non-banded birds with them. Burrows have been occupied, each member of the pair flying in each night to secure it from other prospecting birds, and on or around Christmas Day in 2011 the first chick hatched at the peninsula colony.

Numbers of pairs and eggs have increased slowly: between 2013 and 2015 there were 14–16 pairs incubating eggs at the peninsula and fledging six to eight chicks each season, and 2015 saw the first return to the peninsula of two chicks that had fledged from this site.[10] The increase in numbers is slow, but as the years progress this colony will increase in size and become a viable self-sustaining breeding site.

The Hutton's shearwater project has become a source of pride for the town of Kaikoura, with a huge amount of community involvement. The new peninsula colony (named Te Rae o Atiu, after the headland on which it is located) is surrounded by a predator-proof fence and provides opportunities for visitors to view and learn about this mountain seabird in a more accessible and less fragile setting than the two alpine colonies. The birds and their unique status now feature in lessons taught at the local schools, and 'welcome home' and 'farewell' events, attracting hundreds of people, are held each September and March to celebrate the arrival and departure of the shearwaters from Kaikoura.

The recently created Ka Whata Tu o Rakihouia Conservation Park encompasses the Seaward Kaikoura Range and includes both the Kowhai Valley and Shearwater Stream colonies. The name means 'the uplifted food stores of Rakihouia' and celebrates the collection of seabird eggs from the mountains during Rakihouia's twelfth-century voyage down the east coast of the South Island. The gazetting of this conservation land in 2008 provides further recognition of the significance of the Kaikoura mountains and the rare and unique species that occur there.

The conservation of Hutton's shearwaters matters in these mountains, not just for the survival of this species but also because they offer a view of New Zealand's past and, with the right conservation efforts, a glimpse of the future. To sit in the Hutton's colonies at night, surrounded by the screams and whoops of thousands of shearwaters, is to take a journey back in time to a land untouched by humanity; to a time before the first Māori, before the arrival of Tasman and Cook and the settlers and ecological changes that followed. Only a thousand years ago – a flash in evolutionary time – New Zealand supported populations of giant moa, Haast's eagle, flightless ducks and kiwi, swirling flocks of kākāriki and booming kākāpō, and was home to vast numbers of shearwaters and petrels. These seabirds would not only have dominated the night-time sounds, they would also have overwhelmed the others in terms of biomass and numbers. Prior to humankind's footfall, New Zealand was not the land of the moa, but the land of the seabird.

Epilogue

Nightfall came as usual in the shearwater colony on 13 November 2016, with the Kowhai River providing a constant roar in the otherwise silent valley. Within their burrows the incubating shearwaters waited patiently for their partners to return from sea. Apart from brief movements to preen an errant feather into place or to shuffle and turn the egg to ensure its constant warmth, the birds were still. Outside the burrows the tussocks stirred in the breeze and a solitary chamois sat alert, looking out over a valley bathed in the light of an almost full moon. The bright night stayed the departure of shearwaters from the coast off Kaikoura that night, but shortly before midnight the birds began a fast-legged skitter across the water's surface to lift off and begin their steady climb into the hills. They flew in a direct line, following an aerial highway that had been used for tens of thousands of years by birds returning to their mountain burrows.

This was no ordinary night, however, and as the first birds reached the valley a deafening roar filled the air. The earth shook violently, sending scree and boulders tumbling down the valley and ploughing through the soft ground of the colony. High on the flanks of Mt Saunders a vast rock buttress collapsed and swept down the mountainside, spreading the cordite smell of fresh rockfall across the valley. As the dust cleared and the reverberating echoes faded, the moonlight revealed the damage: three sub-colonies and the shearwaters within them had been buried under thousands of tonnes of rock. The Kowhai River was dammed and silent.

The magnitude 7.8 earthquake that struck at two minutes after midnight on 14 November 2016 was the second largest recorded since European settlement in New Zealand and, tragically, resulted in two human deaths. The quake's epicentre was 60 kilometres to the south of Kaikoura at a depth of 15 kilometres, and the main force of the impact was felt in the Kaikoura and North Canterbury regions. It was followed by thousands of aftershocks. On the coast, the land and seabed moved up to 11 metres horizontally and five metres vertically, and many areas were greatly altered.

In early 2017 the situation within the shearwater colonies is unclear, as the risk of venturing upon the unstable slopes at these sites remains too high. However, aerial photographs taken in the days immediately after the quake show that Impossible, 15 and Hoheria sub-colonies have been fully or partially destroyed. Together these areas made up around 20% of the shearwaters' breeding grounds within the Kowhai Valley, and up to 18,000 birds are likely to have been killed. The extent of damage beyond the destruction of these sub-colonies is unknown, but it is probable that further losses have occurred in other areas of the two colonies. A full assessment will require time on the ground to map out the sub-colony areas and to compare the density of burrows and abundance of birds with previous estimates.

While this event has once more raised urgent concerns for the future of Hutton's shearwater, crucially, one of the major recommendations from earlier studies had been acted upon and a third breeding site had been created on the Kaikoura Peninsula to act as a small but vital insurance population for the more vulnerable mountain colonies. DOC, the Hutton's Shearwater Charitable Trust and the Kaikoura community will continue to move forward with their excellent conservation work. The peninsula sub-colony is unlikely to be able to support more than a few hundred pairs, however, and it may be time to consider establishing a larger colony elsewhere in the Kaikoura ranges.

No doubt events of this magnitude – as a consequence of earthquakes or major avalanches – have occurred in the past, forcing Hutton's shearwaters to find new breeding sites in other alpine tussock areas in the region. Today, however, the scope for birds to establish new colonies by their own means is limited due to the presence of pigs throughout the ranges, and because stoats would rapidly extinguish any small colony of birds. But with advances in predator-proof fencing and predator control, and the knowledge gained from the translocation of the species at the peninsula, the methods and practice already exist for establishing a major new colony.

A new site along the flight path to the existing mountain colonies, such as on the flanks of Mt Fyffe, may attract some of the thousands of birds that have been displaced by the loss of the sub-colonies in the Kowhai Valley or those nesting in areas where population growth is limited by the availability of suitable habitat. A protected fourth colony of several thousand pairs would help secure the conservation of this species and protect the unique breeding habits of this mountain muttonbird. As always, however, such actions require funding and support from a large number of people and organisations, and – crucially – it will need the inspiration and drive of a few key individuals to make it happen – people like Geoff Harrow.

More than a thousand years after Rakihouia's arrival, a ceremony took place on the Kaikoura Peninsula to honour a kaumātua, the Māori name for a tribal elder and keeper of knowledge and traditions. On 20 February 2015, 50 years to the day since Geoff Harrow had set off alone up the Kowhai River and rediscovered Hutton's shearwaters in the Kaikoura mountains, representatives from Ngāti Kuri, Ngāi Tahu, the Hutton's Shearwater Trust, the landowners at Shearwater Stream and DOC, along with naturalists, mountaineers and members of the Kaikoura community, gathered to celebrate this man's long involvement with the species. Geoff was presented with a korowai or feather cloak for his role in inspiring the protection of this unique species, and was recognised as a kaumātua for Hutton's shearwaters. Geoff would be the first to highlight and praise the many people involved in the ongoing conservation of Hutton's shearwaters and the last to mention his own role, but without his involvement in the 1960s and his continued commitment, the species could well have become but a memory in the mountains of Te Whatakai-o-Rakihouia.

The 2016 earthquake was certainly a setback, but I am confident Hutton's shearwaters will survive and provide a living monument to New Zealand's avian past – and future.

Postscript

Conservation efforts to secure the future of Hutton's shearwaters and the unique ecology of their mountain breeding sites continue to be led by the Department of Conservation Te Papa Atawhai and the Hutton's Shearwater Charitable Trust. Ongoing work and other information on the species can be found on the two organisations' websites:

www.huttonsshearwater.org.nz
www.doc.govt.nz/nature/native-animals/birds/birds-a-z/huttons-shearwater-kaikoura-titi

Please consider becoming a member, donor, sponsor or volunteer with the trust and become involved in the conservation of this species.

Notes

1. Arrival in the Kowhai Valley

1 Rattenbury, M.S., Townsend, D.B. & Johnston, M.R. (compilers) (2006), 'Geology of the Kaikoura area', Institute of Geological & Nuclear Sciences 1:250 000 geological map 13. Lower Hutt, New Zealand: GNS Science.

2 Anon (2016), 'The geological history of New Zealand', University of Waikato: http://sci.waikato.ac.nz/evolution/geologicalHistory.shtml

3 Van Dissen, R. & Yeats, R.S. (1991), 'Hope fault, Jordan thrust, and uplift of the Seaward Kaikoura Range, New Zealand', *Geology* 19: 393–96.

2. A gunshot off the Snares Islands

1 Mitchell, H. & Mitchell, M.J. (2004), *History of Māori of Nelson and Marlborough*, Wellington: Huia Publishers; Rāwiri Taonui (2012), 'Canoe traditions: Canoes of the South Island', Te Ara – the Encyclopedia of New Zealand www.TeAra.govt.nz/en/canoe-traditions/page-8

2 *Auckland Star*, 29 March 1920, vol. LI, Issue 76: https://paperspast.natlib.govt.nz/newspapers/AS19200329.2.17; *Poverty Bay Herald* (1920) Death Notice Sigvard Jacob Dannefaerd, 1 April 1920: www.myheritage.com/photo-4000293_10782281_10782281/sigvard-jacob-dannefaerd-death-notice-poverty-bay-herald-apr-1

3 Winsome Shepherd, R., 'Travers, William Thomas Locke', from the Dictionary of New Zealand Biography: www.TeAra.govt.nz/en/biographies/1t105/travers-william-thomas-locke

4 Alan J.D., Tennyson, A.J.D. & Bartle, J.A. (2008), 'Catalogue of type specimens of birds in the Museum of New Zealand Te Papa Tongarewa', *Tuhinga* 19: 185–207.

5 Anon (2014), 'Henry Hammersley Travers', Museum of New Zealand Te Papa Tongarewa: http://collections.tepapa.govt.nz/Topic/2683

6 Miskelly, C. (2011), 'Who wrote that? Forensic analysis of museum specimen labels': http://blog.tepapa.govt.nz/2011/11/01/who-wrote-that-forensic-analysis-of-museum-specimen-labels/; Miskelly, C.M. (2012), 'Discovery and extinction of the South Island snipe (*Coenocorypha iredalei*) on islands around Stewart Island', *Notornis* 59: 15–31.

7 Miskelly, 'Who wrote that?'

8 Miskelly, C.M., Sagar, P.M., Tennyson, A.J.D. & Scofield, R.P. (2001), 'Birds of the Snares Islands, New Zealand', *Notornis* 48: 1–40.

9 Boessenkool, S., Star, B., Scofield, P.R., Seddon, P.J. & Waters, J.M. (2009), 'Lost in translation or deliberate falsification? Genetic analyses reveal erroneous museum data for historic penguin specimens', Proceedings of the Royal Society, B. Biological Sciences, 277: 1057–64.

10 Godman, F.C. (1907–08), 'A monograph of the petrels (Order Tubinares)': https://archive.org/details/monographofp119071910godm
11 Clarke, V.I. & Fleming, C.A. (1948), 'Hutton's shearwater (*Puffinus gavial huttoni* Math.) in New Zealand', *New Zealand Bird Notes* 2(8): 187–88.
12 Tennyson, A.J.D., Miskelly, C.M. & LeCroy, M. (2014), 'Clarification of collection data for the type specimens of Hutton's shearwater *Puffinus huttoni* Mathews, 1912, and implications for the accuracy of historic subantarctic specimen data', *Bulletin of the British Ornithological Club* 134: 242–46.
13 *Otago Daily Times*, 21 January 1890.
14 Rothschild, M. (2008), *Walter Rothschild: The man, the museum and the menagerie*, London: Natural History Museum.
15 The Rothschild Archive (2016), 'Lionel Walter (Walter) Rothschild (1868–1937)': https://family.rothschildarchive.org/people/102-lionel-walter-walter-rothschild-1868-1937
16 Rothschild, *Walter Rothschild.*
17 Ibid.
18 Ibid.
19 Barrow, M.H. (1998), *A Passion for Birds: American ornithology after Audubon*, New Jersey: Princeton University Press.
20 Kloot, T. (1986), 'Mathews, Gregory Macalister (1876–1949)', Australian Dictionary of Biography: http://adb.anu.edu.au/biography/mathews-gregory-macalister-7517/text13111
21 Parton, H.N. (2013), 'Hutton, Frederick Wollaston', from the Dictionary of New Zealand Biography: www.TeAra.govt.nz/en/biographies/2h59/hutton-frederick-wollaston
22 BirdLife International (2016), 'Country profile: Australia': www.birdlife.org/datazone/country/australia
23 Serventy, D.L. (1939), 'The white-breasted petrel of South Australia', *Emu* 39: 95–107.
24 Smithsonian National Museum of Natural History, 'Historical Expeditions: Whitney South Sea Expedition': http://botany.si.edu/colls/expeditions/expedition_page.cfm?ExpedName=31
25 Murphy, M.C. (1952), 'The Manx shearwater, *Puffinus puffinus*, as a species of world-wide distribution', *American Museum Novitates*, 1586: 1–21.
26 Serventy, 'The white-breasted petrel of South Australia'.
27 Whitlock, L.F. (1937), 'A new petrel of the genus Puffinus', *Emu* 37: 116–17.
28 Mathews, G.M. (1937a), 'Description of *Puffinus leptorhynchus*', *Bulletin of the British Ornithological Club* 57: 143; Mathews, G.M. (1937b), 'A new shearwater for Western Australia', *Emu* 37: 114–16.
29 Whitlock, 'A new petrel of the genus Puffinus'.
30 Rasmussen, P.C. & Prŷs-Jones, R.P. (2003), 'History vs mystery: The reliability of museum specimen data', *Bulletin of the British Ornithological Club* 123: 66–94.
31 Serventy, 'The white-breasted petrel of South Australia'.

3. Explorations amidst shearwaters

1 Patrick, B.H. & Cuthbert, R. (1999), 'Lepidoptera and other insects of the Seaward Kaikoura Range', *Records of the Canterbury Museum* 13: 123–27.

4. An ornithological mystery

1 Hillary, E. & Lowe, G. (1956), *East of Everest*, London: Hodder and Stroughton.
2 Ibid.
3 Ibid.
4 Hillary, E. (1999), *View from the Summit*, London: Transworld Publishers.
5 von Tunzelmann, N. (1969), 'Recent New Zealand developments', *Alpine Journal* 74: 70–81.
6 Dell, R.K. (1998), 'Falla, Robert Alexander', from the Dictionary of New Zealand Biography: www.TeAra.govt.nz/en/biographies/4f4/falla-robert-alexander
7 Harrow, G. (1965), 'Preliminary report on discovery of nesting site of Hutton's shearwater', *Notornis* 12: 59–65.
8 Murphy, M.C. (1952), 'The Manx shearwater, *Puffinus puffinus*, as a species of world-wide distribution', *American Museum Novitates* 1586: 1–21.
9 Ibid.
10 Clark, V.I. & Fleming, C.A. (1948), 'Hutton's shearwater (*Puffinus gavia huttoni* Math.) in New Zealand', *Notornis* 2: 187–88.
11 Falla, R.A. (1965), 'Distribution of Hutton's shearwater in New Zealand', *Notornis* 12: 66–70.
12 Ibid.

6. Discovering the nesting grounds

1 G. Harrow, personal communication, 2011.
2 Harrow, G. (1965), 'Preliminary report on discovery of nesting site of Hutton's shearwater', *Notornis* 12: 59–65.
3 G. Harrow, personal communication, 2011.
4 Ibid; Harrow, G. (1976), 'Some observations of Hutton's shearwater', *Notornis* 23: 269–88.
5 McLintock, A.H. (1966), 'Kaikoura Ranges', Te Ara – the Encyclopedia of New Zealand: www.TeAra.govt.nz/en/1966/kaikoura-ranges
6 Tau, T.M. & Anderson, A. (eds) (2008), *Ngāi Tahu: A migration history: The Carrington text*, Wellington: Bridget Williams Books, 146–51.
7 Ibid.
8 Ibid.
9 G. Harrow, personal communication, 2011.
10 Whitaker, A. (1984), '*Hoplodactylus kahutarae* n.sp. (Reptilia: Gekkonidae) from the Seaward Kaikoura Range, Marlborough, New Zealand', *New Zealand Journal of Zoology* 11: 259–70.

11 Harrow, 'Some observations of Hutton's shearwater'.
12 Ibid.
13 Evans, G.R. (1973), 'Hutton's shearwaters initiating local soil erosion in the Seaward Kaikoura Range', *New Zealand Journal of Science* 16: 637–42.
14 'Rotary Club told of mysterious seabird', *Nelson Evening Mail*, 14 April 1967.
15 Wragg, G. (1985), 'The comparative biology of fluttering shearwater and Hutton's shearwater and their relationship to other shearwater species', Master's thesis, University of Canterbury, New Zealand.
16 Sherley, G. (1992), 'Monitoring Hutton's shearwater 1986–1989', *Notornis* 39: 249–61.
17 Paton, B. & Davis, A. (1997), 'Hutton's shearwater recovery plan (*Puffinus huttoni*). Threatened species recovery plan series', Department of Conservation: Wellington.
18 Evans, 'Hutton's shearwaters initiating local soil erosion'; Sherley, 'Monitoring Hutton's shearwater 1986–1989'; Paton & Davis, 'Hutton's shearwater recovery plan'.

7. Alone in the valley

1 Maxwell, G. (1960), *Ring of Bright Water*, London: Longmans.
2 Evans, C.R., 'Sherpa Norbu has close call high in the Himalayas', *Daily Telegraph*, Sydney, 17 June 1954.

8. Searching the transect lines

1 Lyver, P.O. (2000), 'Identifying mammalian predators of sooty shearwaters from bite marks: A tool for focusing wildlife protection', *Mammal Review* 30: 31–44.
2 Cuthbert, R.J. (2003), 'Sign left by introduced and native predators feeding on Hutton's shearwaters (*Puffinus huttoni*)', *New Zealand Journal of Zoology* 30: 163–70.
3 Ibid.
4 Diamond, J. & Bond. A.B. (1999), *Kea, Bird of Paradox: The evolution and behaviour of a New Zealand parrot*, Berkeley and Los Angeles: University of California Press.

9. A famous visitor

1 Warham, J. (1990), *The Petrels: Their ecology and breeding systems*, London: Academic Press.
2 Brooke, M. (1990), *The Manx Shearwater*, London: Poyser.

10. A new season and new questions

1 Cuthbert, R.J. (2003), 'Sign left by introduced and native predators feeding on Hutton's shearwaters (*Puffinus huttoni*)', *New Zealand Journal of Zoology* 30: 163–70.
2 Cuthbert, R.J., Sommer, E.S. & Davis, L.S. (2000), 'Seasonal variation in the diet of stoats (*Mustela erminea*) in a breeding colony of Hutton's shearwaters (*Puffinus huttoni*)', *New Zealand Journal of Zoology* 27: 367–73.

11. The breeding season begins

1 Halse, S.A. (1981), 'Migration by Hutton's shearwater', *Emu* 81: 42–44.
2 Matthiessen, P. (1978), *The Snow Leopard*, New York: Viking Press.
3 Pennycuick, C.J. (1989), *Bird Flight Performance*, Oxford: Oxford Science Publications.
4 Cuthbert, R.J. (1999), 'The breeding ecology and conservation of Hutton's shearwaters (*Puffinus huttoni*)', PhD thesis, University of Otago, New Zealand.
5 Ibid.; Chastel, O., Weimerskirch, H. & Jouventin, P. (1995), 'Influence of body condition on reproductive decision and reproductive success in the Blue Petrel', *Auk* 112: 964–72.
6 Michel, P., Ollason, J.C., Grosbois, V. & Thompson, P.M. (2003), 'The influence of body size, breeding experience and environmental variability on egg size in the northern fulmar (*Fulmarus glacialis*)', *Journal of Zoology London* 261: 427–32.
7 Cuthbert, 'The breeding ecology and conservation of Hutton's shearwaters (*Puffinus huttoni*)'.

12. Living with kea

1 Diamond, J. & Bond. A.B. (1991), 'Social behaviour and the ontogeny of foraging in the kea (*Nestor notabilis*)', *Ecology* 88: 128–44.
2 Diamond, J. & Bond, A.B. (1999), *Kea, Bird of Paradox: The evolution and behaviour of a New Zealand parrot*, Berkeley and Los Angeles: University of California Press.
3 G. Harrow, personal communication, 2011.
4 Ibid.
5 Ibid.
6 Temple, P. (1996), *The Book of the Kea*, Auckland: Hodder Moa Beckett.
7 Worthy, T.H. & Holdaway, R.N. (1996), 'Quaternary fossil faunas, overlapping taphonomies, and palaeofaunal reconstruction in North Canterbury, South Island, New Zealand', *Journal of the Royal Society of New Zealand* 26: 275–361.
8 Diamond & Bond, *Kea, Bird of Paradox*.
9 Ibid.
10 Ibid.

13. Egg-laying and incubation

1 Cuthbert, R.J. & Davis, L.S. (2002), 'Adult survival and productivity of Hutton's shearwaters', *Ibis* 144: 423–32.
2 Cuthbert, R.J. & Davis, L.S. (2002b), 'The breeding biology of Hutton's shearwater', *Emu* 102: 323–29.
3 Cuthbert, R.J., unpublished information.
4 Brooke, M. (1990), *The Manx Shearwater*, London: Poyser.
5 Cuthbert, R.J., unpublished information.
6 Boersma, D.P. (1982), 'Why some birds take so long to hatch', *The American Naturalist* 120: 733–50.
7 Brooke, *The Manx Shearwater*.

14. A perfectly designed killing machine

1 King, C.M & Powell, R.A. (2007), *The Natural History of Weasels and Stoats: Ecology, behavior and management*, Oxford: Oxford University Press.
2 Ibid.
3 Ibid.
4 G. Harrow, personal communication, 2011.

15. Encounters with chamois, falcons and harriers

1 Wodzicki, K. & Wright, S. (1984), 'Introduced birds and mammals in New Zealand and their effect on the environment', *Tuatara* 27: 77–104.
2 Harrow, G. (1976), 'Some observations of Hutton's shearwater', *Notornis* 23: 269–88.
3 Thomson, G.M. (1922), *The Naturalisation of Animals & Plants in New Zealand*, Cambridge: Cambridge University Press.
4 Wodzicki & Wright, 'Introduced birds and mammals in New Zealand'.
5 Nesti, I., Poscillico, M. & Lovari, S. (2010), 'Ranging behaviour and habitat selection of alpine chamois', *Ethology Ecology & Evolution* 22: 215–31; Dalmau, A., Ferret, A., Ruis de la Torre, J.L. & Manteca, X. (2013), 'Habitat selection and social behaviour in a Pyrenean chamois population (*Rupicapra pyrenaica pyrenaica*)', *Journal of Mountain Ecology* 9: 83–102.
6 Hyde, N.H.S. & Worthy, T.H. (2010), 'The diet of New Zealand falcons (*Falco novaeseelandiae*) on the Auckland Islands, New Zealand', *Notornis*, 57: 19–26.
7 Baker-Gabb, D.J. (1986), 'Ecological release and behavioural flexibility in marsh harriers on islands', *Emu* 86: 71–81.
8 Cuthbert, R.J. (2003), 'Sign left by introduced and native predators feeding on Hutton's shearwaters (*Puffinus huttoni*)', *New Zealand Journal of Zoology* 30: 163–70.

16. Hatching and growth of the shearwater chicks

1 Cuthbert, R.J. & Davis, L.S. (2002b), 'The breeding biology of Hutton's shearwater', *Emu* 102: 323–29.
2 Boersma, D.P. (1982), 'Why some birds take so long to hatch', *The American Naturalist* 120: 733–50.
3 Cuthbert, R.J., unpublished information.
4 Ibid.
5 Tickell, W.L.N. (2000), *Albatrosses*, Mountfield: Pica Press.
6 Powlesland, R.G. (2013), 'New Zealand pigeon', in C.M. Miskelly (ed.), *New Zealand Birds Online*: www.nzbirdsonline.org.nz
7 Brooke, M. (1990), *The Manx Shearwater*, London: Poyser; Booth, A.M., Minot, E.O., Imber, M.J. & Fordham, R.A. (2000), 'Aspects of the breeding ecology of the North Island little shearwater *Puffinus assimilis haurakiensis*', *New Zealand Journal of Ecology* 27: 335–45.
8 Cuthbert, R.J. (1999), 'The breeding ecology and conservation of Hutton's shearwaters (*Puffinus huttoni*)', PhD thesis, University of Otago, New Zealand.

9 Ricklefs, R.E., Day, C.H., Huntington, C.E. & Williams, J.B. (1985), 'Variability in feeding rate and meal size of Leach's storm-petrel at Kent Island, New Brunswick', *Journal of Animal Ecology* 54: 883–98.
10 Lack, D. (1968), *Ecological Adaptations for Breeding in Birds*, London: Methuen.
11 Ricklefs, R.E. & Schew, W.A. (1994), 'Foraging stochasticity and lipid accumulation by nestling petrels', *Functional Ecology* 8, 159–70.
12 Cuthbert, 'The ecology of Hutton's shearwaters'.
13 Ibid.
14 Cuthbert, R.J. & Davis, L.S. (2002), 'Adult survival and productivity of Hutton's shearwaters', *Ibis* 144: 423–32.

17. Tracking the valley's stoats – and an unusual grass

1 Cuthbert, R.J. & Sommer, E.S. (2002), 'Home-range and territorial behaviour of stoats (*Mustela erminea*) in a breeding colony of Hutton's shearwaters (*Puffinus huttoni*)', *New Zealand Journal of Zoology* 29: 149–60.
2 Museum of New Zealand Te Papa Tongarewa (2014), 'The mountain ringlet butterfly (*Percnodaimon pluto*)': http://collections.tepapa.govt.nz/topic/983
3 Patrick, B.H. & Cuthbert, R.J. (1999), 'Lepidoptera and other insects of the Seaward Kaikoura Range', *Records of the Canterbury Museum* 13: 123–27.
4 Ibid.
5 H. Spencer, personal communication, 1998.
6 Whitaker, A. (1984), '*Hoplodactylus kahutarae* n.sp. (Reptilia: Gekkonidae) from the Seaward Kaikoura Range, Marlborough, New Zealand', *New Zealand Journal of Zoology* 11: 259–70.
7 Whitaker, T., Shaw, T. & Hitchmough, R. (1999), 'Black-eyed geckos (*Hoplodactylus kahutarae*) on Mt Arthur, Kahurangi National Park', Conservation Advisory Science Notes No. 230, Department of Conservation, Wellington.

18. Piecing together the data

1 Cuthbert, R.J. & Davis, L.S. (2002), 'Adult survival and productivity of Hutton's shearwaters', *Ibis* 144: 423–32.
2 Wooler, R.D., Bradley, J.S., Skira, I.J. & Serventy, D.L. (1989), in I.A. Newton (ed.) *Lifetime Reproduction in Birds*, London: Academic Press, 405–11.
3 Cuthbert & Davis, 'Adult survival and productivity of Hutton's shearwaters'.
4 Brooke, M. (1990), *The Manx Shearwater*, London: Poyser; Warham, J. (1996), *The Behaviour, Population Biology and Physiology of the Petrels*, London: Academic Press.
5 Cuthbert & Davis, 'Adult survival and productivity of Hutton's shearwaters'.
6 Cuthbert, R.J., Fletcher, D. & Davis, L.S. (2001), 'A sensitivity analysis of Hutton's shearwater: Prioritizing conservation research and management', *Biological Conservation* 100: 163–72.
7 Cuthbert & Davis, 'Adult survival and productivity of Hutton's shearwaters'.

8 Brooke, *The Manx Shearwater*; Wooler, R.D., Bradley, J.S. & Croxall, J.P. (1992), 'Long-term population studies of seabirds', *Trends in Ecology and Evolution* 7: 111–14.
9 Cuthbert, R.J. & Davis, L.S. (2002c), 'The impact of predation by introduced stoats on Hutton's shearwaters', *Biological Conservation* 108: 79–92.

19. The true impact of stoats

1 Cuthbert, R.J., Sommer, E.S. & Davis, L.S. (2000), 'Seasonal variation in the diet of stoats (*Mustela erminea*) in a breeding colony of Hutton's shearwaters (*Puffinus huttoni*)', *New Zealand Journal of Zoology* 27: 367–73.
2 Erlinge, S. (1983), 'Demography and dynamics of a stoat *Mustela erminea* population in a diverse community of vertebrates', *Journal of Animal Ecology* 52: 705–26; King, C.M. & Powell, R.A. (2007), *The Natural History of Weasels and Stoats: Ecology, behavior and management*, Oxford: Oxford University Press.
3 Cuthbert, R.J. & Sommer, E.S. (2002), 'Home-range and territorial behaviour of stoats (*Mustela erminea*) in a breeding colony of Hutton's shearwaters (*Puffinus huttoni*)', *New Zealand Journal of Zoology* 29: 149–60.
4 King & Powell, *The Natural History of Weasels and Stoats.*
5 Erlinge, S. (1977), 'Spacing strategy in stoat *Mustela erminea*', *Oikos* 28: 32–42; Sandall, M. (1986), 'Movement patterns of male stoats *Mustela erminea* during the mating season: Differences in relation to social status', *Oikos* 47: 63–70.
6 Cuthbert & Sommer, 'Home-range and territorial behaviour of stoats (*Mustela erminea*)'.
7 Cuthbert, R.J. (2002), 'The role of introduced mammals and inverse density dependent predation in the conservation of Hutton's shearwater', *Biological Conservation* 108: 67–78; Jones, C. (2002), 'A model for the conservation management of a 'secondary' prey: Sooty shearwater (*Puffinus griseus*) colonies on mainland New Zealand as a case study', *Biological Conservation* 108: 1–12.
8 Newton, I. (1998), *Population Limitation in Birds*, London: Academic Press.

20. Beyond the valley's horizon

1 Croll, D.A., Maron, J.L., Estes, J.A., Danner, E.M. & Byrd, G.V. (2005), 'Introduced predators transform subarctic islands from grassland to tundra', *Science*, 307: 1959–61; Bassett, I.E., Elliott, G.P., Walker, K.J., Thorpe, S. & Beggs, J.R. (2014), 'Are nesting seabirds important determinants of invertebrate community composition on subantarctic Adams Island?', *Polar Biology*, 37: 531–40. doi: 10.1007/s00300-014-1454-5; Havik, G., Catenazzi, A. & Holmgren, M. (2014), 'Seabird nutrient subsidies benefit non-nitrogen fixing trees and alter species composition in South American coastal dry forests', *PLOS ONE* 9(1): e86381. doi:10.1371/journal.pone.0086381; Zwolicki, A., Zmudczyńska-Skarbek, K., Richard, P. & Stempniewicz, L. (2016), 'Importance of marine-derived nutrients supplied by planktivorous seabirds to high Arctic tundra plant communities', *PLOS ONE* 11(5): e0154950. doi:10.1371/journal. pone.0154950

2 Worthy, T.H. & Holdaway, R.N. (1995), 'Quaternary fossil faunas from caves on Mt Cookson, North Canterbury, New Zealand', *Journal of the Royal Society of New Zealand*, 25: 333–70; Worthy, T.H. & Holdaway, R.N. (1996), 'Quaternary fossil faunas, overlapping taphonomies, and palaeofaunal reconstruction in North Canterbury, South Island, New Zealand', *Journal of the Royal Society of New Zealand*, 26: 275–361.

3 Holdaway, R.N. (1989), 'New Zealand's pre-human avifauna and its vulnerability', *New Zealand Journal of Ecology* 12: 11–25.

4 Hamilton, J.W. (1849), 'Personal diary: Voyage of the survey ship *Acheron*', cited in Harrow, 'Some observations of Hutton's shearwater', *Notornis* 23: 269–88.

5 *Marlborough Express*, 19 January 1883, Volume XVIII, Issue 16, 2: https://paperspast.natlib.govt.nz/newspapers/marlborough-express/1883/1/19/2

6 Cuthbert, R.J. (2002), 'The role of introduced mammals and inverse density dependent predation in the conservation of Hutton's shearwater', *Biological Conservation* 108: 67–78.

7 Ibid.

8 Clarke, C.M.H. & Dzieciolowski, R.M. (1991), 'Feral pigs in the northern South Island, New Zealand: I. Origin, distribution and density', *Journal of the Royal Society of New Zealand* 21: 237–47.

9 Ibid.

10 Holden, P. (1994), *Wild Boar*, Auckland: Hodder and Stroughton.

11 Ibid.

12 Thomson, G.M. (1922), *The Naturalisation of Animals & Plants in New Zealand*, Cambridge: Cambridge University Press.

13 Oliver, W.R.B. (1925), 'Vegetation of the Poor Knights Islands', *New Zealand Journal of Science and Technology* 7: 376–84.

14 Cruz, J.B. & Cruz, F. (1996), 'Conservation of the dark-rumped petrel *Pterodroma phaepygia* of the Galapagos Islands, 1982–1991', *Bird Conservation International* 6: 23–32.

15 Pavlov, P.M. (1981), 'Feral pigs: Ungulate predators', *New Zealand Journal of Ecology* 4: 132–33.

16 King, C.M. (1984), *Immigrant Killers: Introduced predators and the conservation of birds in New Zealand*, Oxford: Oxford University Press.

17 Cuthbert, 'The role of introduced mammals'.

21. Ongoing conservation efforts and a new beginning

1 Hutton's Shearwater Charitable Trust Newsletter, September 2013, Issue 11, ISSN 1179-5646.

2 Sommer, E., Bell, M., Bradfield, P., Dunlop, K., Gaze, P., Harrow, G., McGahan, P., Morrissey, M., Walford, D. & Cuthbert, R. (2009). Population trends, breeding success and predation rates of Hutton's shearwater *Puffinus huttoni*: A 20-year assessment. *Notornis*, 56: 144–53.

3 Hutton's Shearwater Charitable Trust Newsletter, June 2016, Issue 18, ISSN 1179-5646.

4 Ibid.

5 Ibid.

6 Hutton's Shearwater Charitable Trust Newsletter, September 2013, Issue 11.

7 Mills. J.A., Yarral. J.W., Bradford-Grieve, J.M., Uddstrom, M.J., Renwick, J.A. & Merilä, J. (2008), 'The impact of climate fluctuation on food availability and reproductive performance of the planktivorous red-billed gull *Larus novaehollandiae scopulinus*', *Journal of Animal Ecology* 77: 1129–42.

8 Miskelly, C.M., Taylor, G.A., Gummer, H. & Willams, R. (2009), 'Translocations of eight species of burrow-nesting seabirds (genera Pterodroma, Pelecanoides, Pachyptila and Puffinus: Family Procellariidae)', *Biological Conservation*, 142: 1965–80.

9 Miskelly, C.M., Sagar, P.M., Tennyson, A.D. & Scofield, P.R. (2001), 'Birds of the Snares Islands, New Zealand', *Notornis* 48: 1–40.

10 Hutton's Shearwater Charitable Trust Newsletter, September 2013, Issue 11.

Bibliography

Newspapers

Auckland Star
Daily Telegraph, Sydney
Poverty Bay Herald
Marlborough Express
Nelson Evening Mail
Otago Daily Times

Books, journals and websites

Alan J.D., Tennyson, A.J.D. & Bartle, J.A. (2008), 'Catalogue of type specimens of birds in the Museum of New Zealand Te Papa Tongarewa', *Tuhinga* 19: 185–207.

Anon (2016), 'The geological history of New Zealand', University of Waikato: http://sci.waikato.ac.nz/evolution/geologicalHistory.shtml

____ (2014), 'Henry Hammersley Travers', Museum of New Zealand Te Papa Tongarewa: http://collections.tepapa.govt.nz/Topic/2683

Baker-Gabb, D.J. (1986), 'Ecological release and behavioural flexibility in marsh harriers on islands', *Emu* 86: 71–81.

Barlow, V. (1994), *Tikanga Whakaaro: Key concepts in Māori culture*, Auckland: Oxford University Press.

Barrow, M.H. (1998), *A Passion for Birds: American ornithology after Audubon*, New Jersey: Princeton University Press.

Bassett, I.E., Elliott, G.P., Walker, K.J., Thorpe, S. & Beggs, J.R. (2014), 'Are nesting seabirds important determinants of invertebrate community composition on subantarctic Adams Island?', *Polar Biology*, 37: 531–40. doi: 10.1007/s00300-014-1454-5

BirdLife International (2016), 'Country profile: Australia': www.birdlife.org/datazone/country/australia

Boersma, D.P. (1982), 'Why some birds take so long to hatch', *The American Naturalist* 120: 733–50.

Boessenkool, S., Star, B., Scofield, P.R., Seddon, P.J. & Waters, J.M. (2009), 'Lost in translation or deliberate falsification? Genetic analyses reveal erroneous museum data for historic penguin specimens', Proceedings of the Royal Society, B. Biological Sciences, 277: 1057–64.

Booth, A.M., Minot, E.O., Imber, M.J. & Fordham, R.A. (2000), 'Aspects of the breeding ecology of the North Island little shearwater *Puffinus assimilis haurakiensis*', *New Zealand Journal of Ecology* 27: 335–45.

Brooke, M. (1990), *The Manx Shearwater*, London: Poyser.

Chastel, O., Weimerskirch, H. & Jouventin, P. (1995), 'Influence of body condition on

reproductive decision and reproductive success in the Blue Petrel', *Auk* 112: 964–72.
Clark, V.I. & Fleming, C.A. (1948), 'Hutton's shearwater (*Puffinus gavia huttoni* Math.) in New Zealand', *Notornis* 2: 187–88.
Clarke, C.M.H. & Dzieciolowski, R.M. (1991), 'Feral pigs in the northern South Island, New Zealand: I. Origin, distribution and density', *Journal of the Royal Society of New Zealand* 21: 237–47.
Croll, D.A., Maron, J.L., Estes, J.A., Danner, E.M. & Byrd, G.V. (2005), 'Introduced predators transform subarctic islands from grassland to tundra', *Science*, 307: 1959–61.
Cruz, J.B. & Cruz, F. (1996), 'Conservation of the dark-rumped petrel *Pterodroma phaepygia* of the Galapagos Islands, 1982–1991', *Bird Conservation International* 6: 23–32.
Cuthbert, R.J. (1999), 'The breeding ecology and conservation of Hutton's shearwaters (*Puffinus huttoni*)', PhD thesis, University of Otago, New Zealand.
____ (2002), 'The role of introduced mammals and inverse density dependent predation in the conservation of Hutton's shearwater', *Biological Conservation* 108: 67–78.
____ (2003), 'Sign left by introduced and native predators feeding on Hutton's shearwaters (*Puffinus huttoni*)', *New Zealand Journal of Zoology* 30: 163–70.
Cuthbert, R.J. & Davis, L.S. (2002), 'Adult survival and productivity of Hutton's shearwaters', *Ibis* 144: 423–32.
Cuthbert, R.J. & Davis, L.S. (2002b), 'The breeding biology of Hutton's shearwater', *Emu* 102: 323–29.
Cuthbert, R.J. & Davis, L.S. (2002c), 'The impact of predation by introduced stoats on Hutton's shearwaters', *Biological Conservation* 108: 79–92.
Cuthbert, R.J., Fletcher, D. & Davis, L.S. (2001), 'A sensitivity analysis of Hutton's shearwater: Prioritizing conservation research and management', *Biological Conservation* 100: 163–72.
Cuthbert, R.J. & Sommer, E.S. (2002), 'Home-range and territorial behaviour of stoats (*Mustela erminea*) in a breeding colony of Hutton's shearwaters (*Puffinus huttoni*)', *New Zealand Journal of Zoology* 29: 149–60.
Cuthbert, R.J., Sommer, E.S. & Davis, L.S. (2000), 'Seasonal variation in the diet of stoats (*Mustela erminea*) in a breeding colony of Hutton's shearwaters (*Puffinus huttoni*)', *New Zealand Journal of Zoology* 27: 367–73.
Dalmau, A., Ferret, A., Ruis de la Torre, J.L. & Manteca, X. (2013), 'Habitat selection and social behaviour in a Pyrenean chamois population (*Rupicapra pyrenaica pyrenaica*)', *Journal of Mountain Ecology* 9: 83–102.
Dell, R.K. (1998), 'Falla, Robert Alexander', from the Dictionary of New Zealand Biography: www.TeAra.govt.nz/en/biographies/4f4/falla-robert-alexander
Diamond, J. & Bond, A.B. (1999), *Kea, Bird of Paradox: The evolution and behaviour of a New Zealand parrot*, Berkeley and Los Angeles: University of California Press.
Diamond, J. & Bond. A.B. (1991), 'Social behaviour and the ontogeny of foraging in the kea (*Nestor notabilis*)', *Ecology* 88: 128–44.
Erlinge, S. (1977), 'Spacing strategy in stoat *Mustela erminea*', *Oikos* 28: 32–42.

____ (1983), 'Demography and dynamics of a stoat *Mustela erminea* population in a diverse community of vertebrates', *Journal of Animal Ecology* 52: 705–26.
Evans, G.R. (1973), 'Hutton's shearwaters initiating local soil erosion in the Seaward Kaikoura Range', *New Zealand Journal of Science* 16: 637–42.
Falla, R.A. (1965), 'Distribution of Hutton's shearwater in New Zealand', *Notornis* 12: 66–70.
Godman, F.C. (1907–08), 'A monograph of the petrels (Order Tubinares)': https://archive.org/details/monographofp119071910godm
Halse, S.A. (1981), 'Migration by Hutton's shearwater', *Emu* 81: 42–44.
Hamilton, J.W. (1849), 'Personal diary: Voyage of the survey ship *Acheron*', cited in Harrow, 'Some observations of Hutton's shearwater', *Notornis* 23: 269–88.
Harrow, G. (1965), 'Preliminary report on discovery of nesting site of Hutton's shearwater', *Notornis* 12: 59–65.
____ (1976), 'Some observations of Hutton's shearwater', *Notornis* 23: 269–88.
Havik, G., Catenazzi, A. & Holmgren, M. (2014), 'Seabird nutrient subsidies benefit non-nitrogen fixing trees and alter species composition in South American coastal dry forests', *PLOS ONE* 9(1): e86381. doi:10.1371/journal.pone.0086381
Hillary, E. (1999), *View from the Summit*, London: Transworld Publishers.
Hillary, E. & Lowe, G. (1956), *East of Everest*, London: Hodder and Stroughton.
Holdaway, R.N. (1989), 'New Zealand's pre-human avifauna and its vulnerability', *New Zealand Journal of Ecology* 12: 11–25.
Holden, P. (1994), *Wild Boar*, Auckland: Hodder and Stroughton.
Hutton's Shearwater Charitable Trust Newsletter, September 2013, Issue 11.
Hutton's Shearwater Charitable Trust Newsletter, April 2015, Issue 15.
Hutton's Shearwater Charitable Trust Newsletter, June 2016, Issue 18.
Hyde, N.H.S. & Worthy, T.H. (2010), 'The diet of New Zealand falcons (*Falco novaeseelandiae*) on the Auckland Islands, New Zealand', *Notornis*, 57: 19–26.
Jones, C. (2002), 'A model for the conservation management of a 'secondary' prey: Sooty shearwater (*Puffinus griseus*) colonies on mainland New Zealand as a case study', *Biological Conservation* 108: 1–12.
King, C.M. (1984), *Immigrant Killers: Introduced predators and the conservation of birds in New Zealand*, Oxford: Oxford University Press.
King, C.M & Powell, R.A. (2007), *The Natural History of Weasels and Stoats: Ecology, behavior and management*, Oxford: Oxford University Press.
Kloot, T. (1986), 'Mathews, Gregory Macalister (1876–1949)', Australian Dictionary of Biography: http://adb.anu.edu.au/biography/mathews-gregory-macalister-7517/text13111
Lack. D. (1968), *Ecological Adaptations for Breeding in Birds*, London: Methuen.
Lyver, P.O. (2000), 'Identifying mammalian predators of sooty shearwaters from bite marks: A tool for focusing wildlife protection', *Mammal Review* 30: 31–44.
Mathews, G.M. (1937a), 'Description of *Puffinus leptorhynchus*', *Bulletin of the British Ornithological Club* 57: 143.

____ (1937b), 'A new shearwater for Western Australia', *Emu* 37: 114–16.

Matthiessen, P. (1978), *The Snow Leopard*, New York: Viking Press.

Maxwell, G. (1960), *Ring of Bright Water*, London: Longmans.

McLeod, D., (ed.) (1972), *Alone in a Mountain World: A high country anthology*, Wellington: A.H. & A.W. Reed.

McLintock, A.H. (1966), 'Kaikoura Ranges', Te Ara – the Encyclopedia of New Zealand: www.TeAra.govt.nz/en/1966/kaikoura-ranges

Michel, P., Ollason, J.C., Grosbois, V. & Thompson, P.M. (2003), 'The influence of body size, breeding experience and environmental variability on egg size in the northern fulmar (*Fulmarus glacialis*)', *Journal of Zoology London* 261: 427–32.

Milkanowski, J. (2016), 'A natural history of Walter Rothschild: One very rich man's zoological obsessions': https://theawl.com/a-natural-history-of-walter-rothschild-e5aec44734bb#.5eqw88z8s

Mills. J.A., Yarral. J.W., Bradford-Grieve, J.M., Uddstrom, M.J., Renwick, J.A. & Merilä, J. (2008), 'The impact of climate fluctuation on food availability and reproductive performance of the planktivorous red-billed gull *Larus novaehollandiae scopulinus*', *Journal of Animal Ecology* 77: 1129–42.

Miskelly, C.M. (2011), 'Who wrote that? Forensic analysis of museum specimen labels': http://blog.tepapa.govt.nz/2011/11/01/who-wrote-that-forensic-analysis-of-museum-specimen-labels/

____ (2012), 'Discovery and extinction of the South Island snipe (*Coenocorypha iredalei*) on islands around Stewart Island', *Notornis* 59: 15–31.

Miskelly, C.M., Sagar, P.M., Tennyson, A.D. & Scofield, P.R. (2001), 'Birds of the Snares Islands, New Zealand', *Notornis* 48: 1–40.

Miskelly, C.M., Taylor, G.A., Gummer, H. & Willams, R. (2009), 'Translocations of eight species of burrow-nesting seabirds (genera Pterodroma, Pelecanoides, Pachyptila and Puffinus: Family Procellariidae)', *Biological Conservation*, 142: 1965–80.

Murphy, M.C. (1952), 'The Manx shearwater, *Puffinus puffinus*, as a species of world-wide distribution', *American Museum Novitates* 1586: 1–21.

Museum of New Zealand Te Papa Tongarewa (2014), 'The mountain ringlet butterfly (*Percnodaimon pluto*)': http://collections.tepapa.govt.nz/topic/983

Nesti, I., Poscillico, M. & Lovari, S. (2010), 'Ranging behaviour and habitat selection of alpine chamois', *Ethology Ecology & Evolution* 22: 215–31.

Newton, I. (1998), *Population Limitation in Birds*, London: Academic Press.

Oliver, W.R.B. (1925), 'Vegetation of the Poor Knights Islands', *New Zealand Journal of Science and Technology* 7: 376–84.

Parton, H.N. (2013), 'Hutton, Frederick Wollaston', from the Dictionary of New Zealand Biography: www.TeAra.govt.nz/en/biographies/2h59/hutton-frederick-wollaston

Paton, B. & Davis, A. (1997), 'Hutton's shearwater recovery plan (*Puffinus huttoni*). Threatened species recovery plan series', Wellington: Department of Conservation.

Patrick, B.H. & Cuthbert, R. (1999), 'Lepidoptera and other insects of the Seaward Kaikoura Range', *Records of the Canterbury Museum* 13: 123–27.

Pavlov, P.M. (1981), 'Feral pigs: Ungulate predators', *New Zealand Journal of Ecology* 4: 132–33.
Pennycuick, C.J. (1989), *Bird Flight Performance*, Oxford: Oxford Science Publications.
Powlesland, R.G. (2013), 'New Zealand pigeon', in C.M. Miskelly (ed.) *New Zealand Birds Online*: www.nzbirdsonline.org.nz
Rasmussen, P.C. & Prŷs-Jones, R.P. (2003), 'History vs mystery: The reliability of museum specimen data', *Bulletin of the British Ornithological Club* 123: 66–94.
Rattenbury, M.S., Townsend, D.B. & Johnston, M.R. (compilers) (2006), 'Geology of the Kaikoura area', Institute of Geological & Nuclear Sciences 1:250 000 geological map 13. Lower Hutt, New Zealand: GNS Science.
Revolvy (2016), 'Lionel Walter Rothschild': www.revolvy.com/main/index.php?s=Walter%20Rothschild&item_type=topic
Ricklefs, R.E., Day, C.H., Huntington, C.E. & Williams, J.B. (1985), 'Variability in feeding rate and meal size of Leach's storm-petrel at Kent Island, New Brunswick', *Journal of Animal Ecology* 54: 883–98.
Ricklefs, R.E. & Schew, W.A. (1994), 'Foraging stochasticity and lipid accumulation by nestling petrels', *Functional Ecology* 8, 159–70.
Rothschild, M. (2008), *Walter Rothschild: The man, the museum and the menagerie*, London: Natural History Museum.
Sandall, M. (1986), 'Movement patterns of male stoats *Mustela erminea* during the mating season: Differences in relation to social status', *Oikos* 47: 63–70.
Serventy, D.L. (1939), 'The white-breasted petrel of South Australia', *Emu* 39: 95–107.
Sherley, G. (1992), 'Monitoring Hutton's shearwater 1986–1989', *Notornis* 39: 249–61.
Shipton, E. (1943), *Upon That Mountain*, London: Hodder and Stoughton.
Smithsonian National Museum of Natural History, 'Historical Expeditions: Whitney South Sea Expedition': http://botany.si.edu/colls/expeditions/expedition_page.cfm?ExpedName=31
Sommer, E., Bell, M., Bradfield, P., Dunlop, K., Gaze, P., Harrow, G., McGahan, P., Morrissey, M., Walford, D. & Cuthbert, R. (2009), 'Population trends, breeding success and predation rates of Hutton's shearwater *Puffinus huttoni*: A 20-year assessment', Notornis, 56: 144–53.
Tau, T.M. & Anderson, A. (eds) (2008), *Ngāi Tahu: A migration history: The Carrington text*, Wellington: Bridget Williams Books, 146–51.
Temple, P. (1996), *The Book of the Kea*, Auckland: Hodder Moa Beckett.
Tennyson, A.J.D., Miskelly, C.M. & LeCroy, M. (2014), 'Clarification of collection data for the type specimens of Hutton's shearwater *Puffinus huttoni* Mathews, 1912, and implications for the accuracy of historic subantarctic specimen data', *Bulletin of the British Ornithological Club* 134: 242–46.
The Rothschild Archive (2016), 'Lionel Walter (Walter) Rothschild (1868–1937)': https://family.rothschildarchive.org/people/102-lionel-walter-walter-rothschild-1868-1937
Thomson, G.M. (1922), *The Naturalisation of Animals & Plants in New Zealand*, Cambridge: Cambridge University Press.

Tickell, W.L.N. (2000), *Albatrosses*, Mountfield: Pica Press.

Van Dissen, R. & Yeats, R.S. (1991), 'Hope fault, Jordan thrust, and uplift of the Seaward Kaikoura Range, New Zealand', *Geology* 19: 393–96.

von Tunzelmann, N. (1969), 'Recent New Zealand developments', *Alpine Journal* 74: 70–81.

Warham, J. (1990), *The Petrels: Their ecology and breeding systems*, London: Academic Press.

____ (1996), *The Behaviour, Population Biology and Physiology of the Petrels*, London: Academic Press.

Whitaker, A. (1984), '*Hoplodactylus kahutarae* n.sp. (Reptilia: Gekkonidae) from the Seaward Kaikoura Range, Marlborough, New Zealand', *New Zealand Journal of Zoology* 11: 259–70.

Whitaker, T., Shaw, T. & Hitchmough, R. (1999), 'Black-eyed geckos (*Hoplodactylus kahutarae*) on Mt Arthur, Kahurangi National Park', Conservation Advisory Science Notes No. 230, Department of Conservation, Wellington.

Whitlock, L.F. (1937), 'A new petrel of the genus Puffinus', *Emu* 37: 116–17.

Winsome Shepherd, R., 'Travers, William Thomas Locke', from the Dictionary of New Zealand Biography: www.TeAra.govt.nz/en/biographies/1t105/travers-william-thomas-locke

Wodzicki, K. & Wright, S. (1984), 'Introduced birds and mammals in New Zealand and their effect on the environment', *Tuatara* 27: 77–104.

Wooler, R.D., Bradley, J.S. & Croxall, J.P. (1992), 'Long-term population studies of seabirds', *Trends in Ecology and Evolution* 7: 111–14.

Wooler, R.D., Bradley, J.S., Skira, I.J. & Serventy, D.L. (1989), in I.A. Newton (ed.) *Lifetime Reproduction in Birds*, London: Academic Press, 405–11.

Worthy, T.H. & Holdaway, R.N. (1995), 'Quaternary fossil faunas from caves on Mt Cookson, North Canterbury, New Zealand', *Journal of the Royal Society of New Zealand*, 25: 333–70.

Worthy, T.H. & Holdaway, R.N. (1996), 'Quaternary fossil faunas, overlapping taphonomies, and palaeofaunal reconstruction in North Canterbury, South Island, New Zealand', *Journal of the Royal Society of New Zealand* 26: 275–361.

Wragg, G. (1985), 'The comparative biology of fluttering shearwater and Hutton's shearwater and their relationship to other shearwater species', Master's thesis, University of Canterbury, New Zealand.

Zwolicki, A., Zmudczyńska-Skarbek, K., Richard, P. & Stempniewicz, L. (2016), 'Importance of marine-derived nutrients supplied by planktivorous seabirds to high Arctic tundra plant communities', *PLOS ONE* 11(5): e0154950. doi:10.1371/journal.pone.0154950

Index

Page numbers in **bold** refer to illustrations.